THE EVERYTHING®
Shakespeare
Book

Dear Reader,

When a man called Shakespeare died in 1616 the news journals of the day did not herald his passing. He was, after all, just a playwright of popular plays, not an icon of great works of literary art. It wasn't until 1769 when director David Garrick held the First Shakespeare Jubilee in the Bard's birthplace, Stratford-upon-Avon, to showcase the plays, that Shakespeare's genius began to be recognized.

It wasn't long after that when doubts began to emerge about the true authorship of Shakespeare's plays. Detractors began to say, "Would you ask me to believe that this rural clod from Stratford was transformed into a literary genius by a divine bolt of lightning?"

Even now, we might ask ourselves: "Who is Shakespeare?"

Everyone agrees that Homer penned *The Iliad*. Yet, to accept Shakespeare as the author of the most poetic masterpieces in the English language has caused endless—and many times furious and vindictive—debates. Those who doubt Shakespeare's authorship are called "anti-Stratfordians." They argue that a "country bumpkin" from Stratford-upon-Avon could never have penned the plays. Famous doubters include Mark Twain, Ralph Waldo Emerson, and Charlie Chaplin.

That thought can also apply to William Shakespeare. And that is the purpose of *The Everything® Shakespeare Book, 2nd Edition*. It not only delves into the great works of Shakespeare—from his poetry to his plays—but it also seeks to reveal the truth about this man from Stratford-upon-Avon.

It's a story Shakespeare would have loved to write.

Cork Milner

Welcome to the EVERYTHING® Series!

These handy, accessible books give you all you need to tackle a difficult project, gain a new hobby, comprehend a fascinating topic, prepare for an exam, or even brush up on something you learned back in school but have since forgotten.

You can choose to read an *Everything*® book from cover to cover or just pick out the information you want from our three useful boxes: e-questions, e-facts, e-quotes.

We give you everything you need to know on the subject, but throw in a lot of fun stuff along the way, too.

We now have more than 400 *Everything*® books in print, spanning such wide-ranging categories as weddings, pregnancy, cooking, music instruction, foreign language, crafts, pets, New Age, and so much more. When you're done reading them all, you can finally say you know *Everything*®!

QUESTIONS?
Answers to
common questions

FACTS
Important snippets
of information

QUOTE
Words of wisdom
from experts
in the field

DIRECTOR OF INNOVATION Paula Munier

EDITORIAL DIRECTOR Laura M. Daly

EXECUTIVE EDITOR, SERIES BOOKS Brielle K. Matson

ASSOCIATE COPY CHIEF Sheila Zwiebel

ACQUISITIONS EDITOR Lisa Laing

DEVELOPMENT EDITOR Katie McDonough

PRODUCTION EDITOR Casey Ebert

Visit the entire Everything® series at *www.everything.com*

THE
EVERYTHING®
SHAKESPEARE
BOOK
2nd Edition

Celebrate the life, times, and works
of the world's greatest storyteller

Cork Milner

avon, massachusetts

An Everything® Series Book.
Everything® and everything.com® are registered trademarks of F+W Publications, Inc.

Published by Adams Media, an F+W Publications Company
57 Littlefield Street, Avon, MA 02322 U.S.A.
www.adamsmedia.com

ISBN 10: 1-59869-453-7
ISBN 13: 978-1-59869-453-6

Printed in the United States of America.

J   I   H   G   F   E   D   C   B   A

Library of Congress Cataloging-in-Publication Data
available from the publisher.

This publication is designed to provide accurate and authoritative information with regard to the subject matter covered. It is sold with the understanding that the publisher is not engaged in rendering legal, accounting, or other professional advice. If legal advice or other expert assistance is required, the services of a competent professional person should be sought.

—From a *Declaration of Principles* jointly adopted by a Committee of the American Bar Association and a Committee of Publishers and Associations

Many of the designations used by manufacturers and sellers to distinguish their products are claimed as trademarks. Where those designations appear in this book and Adams Media was aware of a trademark claim, the designations have been printed with initial capital letters.

This book is available at quantity discounts for bulk purchases.
For information, please call 1-800-289-0963.

Contents

Shakespeare's Problem Comedies / 167

Shakespeare's Tragic Comedies / 181

Acknowledgments

My thanks to Lisa Laing, Project Editor of Adams Media, for her professional editing and technical direction in completing this book.

To my agent, Bob Diforio, who convinced me that my love for the words of Shakespeare made *The Everything® Shakespeare Book* an exceptional writing project.

Top Ten Things You Didn't Know about William Shakespeare

1. The first record of the name "Shakespeare" is one of William Saksper of Gloucestershire who in 1248 was hanged for robbery.

2. On April 26, 1564, the Stratford parish register records the baptism of "Gulielmus filius Johannes Shakspere" ("William, son of John Shakespere").

3. Episcopal records in the diocese of Worcester register the marriage of "Willelmum Shaxpere" in 1582. The groom was eighteen, the bride, "Anne Hathway," twenty-six. One can assume it was a "shotgun" wedding, as six months after the marriage, Susanna Shakespeare was christened.

4. Shakespeare's name was spelled (or shall we say misspelled) a variety of ways during his lifetime: Shackespere, Shaxpere, and even Shaeaxsperre.

5. There are only six known signatures of Shakespeare, three of them on his last will and testament. They are valued at over $5 million each. The last signature was sold in 1844 for the equivalent of $180. There are no known copies of his plays written in his hand. Their value would be priceless.

6. Shakespeare's family line ceased to exist with the death of his granddaughter, Elizabeth. His sister, Joan, survived him by many years and through her descendants the Shakespeare name still lives on.

7. No known portraits were painted during Shakespeare's lifetime. The most well-known likeness, the Droeshout Engraving, which appears on the title page of the First Folio, was done by Martin Droeshout, who was only fifteen when Shakespeare died.

8. George Bernard Shaw, who deplored what he thought was Shakespeare's bloated reputation, invented the word bardolatry, hence the term "Bard." Shaw thought Shakespeare's ideas were "platitudinous fludge."

9. There have been over fifty claimants to Shakespeare's literary crown, the most prominent being Sir Francis Bacon and Edward de Vere. There are also such absurd contenders as Queen Elizabeth I, Sir Walter Raleigh, and Daniel Defoe.

10. Mark Twain was the most verbal of the doubters that Shakespeare, a "Stratford rustic," wrote great plays. He termed all believers (known as "the Stratfordians"), as "Stratfordolators, Shakespearoids and blatherskites."

Introduction

▶ MANY A POTENTIAL FAN has been turned off by being forced to read Shakespeare in school or by being dragged to see a badly staged and acted version of one of Shakespeare's plays. Nearly all of us as schoolchildren were forced to endure turgid study sessions of Shakespeare plays because it was "good for us."

Admittedly, reading a play by Shakespeare can be puzzling. Many of the words are foreign to us. In *Henry IV, Part II* we have this tirade: "Away, you scullion! You rampallion." (Ruffian.) "You fustilarian!" (A made-up word like "fussy.") "I'll tickle your catastrophe!" (A popular phrase of the time.)

The phrasing can also be confusing. When Juliet calls from the balcony and laments, "Wherefore art thou Romeo?" the reader assumes she means, "Where?" Yet, Juliet is saying, "Why are you Romeo?" In other words, "Why must you be an enemy of my family, which will keep us apart."

But seeing a play performed, either onstage or as a movie, is a joy. Some producers have staged lavish versions of Shakespeare's plays with great actors who take what seems to be incomprehensible language and make it sing.

Take director Laurence Olivier's *Henry V*, in which he also starred. Olivier said he designed the film for "people who believed that Shakespeare was not for the likes of them."

After watching Sir John Gielgud's stage performance in *Hamlet*, a critic wrote, "The voice of John Gielgud introduced me to classical acting and now I can't read *Hamlet* without hearing it."

Of course, there are some performances that go beyond the bounds of good taste, such as James Cagney acting in a 1935 movie version of *A Midsummer Night's Dream*. He was said to be a "cross between a Chicago Hood and the Ugly Duckling."

Mickey Rooney, who played Puck at age fifteen in *A Midsummer Night's Dream*, said later, "I never read Shakespeare before or since."

Other movie stars have attempted Shakespeare on the screen to less than glowing reviews, such as actor Tony Curtis as the evil Iago in *Othello*. Walter Matthau was just as ill-cast in the same part. Humphrey Bogart didn't fare any better in a radio adaptation of *Henry IV*.

No doubt Orson Welles presented the most original performance of *Macbeth* when he staged the play in Haiti during the nineteenth century and titled it "Voodoo *Macbeth*." Although it was a success, one has to wonder what Shakespeare would have thought seeing his play lifted from Scottish heath and dropped on an island.

Even with the vast number of interpretations of the plays, there is no question that studying Shakespeare requires some effort. But it is worth the mental effort. He takes us into a different world, introduces us to deviant people, and makes us listen to them talk in a way that at first seems almost incomprehensible. But his characters are, in fact, remarkable and recognizable. Just pick up the newspaper or turn on the television, and chances are you'll recognize people in the modern world who bear a resemblance to Shakespearean characters.

Shakespeare's genius was to capture, perhaps for the first time in the English language, the deep and troubling complexities and passions that we are all slave to.

Shakespeare also helped to invent the language we now know as English. He wrote at a time when English was evolving from a form called Middle English, which was part Germanic and part French, into the language we recognize today. He invented words and played with the language. Even audiences in his day did not understand everything he wrote any better than we do today. He was a poet with a poet's sensibilities, and his use of speech and his inventiveness reflect that.

So, let's investigate the world of the man who proclaimed in *As You Like It*: "All the world's a stage, and all the men and women merely players." Let's see if he can't teach us a thing or two about ourselves and the world around us.

CHAPTER 1

Shakespeare's World

Shakespeare is an enigma. In Elizabethan times, literacy was dramatically on the rise but those people who could write seldom wrote about the living. As a result, there are few reliable stories about Shakespeare's life. Yet, a bit of detective work in church records and legal documents, as well as a few personal reminiscences from his contemporaries, can give us the "bones" of a skeletal life story to which we can add some "meat."

A Bare Bones Biography

Biography in the modern sense was unknown to the Elizabethans. Kings and queens, statesmen and military heroes' lives were recorded, but a man of middle class, an actor and writer of plays, of him little was written. We are not even sure of the exact date of Shakespeare's birth.

Mark Twain, who strongly denounced the man called Shakespeare as the author of the plays listed under his name, compared the creation of Shakespeare's biography to the "reconstruction of a dinosaur from a few bits of bone stuck together with plaster."

Here are the facts, and only the facts:

- Holy Trinity Church in Stratford-upon-Avon does not record Shakespeare's birth date. But the parish register lists his christening on April 26, 1564. Baptisms usually took place about three days after a child's birth because infants often died in those first two days. We can calculate that he was most probably born on April 23.
- In 1582, a marriage license was granted to one "Willelmun Shaxpere." His bride, "Anne Hathwey," was eight years his senior and from the nearby village of Shottery. Six months after the marriage, church records show Susanna Shakespeare was christened.
- There is some confusion with Anne's name. The church register reads "Annam Whateley de Temple Grafton." But the bond of marriage lists the bride as "Anne Hathwey" of Stratford. (It has been assumed that Whateley was a scribal error rather than a second woman in Shakespeare's young life.) Anne Hathaway's name was also registered as "Agnes" Hathwey. Anne was a common variation of Agnes.
- Two years after the marriage of William and Anne, on February 2, 1585, the twins, Hamnet and Judith, were baptized. They were named in honor of two close family friends, the baker Hamnet Sadler and his wife Judith. Eleven years later, one of the twins, Hamnet, died.

- Shakespeare's father, John, was a respected glove maker and wool merchant. His social position rose over twenty years from chamberlain to high bailiff, what we would call mayor.
- Shakespeare turned twenty-one in 1585. For the next seven years, until 1592, there are no official records of where he went or what he did. He is mentioned in 1592 when a London dramatist, Robert Green, referred to him as "Shake-scene" and called him an "upstart crow, beautified with our feathers."
- In the early years in London, Shakespeare worked as an actor, later in his career playing the Ghost in *Hamlet* and Adam in *As You Like It*.
- Shakespeare's first tragedy, *Titus Andronicus,* and his first comedy, *The Comedy of Errors*, were enthusiastically received by the London audience, as was his first history, *Henry VI.*
- In 1611 Shakespeare left London and retired to New Place, his home in Stratford-upon-Avon.
- In 1616 Shakespeare died. He was fifty-two. His tomb is in Holy Trinity Church, Stratford.
- Anne Hathaway Shakespeare died in 1623, at the age of sixty-eight. She is also entombed In Holy Trinity Church.

Spelling was also hit or miss in Elizabethan days before English was standardized; so Shakespeare's name can be found spelled as Shackerpere, Shaxpeare, and many other variations. One researcher, George Wise, published a tome titled *The Autograph of William Shakespeare*, in which he listed 400 ways of spelling the name, such as Scheackespyrr and Schaeaxspierre. There are six different versions of Shakespeare's actual signature.

The Early Years

It is commonly agreed that England's greatest poet and playwright was born April 23, 1564, and that he died on the same day of the same month, St. George's Day, April 23, 1616. Hospice workers today report men and women from all classes often cling to life until a special date. Given Shakespeare's obvious love of symmetry, it seems likely he would try to shape his ending to match his beginning, giving scholars further reason to believe he was born on April 23. His birthplace was Stratford-upon-Avon, in the county of Warwickshire, about 100 miles north of London.

In the mid-sixteenth century, Stratford was a market town of some 1,500 people and was considered a large town. In the agrarian society of the time, villages were limited in size by the productivity of the surrounding countryside. As rising business centers, such towns made use of rivers and streams to transport local produce such as wool, cheese, and grain. The population of London at the time of Shakespeare's birth was about 200,000 and rapidly growing. By his death, more than 400,000 people lived in London.

Shakespeare's Family

Shakespeare was the eldest son of a glove maker and prosperous merchant, John Shakespeare, and the third child of eight. John was an established glove maker and leather dresser. Shakespeare's mother's maiden name was Mary Arden, and her family was from the gentry—that is, they were landlords rather than tenants and lived off the income of their real estate. Along with the properties that Mary brought to the marriage, and the income of John's leather and tanning business, which was a respectable trade, they were comparatively well off.

John was active in local government and was appointed to jobs of increasing responsibility, culminating in his election as bailiff, or mayor, of Stratford. Then, John's fortunes began to decline. In 1586 he was replaced as an alderman. By 1592, he was being rebuked in writing for not attending church and was in fear of being jailed for debt.

Historians speculate that John may have held onto old Roman Catholic beliefs (his mother was from a Catholic family) and suffered for it. England had broken with the Roman Catholic Church. Henry VIII declared himself the head of state and the "Church of England," what we now call Anglicanism in England and Episcopalianism in the United States. Henry began tearing down monasteries and reclaiming Church property. After Henry died, his son Edward VI attempted to introduce the more radical Protestantism of the Reformation. He began executing Roman Catholics. Edward, however, died after four years on the throne. His older sister began her reign as Queen Mary in 1553. In a bloody upheaval, Mary tried to reintroduce

Catholicism by executing many Protestants. After Mary's death in 1558, her half sister Elizabeth, the daughter of Anne Boleyn, became queen. Queen Elizabeth embraced the Church of England as the national religion with herself, like her father Henry VIII, as the head of state and religion. Unlike her half siblings Edward and Mary, Elizabeth strove for religious moderation. She would reign over England for forty-five years, leaving the throne to her cousin James in 1603.

QUESTION?

Were Shakespeare's parents educated?
John, in his position as Stratford's bailiff, should have been able to read and write, but he signed all documents with his glover's mark (two compasses) instead of his name. Scholars, however, now speculate that such trade marks may have carried more weight than a signature and so do not necessarily reflect illiteracy. Mary Shakespeare used as her mark a running horse. Though she came from a prosperous family, given the status of women when she was born, it is unlikely she was literate by today's standards.

Shakespeare's Education

As the son of a local official, Shakespeare would have been entitled to free schooling (mandatory schooling was not yet the law), and it is likely he was educated at Stratford Grammar School, which had a reputation as an excellent school. After a few years of training in basic literacy, boys of well-off families spent the rest of their education learning to read, recite, and speak Latin and possibly some Greek. The influence of Latin authors such as Pliny, Ovid, Seneca, Plautus, and Terence as well as Greek authors Homer and Plutarch, are clear in Shakespeare's plays.

Young William did not go on to a university, but the grammar school curriculum should have given him a formidable linguistic and literary education. As was common at the time, he attended classes from dawn to dusk six days a week and was probably whipped if he was inattentive or lazy in his studies. Some researchers think that the character of Sir Hugh Evans, in

The Merry Wives of Windsor, is a caricature of Shakespeare's old headmaster, Thomas Jenkins.

Ben Jonson, who received honorary degrees from Oxford and Cambridge, and who would become Shakespeare's close friend in later years, once referred to Shakespeare's grammar schooling by saying, "He had small Latin and less Greek." Jonson, however, would have made that judgment against very high standards.

Marriage and Children

When Anne became pregnant, the couple was forced to ask for a waiver of the banns from the bishop of Worcester so that the wedding could take place quickly before the holiday season, when marriages weren't performed. There was good reason for this rush to the altar: William and Anne's daughter Susanna was born six months later. Historians estimate that one in three Elizabethan brides was pregnant on her wedding day, so this situation was not out of the ordinary. Shakespeare's father probably urged the marriage on because of the financial improvements to his family that would result from the union to Anne, whose father was a well-to-do farmer and landlord.

In Elizabethan times marriage was considered more a business proposition than a union of two people who had fallen in love. Though one can certainly imagine young William's excitement taking the short walk from Stratford to Anne's home in Shottery for a rendezvous of passion with an "older" woman, settling into married life and having children would have been considered love enough by the larger community.

Not a lot is known of Shakespeare between the ages of eighteen and twenty-five. Some stories say he had to flee Stratford after being caught poaching deer on a nobleman's estate, while others, less fanciful, have him working as a schoolmaster, either in a small town or for the family of a local nobleman.

Plays were performed in grammar school and Shakespeare may have taken part in these performances, honing his taste for acting. Traveling players often acted in Stratford. The Earl of Leicester's players performed there, and in 1576 (when Shakespeare was twelve) the Earl of Worcester's and the Earl of Warwick's troupes were there. With his budding interest in the theater, Shakespeare no doubt met these players.

Shakespeare in London

Sometime after 1585, Shakespeare left his home and family to travel to London perhaps as a member of the Queen's Men, an elite troupe of actors who performed in Stratford in 1587. For seven years—termed the "Lost Years"—there are no official records of what he did.

His wife, Anne, no doubt, had great fear of his departure. For a country person, Anne had to look upon London as a terribly huge place where pickpockets strolled, country cousins were made fun of, and cats clawed over the remains of fish tossed from above to the street. The odious contents of chamber pots were also splashed into the street and added to the stench.

There was also a deadly fear of the plague, which ravaged London in 1564, 1592–93, 1603, and 1623. In 1593 at least 100,000 victims in England succumbed to the scourge. People stuffed rosemary in their ears as a desperate preventative. "The scourge of God is descended upon the wickedness of the city!" preachers ranted from street-side pulpits as carts carried away the dead.

Life in Theater

It is unlikely, but commonly believed, that Shakespeare's first job in the theater was holding horses at the stage door. He may have been some sort of stage manager. As he began journeyman play editing and copying, and collaborating with other playwrights and actor managers, he learned his craft. He also performed as an actor.

We don't know exactly what roles Shakespeare played, but authorities on Shakespeare think he probably played "cameo" roles, such as the Ghost in *Hamlet*, and Chorus in *King Henry V.* He seemed to play older men. He was also in the cast list of a Ben Jonson play, *Everyman in his Humour.*

Producer Philip Henslowe, the leading impresario of the Rose Theatre, who was noted for keeping complete records of the theater, recorded what plays were preformed and what actors were paid. Strangely, he failed to list any payment to Shakespeare for his plays. London's premiere acting company, the Lord Chamberlain's Men, did record warrants for payment and Shakespeare was a full-fledged professional in the company, where he served as both actor and playwright.

The acting troupe did well, no doubt partly as a result of their in-house writer, possibly performing for Queen Elizabeth I herself. They also put on productions for law school professors and students at the Inns of Court.

Shakespeare wasn't above taking someone's idea if he liked it and rewriting it for himself and his company. The playwright's version, of course, would have been uniquely his. For example, the *King Lear* story did not originally contain Cordelia or the Fool, two characters we find most interesting. In those days, plagiarism wasn't a crime. A lot of his work, for example the stories of *Macbeth, King Lear,* and *Hamlet,* can be traced back to stories by Holinshed, to the anonymous author of a play called *King Leir,* and to a lost tragedy written by Thomas Kyd. He borrowed other plots from Chaucer, Plutarch, familiar folktales, and many Italian novellas.

By 1592, no more than seven years after his arrival, he was well established as an actor/playwright in London. A bitter rival, Robert Greene, who was a university-trained writer, resented the "uneducated" lowlifes like Shakespeare becoming more successful than he. Reacting to this, he accused Shakespeare of stealing techniques from other playwrights to further his own career, and added, "there is an upstart crow, beautified with our feathers [that is, he stole our stuff], that with his Tygers hart wrapt in a Players hyde [a possible reference to a line from *King Henry VI, Part III,* an early play, but also referring to Shakespeare as an untalented person pretending to be a playwright and actor], supposes he is as well able to bombast out blanke verse as the best of you [that is, he thinks he is a very good writer]; and being an absolute Johannes fac totum [that is, Jack-of-all-trades (and the rest of the insult implies a master of none)], is in his own conceit the only Shake-scene in a country [in other words, he *really* thinks he is England's best playwright]."

In 1592 the plague broke out again and the authorities in London closed all the theaters because of the risk of spreading infection in the audiences. While other players went on tour, Shakespeare gained a noble patron, Henry Wriothesley, Earl of Southampton. The playwright turned to writing poetry, considered a higher art than writing plays. Shakespeare published two major lyric works, *Venus and Adonis* in 1593 and *The Rape of Lucrece* in 1594, both dedicated to Southampton. Shakespeare may also have written his long sonnet sequence during this period, dedicating it to an "H. W."

When the theaters reopened in 1594, the thirty-year-old actor/playwright joined an acting company, led by actor Richard Burbage, called the Lord Chamberlain's Men. This company first performed in a space simply called "The Theatre." In 1599 they would open the Globe, built from the Theatre's timbers. It held about 3,000 people—a huge place for its day—charging a penny for the standing room only groundlings, another penny to enter the covered galleries, and another penny for a cushion. More than half of Shakespeare's plays were performed for the first time in the Globe Theatre.

Profile of Shakespeare

By some accounts Shakespeare was a good-looking, witty young man, probably not unlike Joseph Fiennes's portrayal of him in the 1998 movie *Shakespeare in Love.*

Shakespeare could be intense, had a real eye for the dramatic in a situation, was extremely knowledgeable about stagecraft, and likely paid great attention to the world and the people around him, initially listening more than talking.

Shakespeare would likely have been the quiet one in a crowd at first, the one who sat in the corner entertaining himself and perhaps a friend or two by watching everyone coming and going in a room and making pithy, witty comments, probably in a low voice. But once the party got going, he was likely just as loud and passionate as others. Pity the poor man who had to get into an argument with Shakespeare. A nimble mind, a way with words, and a sharp tongue no doubt helped him win a lot more arguments than perhaps he should have won.

What Did Shakespeare Look Like?

We have all seen his likeness; the portrait of the bald man with a wispy mustache and prickly hair under his lip, big black eyes staring at—nothing. This image is from the Droeshout Engraving and first appeared on the title page of the First Folio, the original collection of Shakespeare's plays. Yet, is it a correct representation of the man? The engraver, Martin Droeshout, was fifteen when Shakespeare died, so the portrait certainly didn't come from life, nor do we know if the engraver and playwright ever met.

The Chandos portrait is far more romantic, offering an idealized face of the playwright wearing a gold earring. Richard Burbage, the best-known actor in Shakespeare's company and an artist, was once thought to have painted it, though the more likely artist is one John Taylor. It is called the Chandos portrait because it eventually came to be in the possession of the Duke of Chandos.

Shakespeare's colleague Ben Jonson evidently thought it a good like-ness, as he wrote in his poem in the First Folio:
It was for Gentle Shakespeare's cut;
Wherein the Graver had a strife
With Nature to out-do the life.

The worst likeness is no doubt the Janssen bust, which is in Holy Trinity Church in Stratford and is placed near Shakespeare's tomb. He is shown as a bloated figure, the features puffy, which could be a reflection of his illness in the last years of his life.

Shakespeare's Fees from His Writing

Most of the records that mention Shakespeare deal with lawsuits. He was a businessman and the theater was the movie house of its time. Shakespeare was both a "sharer" in the acting company and a "housekeeper," or part owner of the theater building itself. As such, he received 10 percent of all profits. He was careful with his money (perhaps as a result of lessons learned from his father's misfortunes). He earned fees not only from writing plays and from their production, but also from investments in real estate. He did not own his plays—those were owned by the Lord Chamberlain's Men, later known as the King's Men. But since Shakespeare gained from the company's buying his play as well as producing it, his profit was greater than those playwrights who were not sharers. He became a very wealthy man.

We have no evidence that he traveled abroad, although it is certainly possible given his knowledge of other countries and the things he wrote about in his plays.

Was Shakespeare a Womanizer?

Certainly the movie *Shakespeare in Love* showed him involved in an amorous relationship. One can easily suppose that as an actor he had access to many sexual companions. A law student named John Manningham wrote this in his diary in 1601 when Shakespeare was age thirty-six:

Upon a time when Burbage played Richard III there was a citizen grew so far in liking him that, before she went from the play, she appointed him to come that night unto her by the name of Richard the Third. Shakespeare, overhearing their conclusion, went before, was entertained and at his game ere Burbage came. Then, message being brought that Richard the Third was at the door, Shakespeare caused return to be made that William the Conqueror was before Richard the Third.

This anecdote may only be that—a funny story. But what is known to be fact is that Shakespeare addresses most of his love sonnets to a young man and some to a "dark lady." What those facts mean is more debatable.

Performing for Royalty

Shakespeare wrote and performed for both Queen Elizabeth and her successor, King James. He also had a royal patron. These circumstances no doubt helped him write convincingly about royalty. It is not a stretch of the imagination to think that as the leading playwright and poet of his time, he was often in the company of leading political and social figures of the time, whether aristocrats or not.

In 1603, Queen Elizabeth I died and James VI of Scotland became James I of England. He took Burbage and company under his sponsorship, renaming the company the King's Men. James commanded more court productions from this premier troupe than did Queen Elizabeth. For him in particular, Shakespeare wrote "that Scottish play," *Macbeth*.

The Works

Shakespeare wrote for nearly twenty years, and at the height of his powers could have written as many as two or even three plays a year. He began writing dramas in the late 1580s and of the thirty-eight to forty plays that comprise the Shakespeare canon, thirty-six were published in the First Folio of 1623. Eighteen plays had been published in his lifetime in quarto versions, smaller and cheaper publications than a folio. The earliest quartos were *King Henry VI, King Richard III, Titus Andronicus,* and *Love's Labour's Lost,* followed by *The Comedy of Errors, King Richard II, The Two Gentlemen of Verona,* and *Romeo and Juliet.* Then followed *The Taming of the Shrew, King John, The Merchant of Venice, A Midsummer Night's Dream, All's Well That Ends Well, King Henry IV, The Merry Wives of Windsor, King Henry V, Much Ado About Nothing, As You Like It, Twelfth Night, Julius Caesar, Hamlet, Troilus and Cressida, Othello, Measure for Measure, Macbeth, King Lear, Timon of Athens, Pericles, Antony and Cleopatra, Coriolanus, Cymbeline, The Winter's Tale, The Tempest, King Henry VI,* and *The Two Noble Kinsmen.* Since a company saw no benefit from publishing a play while it was still in production, and since some of these quartos were actually pirated, the order of composition and performance does not often match up with the date of publication. The play *Cardenio,* moreover is claimed by some to exist under a different name (*The Second Maiden's Tragedy*) and by others to exist only in fragments or late adaptations. One must question how one man in a comparatively short period of time wrote so many extraordinary plays. Virginia Woolf may have answered this question when she wrote, "He writes at a speed that is quicker than anybody else's quickest."

CHAPTER 2

The Elizabethan Stage

In order to appreciate both what Shakespeare wrote and why the plays are as brilliant as they are so frequently said to be, it's useful to know something about the Elizabethan stage and how it developed. It is also important to note that Shakespeare and his contemporaries invented what we now consider the first professional, not to mention commercially successful, modern theater. Today's Broadway shows are the direct descendents of the early plays presented in Elizabethan theaters.

Elizabethan Theater in Shakespeare's Time

The plays performed by traveling actors that Shakespeare had seen in Stratford-upon-Avon were far different from what he found upon his arrival in London. The religious pageants and morality plays of the Middle Ages had evolved into full-fledged secular drama. More importantly, London provided the first established spaces especially constructed for playing. It was James Burbage, father to Richard, who opened the first public theater in Shoreditch in 1577. Two important new plays written by university men in 1564 (the year of Shakespeare's birth) were beginning to have an impact on public theater. These were *Ralph Roister Doister* (the first regular comedy in English) and *Gorboduc* (the first regular tragedy in English); blank verse and imaginative stories freed the minds of young playwrights even as an established, reliable playing space spurred on production of new plays.

FACT

Elizabethan audiences cheered at public executions where victims were put to death by hanging. To add more gore to these "death performances," enemies of the Crown were "drawn and quartered," in which the body was sliced open and the entrails put on display. Traitors were beheaded, their heads held aloft by the executioner, then left to rot on pikes as a warning to others who might defy the power of the monarch. Shakespeare's plays had to please these same people. The Globe, in fact, followed the design of a bear-baiting pit.

Drama in England began with folk festivals and religious liturgy. Songs and dances and performances known as "mummings" (the source for the "Mummers Parade" in New Orleans) helped farming communities celebrate the turn of the seasons. Those same people would encounter a higher art in church, in ceremonies like that marked by the tenth-century Quem Queritas tropes. "Quem queritas" means "Whom do you seek," the words spoken by a New Testament angel to the three women who approach the empty tomb on Easter Sunday. In a chanted exchange, different voices continue the story. Though the text was in Latin, dialogue had been born.

Eventually, entire plots drawn from the Bible and set in English were performed inside churches. These began a tradition of plays that were played out in great "cycles" of stories whose scenes would be mounted on pageant wagons brought from town to town. As the performances grew more comic and more sensational, the Church grew nervous and moved the new plays outdoors. Other plays that taught moral lessons moved to inn yards on moving scaffolds. Though the subject matter of these public plays would remain religious, a new direction had been taken. The theater had gone public both in space and in language.

Morality Plays and Mystery Cycles

Though medieval plays clearly foreshadow the future, they also reflected their own times. The players were still amateurs, members of specific trade guilds who volunteered to help with seasonal performances. Shakespeare smilingly acknowledged those actors when he drew the working-class characters of *A Midsummer Night's Dream* who rehearse a play within the play. Bottom is a weaver while other characters are identified by such crafts as tinker (a metal worker), carpenter, and joiner (one who built furniture).

Public morality plays used symbolic characters to get their points across. The characters became known collectively as Vices and Virtues (Hal teasingly calls Falstaff a Vice in *Henry IV*). Players wore costumes which identified them as specific vices and virtues like Pride or Humility, Anger or Temperence. The human protagonists were Everyman or Mankind figures.

At the beginning of the sixteenth century, private performances for noble folk were held in great dining halls lit by tall candles. A curtain ran behind the boards, forming an area hidden from public view where the actors could change costumes and make ready their entrances and exits. They used few props and little scenery and often schoolboys took part. These plays, called *interludes*, reflected a growing interest in nonreligious subject matter among the educated classes.

As the public theater developed throughout the reign of Queen Elizabeth I and went from a traveling entertainment to something housed in a permanent structure, distinctive stories about recognizable characters with sometimes ambiguous purposes and personalities developed.

The Players

Actors, or as they were called, players, were all men, both in the medieval and the Renaissance worlds. Women were forbidden to step on the stage, so boys played women's roles, as in Japenese Kabuki and No theater. Henry VIII's break with the Roman Catholic Church soon made mystery and morality plays illegal, though they may still have been performed in country towns by actors on the verge of becoming professional. Some had probably worked as troubadours and jugglers, dancer, singers, and storytellers. Some had been guild performers who preferred acting to their artisan's craft. Then, in 1573, the Queen passed laws that restricted entertainment and required all players to be licensed, which also meant that all players must be sponsored by a member of either the royal or legal court. The best of the traveling men were organized into companies of players sponsored by lords and other prominent men. Many, like Shakespeare, were the sons of merchants drawn to a new trade, a trade that was also an art. Yet despite the rise of professional acting, actors were generally considered to be among the lowest of the low in society, akin to the cutpurses (thieves), vagabonds, and beggars who worked the theater crowds.

QUESTION?

When were women finally allowed to act?
In 1642, more than twenty-five years after Shakespeare's death, the Puritans shut down the theaters for twenty years; when they reopened during the restoration of the monarchy under King Charles II, women were finally allowed to perform onstage. The first woman appeared on a public stage in 1660.

As the theater developed, Elizabethan actors became skilled in singing, dancing, swordsmanship, throwing knives and axes, juggling, and performing sleight-of-hand tricks. There were no stunt doubles or stand-ins. If a playwright needed a song, a player would sing it. If he needed a thrilling sword fight, there was no fumbling, clumsy jabbing, and poking at arm's length; the players gave the playwright and the audience the real thing—without anyone getting killed. The only other skill one needed in order to become an actor was the ability to memorize lines.

FACT

Journeyman actors were paid about six pennies a day, £6 a year, the typical salary of a guild apprentice. They could earn more while touring and there were occasional bonuses, but only the truly famous actors, men like Richard Burbage and Edward Alleyn could become rich on acting alone. And even they earned much of their income as part owners of the companies they served.

These lines from *Hamlet* re-create what acting troupes were like during Shakespeare's time and what was expected of the actors:

Hamlet: Speak the speech, I pray you, as I pronounced it to you, trippingly on the tongue. But if you mouth it, as many of your players do, I had as lief the town-crier spoke my lines. Nor do not saw the air too much with your hand, thus; but use all gently: for in the very torrent, tempest, and, as I may say, whirlwind of your passion, you must acquire and beget a temperance that may give it smoothness. O, it offends me to the soul to hear a robustious peri-wig-pated fellow tear a passion to tatters, to very rags, to split the ears of the groundlings, who, for the most part, are capable of nothing but inexplicable dumb shows and noise. . . . Pray you, avoid it. . . . Be not too tame neither, but let your own discretion be your tutor. Suit the action to the word, the word to the action, with this special observance, that you o'erstep not the modesty of nature. For anything so overdone is from the purpose of playing, whose end, both at the first and now, was and is, to hold, as 'twere, the mirror up to nature, to show virtue her own feature, scorn her own image, and the very age and body of the time his form and pressure. Now this overdone or come tardy off, though it make the unskilful laugh, cannot but make the judicious grieve, the censure of the which one must in your allowance o'erweigh a whole theatre of others. . . . And let those that play your clowns speak no more than is set down for them; for there be of them that will themselves laugh, to set on some quantity of barren spectators to laugh too, though in the mean time some necessary question of the play be then to be considered. That's villainous, and shows a most pitiful ambition in the fool that uses it.

The Playwrights

The playwrights were sometimes trained at university, as was the very popular Christopher Marlowe. Others, like Shakespeare and Marlowe's roommate Thomas Kyd, had no advanced degrees. Nor did they need them to perfect their art. Books were becoming increasingly accessible. The self-educated playwright could easily obtain a copy of Holinshed's history book, *Chronicles of England, Scotland, and Ireland*, North's translation of the Greek writer-philosopher Plutarch's *Lives of the Noble Greeks and Romans*, Florio's translation of the *Frenchman Montaigne*, and many French and Italian romances that were making their way into England, sometimes in English but also in French and Italian made more accessible by the realities of trade and the need to speak business languages.

Shakespeare was particularly influenced by Golding's translation of the *Metamorphoses*, not to mention translations of the Bible. It's from *Metamorphoses* that Shakespeare found the seeds of *Romeo and Juliet* and *A Midsummer Night's Dream*. He transformed the *Chronicles* not only into history plays like *Richard II* but also into those dark tales of tragedy, *King Lear* and *Macbeth*.

Publishing and Plagiarism

Copyright laws did not exist in Shakespeare's time, and playwrights were free to borrow plots and dialogue from other sources. Dialogue in the three *Henry VI* plays, for example, was borrowed directly from the *Chronicles*. Some of Shakespeare's Roman plays, such as *Julius Caesar* and *Antony and Cleopatra*, reveal their debt to North's translation of Plutarch's *Lives of the Noble Greeks and Romans*. Playwrights thought nothing of wholesale adapting or filching of events, characterization, and even lines from previous works.

As a result, there was no real incentive for acting companies to publish the plays they commissioned until they had stopped acting the play. The versions sold to printers were called *quartos* and about half of Shakespeare's plays were first published this way, sometimes in pirated editions like the Bad Quarto of *Hamlet*. Not until his friend and rival Ben Jonson oversaw the publishing of his own folio of dramas was publishing plays treated with some care and respect.

A number of Shakespeare's contemporaries loom large and occasionally their plays are still performed. In Shakespeare's day, his chief competitors were Christopher Marlowe early in his career, Ben Jonson throughout, and John Webster toward the end. Now considered to be Shakespeare's greatest dramatic rival, Marlowe died in a pub at the age of twenty-nine. Probably the victim of an assassination disguised as a brawl, Marlowe had worked as a spy for the queen. He left behind several famous plays: *Doctor Faustus* (the text of which is corrupted and has to be reassembled by whoever produces it), *Edward II*, *The Jew of Malta*, and *Tamburlaine I* and *II*. Shakespeare laments the death of Marlowe in his comedy *As You Like It*.

Shakespeare's work was popular in his lifetime but not well regarded in the eighteenth century. But from the nineteenth century on, his plays have been an important part of most classical education. His work continues to challenge modern-day actors and directors who strive to find relevance and meaning in the past for contemporary audiences. Shakespeare's knowledge of people combined with his poetic skill made him a great playwright. In building his plays he seldom wrote a speech that did not advance the action, develop a character, or help the imagination of the spectator.

QUESTION?

Why do many of Shakespeare's plots seem far-fetched?
The Elizabethans did not go to the theater to see real life. They wanted to be carried away to other times and places or to a land of fancy. The imaginative reader today loves him for the same reason.

Little Fame, Little Glory

Just as it is today, the actors, not the authors, were the stars that drew the audiences. Usually, playwrights would propose their ideas to the shareholders of a theater. The shareholders, or those like Philip Henslowe who owned theaters outright, might also commission plays on given subjects. The queen could also request certain kinds of plays. It was not uncommon for several writers to write about the same idea and it was not uncommon for two or more authors to work together on the same play. Records show that anywhere from £4 to £8 was paid for a typical Elizabethan play.

Once sold, a play became the property of the company. Authors of successful plays—ones that ran more than the average ten performances per season—might get bonuses. A theater like the Globe provided a good annual profit of several hundred pounds—a comfortable amount for Elizabethans even divided among the shareholders. In order to explain how much wealth an actor or playwright or theatergoer had, many have looked to inflation within the Eliabethan period and the centuries that followed. Our own economy moves so quickly, however, that it is almost impossible to reach a settled exchange rate. Equivalencies are also hard to determine given shifts in economic theory. On the one hand, the average working man made six pennies a day. Entrance to the theater cost one pence, one-sixth a day's wage, One penny also bought six eggs, while six pennies bought a pipe of tobacco. What seems of special interest is that the ordinary man would often have to choose wisely between necessities and luxuries. Nevertheless, more than 30 percent of Lonodoners went to the theater once a week.

The Master of Revels

Anyone involved in the production of plays in Elizabethan England, from the playwright to the theater owners, knew that the Master of Revels was the man to impress—and fear. It was he who auditioned acting troupes, selected the plays they would perform for the court, and controlled the scenery and costumes to be used in each production. During the reign of James I, the Master of Revels reached the apex of his power and had complete authority over both the production and the publication of plays.

The Master of Revels, deputy to the Lord Chamberlain, headed the Revels Office, the department of the royal household responsible for the coordination of theatrical entertainment at court. Performing at court was the goal of every Elizabethan theater company. When the Master of Revels organized an upcoming season of performances he would summon the acting troupes so that they could audition before him and his three subordinate officers. The Master would then choose which companies would perform and which plays they would be allowed to produce. If the Master saw fit, he deleted lines or passages and even requested that entire scenes be inserted into the original material.

FACT

The Master of Revels's power also included issuing licenses to plays destined for public theaters. This power led to a gradual corruption of the office since fees were involved and bribes were inevitably offered. Most importantly, the Master came to function as a public censor, requiring any unsuitable or politically offensive lines to be removed from a play before he would issue a license through the Stationers' Register. Following the English Civil War in 1642, the Puritan government closed all the theaters and the Office of the Revels became useless. It was formally terminated in 1737.

Once the Master of Revels selected the plays to be produced before the royal court, he arranged for all the required costumes and scenery to be created by his own seamstresses and workmen. Much time and money was spent on the elaborate wardrobes, and only the finest fabrics were used.

To Play or Not to Play

As professional theater developed, actors began to be able to support themselves through their craft A large part of this independence was due to the growth of theaters in London, a thriving city nestled against the banks of the River Thames since the days of the Romans. As the sixteenth century drew to a close, ships sailed up the Thames from foreign ports and departed on the turn of the tide as London sent its sons and daughters as far afield as newly colonized Virginia in the New World, while welcoming travelers from all over the known world.

The Effects of War on Shakespeare's Writing

Newly Anglican (i.e., Protestant) London was the capital of a nation at war, engaged in a drawn-out fight with the Catholic Spanish Empire that controlled a great deal of Europe, either directly or by alliance. The Lowlands of the Netherlands (Holland and Flanders) were the battlefields of constant engagements between the armies of Spain and small companies of French and English men who joined with Dutch forces to hold them back.

At sea, meanwhile, Sir Francis Drake and Sir Walter Raleigh were harrying Spanish ships bringing back gold and exotic trade goods from the New World. Although really pirates or privateers, they received a royal blessing from Queen Elizabeth, who turned a blind eye as long as money filled the royal coffers. It all came to a head in 1588, when, with the help of a storm, the English smashed a vastly superior Spanish Armada. The war dragged on, though, and the English lost Calais to the Spanish in 1596. For days, it was said, you could hear the sounds of the cannons as far as London.

Shakespeare wrote a lot about a nation at war or existing in an uneasy peace, during which religious strife and bigotry could result in a treason trial and one's head being stuck on a pike at Traitor's Gate. As the medieval guilds began to flounder, unemployment grew, and beggars and homeless people filled the streets and prisons of towns and cities. A kind of "baby boom" also took place as the country recovered from the ravages of the Black Death over the previous 100 years.

But the riches of the Renaissance began to pour forth, and the notion of being an Englishman was steadily taking hold. This growing pride in nationhood and military might, particularly after the defeat of the Armada, is a key to understanding a lot of Shakespeare's work.

The Queen's Protection

Presiding over the growth of art and drama and maritime adventure was the aging queen. Elizabeth was childless and unmarried; her advancing age and the likelihood that the throne would soon stand empty threatened the peace and security of the nation with potential civil wars or the imposition of foreign potentates. Shakespeare touched all of these anxieties in his plays but did so with sufficient subtlety to avoid royal anger.

Most plays were staged during the daytime and literally could not hide from those come to assess the loyalty of players, playwrights, and audience alike. London's city alderman and constables feared that the theaters would become meeting places for mobs and disaffected groups, as well as dangerous centers of infection in times of plague. Events seemed to justify such concerns: The Earl of Essex and his men attended a performance of *Richard II* as a source of inspiration for their attempted coup against Queen Elizabeth. Unlike Essex, Shakespeare and company suffered no serious harm, though they were forced to remove from production the scene in which Richard hands over his crown to those who came to seize it.

Meanwhile, disease was constantly forcing the theaters to close and the acting troupes to take to the road. The actors were allowed to follow their vocation under sufferance simply because the rich, particularly the queen, demanded their entertainment.

Attacking Moral Purity

The Protestant clergy considered the theater an attack on the moral purity of the populace, particularly the young. In 1583 in his *The Anatomie of Abuses*, religious leader Philip Stubbes declared that far from teaching men and women how to be better people, plays offered instruction in how to lie, cheat, steal, and deceive.

Philip Stubbs said: "If you will learn to jest, laugh and leer, to grin, to nod, and mow [fornicate]; if you will learn to play the vice, to swear, tear, and blaspheme both Heaven and Earth; if you will learn to become a bawd, unclean, and to devirginate maids, to deflower honesty wives; if you will learn to murder, flay, kill, pick, steal, rob, and row."

Most companies consisted of about a dozen or so regular players and were required by law to have the patronage of an aristocrat or member of the law court. That explains company names which range from Lord Leicester's Men to the Admiral's Men. Shakespeare himself joined a troupe called the Lord Chamberlain's Men with acting stars such as Richard Burbage. The troupe was renamed the King's Men when James I came to the throne.

Choice Theaters

In 1576 James Burbage, a former carpenter and then the actor/manager of Lord Leicester's Men, leased a piece of land in Shoreditch, just north of the London city limits, and built the first permanent theater called, appropriately enough, the Theatre. (Burbage's son, Richard, later headed a company of actors with Shakespeare.) A second theater, The Curtain, was built nearby the next year. Building permanent theaters within the London city limits was prohibited.

Other theaters on the south bank of the Thames soon followed, including the Rose and the Swan. Builders of permanent theaters thus continued to avoid the interference of the local authorities, joining other adult entertainments in the Elizabethan equivalent of a "red-light" district. Here you could also find brothels, gambling dens, and bear-baiting arenas

FACT

It was once thought that as people entered the Globe Theatre, they would drop their admission fee into a box, leading to our modern term for the box office at the front of the theater. But in fact, "gatherers" collected fees at the entrances to various levels of the Globe. This was the one job allowed women at the Globe.

In 1598, Richard Burbage lost the lease to his father's theater, which fell into disrepair. In the dead of night, he and his players had to sneak the building timbers off the property before the landowner confiscated them. They dismantled the building, transported it piece by piece across the frozen River Thames, and reassembled it on the south bank of the river and called it the Globe.

Different companies adopted particular theaters as their "homes" even if they toured the countryside and gave performances in the houses of noble patrons. The Blackfriars, for instance, was a small indoor theater that housed a troupe of boy actors, offering highbrow theater for nobles (as did other boy companies) until it was taken over by Shakespeare's King's Men in 1608. This immediately became the company's winter home and then its principal theater when the Globe burned down in 1613. Scholars speculate that some of Shakespeare's later plays, particularly those such as *The Tempest* and *The Winter's Tale,* which called for special effects, may have been composed for the more intimate setting of the Blackfriars, and its richer, perhaps more sophisticated audiences.

Stage Construction

The Globe stage had little scenery, no front curtain to hide the bare stage, and little or no stage machinery for special effects until after they had been acquired for Blackfriars A chorus, or dialogue between characters, established the scene. Entrances and exits were through two doorways to the "tiring house" (a contraction of "attiring house") backstage.

The Stage

The theater was by no means a drab affair. A lack of scenery was compensated for by magnificent costumes. Even if the play was supposed to take place in ancient Egypt (*Antony and Cleopatra*), or some mythical far-off Island Kingdom, the audiences knew that the plays were really about themselves, and so there was little attempt to make the costumes fit the time or style of the setting. Not only did a wealthy company not spend great sums of money on costumes, but theatrical goups also inherited discarded fashions from their wealthy patrons.

FACT

Battle scenes were accompanied by loud bangs and smoke, with braying trumpets sounding the start and announcing the arrival of important characters. Music played a large part in Elizabethan theater, and often incidental music that included jigs and reels and clowning was used, even when the main event was a tragic play such as *King Lear*.

The "dead" were carried off in dramatic flourishes because there was no other way to get the bodies off the stage. Intimate scenes like the murder of Desdemona in *Othello* may have been played in a space behind the central door, covered by a curtain. There might also be an open gallery or balcony high up on the back wall of the stage.

The area in front of the stage was left open to the elements, but a roof covered the rear stage. The exposed underside would sometimes be painted with a moon and stars. A trapdoor in the stage would allow a "ghost," such as in *Macbeth*, to arise, or for the gravediggers to throw up bones in *Hamlet*.

The Audience

Unlike the modern theater, where the expensive seats put you almost on the stage, and certainly near the front of the theater, the "cheap seats" weren't seats at all, but a courtyard open to the sky in front of the stage where the "groundlings" stood. They were a mixed group composed of apprentices and merchants as well as tourists and the stray nobleman. These patrons drank freely and spoke openly during performances. Prostitutes and cutpurses worked the crowd.

The groundlings stood in a rough circle some sixty feet or more in length in front of a stage that stood some five feet off the ground, was about forty feet in width, and had a jettylike piece that jutted into the audience as much as twenty feet or more. The vertical walls of the theater in front of the stage had a number of "boxes," or galleries, that were reached by steep staircases. On a good day, a packed house could have upwards of 3,000 people in the audience.

Given the nature of the audience, we can presume that feedback was instantaneous, with shouts of encouragement and applause for what worked, and boos and rotten fruit and vegetables thrown onstage for what didn't work. The groundlings would have paid a penny, which was roughly one-sixth of a day's wages, to see the play, and they wanted value for their money. The price was six times that for the boxed seats. Due both to terrible inflation at different moments of the sixteenth century as well as to modern changes in economic systems, it is very difficult to establish monetary equivalencies between our world and Shakespeare's. But given that a penny could buy either entrance to the theater or six eggs, it seems that theater attendance was something of an affordable luxury for the working-class citizens of London. Perhaps Shakespeare was thinking of these determined and diverse theatergoers when he wrote in *As You Like It*:

> *All the world's a stage,*
> *And all the men and women are merely players.*
> *They have their exits and entrances,*
> *And one man in his time plays many parts*

CHAPTER 3

Shakespeare's Rivals

Shakespeare was not the first playwright to come to London seeking fame and fortune. By the time he arrived in 1587, Christopher Marlowe had left his studies at Cambridge and was living in London and had already written *Tamburlaine the Great*, a two-part play that was performed the same year and published in 1590. It was this play, filled with gorgeous imagery and powered by a driving character, that won him acclaim from theatergoers as well as accolades from other emerging playwrights.

Christopher Marlowe

Christopher Marlowe (1564–1593), unlike Shakespeare, was a highly educated man. He was, however, the son of a shoemaker. On January 14, 1579, he entered the King's School, Canterbury, as a scholarship student and in 1584 received his Bachelor of Arts degree. He even began study for a master's degree in divinity.

FACT

During the last fifteen years of the sixteenth century, a group of playwrights, whom Victorian critic George Saintsbury named "The University Wits," began writing plays for the popular stage which reflected their classical education. One of the pioneers was John Lyly. Others included Thomas Lodge, George Peele, Christopher Marlowe, Robert Greene, and Thomas Nashe. Only one of the "Wits," Thomas Kyd, though not university-trained, was an important part of this group and wrote the most successful play of the period, *The Spanish Tragedy*.

Christopher Marlowe was not a diligent student at Cambridge. He was known to disappear frequently from his classes and was once imprisoned for a fight. After graduation, he was linked to counterfeiting schemes in the Netherlands. Later he was accused of heresy, a crime punishable by death. Marlowe had joined a group of radical thinkers who speculated about the existence of God. Just beneath the surface of his plays we can find forbidden views on God, authority, and sexuality. But Marlowe's prompt release from prison on bail has supported suspicions that he was also a spy often on "the Queen's business." The fact that he was murdered in a supposed barroom fight while awaiting trial adds fuel to that speculation. Dead men don't talk.

QUOTE

Robert Greene, in his essay, Greenes groats-worth of witte, calls Marlowe a "famous gracer of Tragedians" and reproved him for having said "There is no god."

Marlowe's Playwrighting Career

The young poet, quick of wit and pen, soon found himself associating with playwrights and poets, even adventuring soldiers such as Sir Walter Raleigh. He often frequented the taverns of London with the likes of Robert Greene and Thomas Nashe. His flamboyant appearance and bejeweled costumes soon set him aside from his more traditionally clothed companions.

In a playwrighting career that lasted not much more than six years, Marlowe's achievements were remarkable. He translated Ovid's *Amores* (The Loves) and the first book of Lucan's *Pharsalia* from Latin. He also cowrote the play *Dido, Queen of Carthage* (published in 1594 with Thomas Nashe). His unfinished *Hero and Leander* is considered to be one of the finest examples of nondramatic Elizabethan poetry.

FACT

Scholars are not in agreement about the order of Marlowe's plays after *Tamburlaine*. Many have concluded that *Doctor Faustus* was next, followed by *Edward II* and *The Massacre at Paris*. Marlowe's last play may have been *The Jew of Malta*.

Doctor Faustus is Marlowe's most famous play, as much for its dramatization of a familiar story—a man who makes a contract with the devil—as for its beautiful verse and odd moments of comedy. Unfortunately, it has survived only in a corrupt version. No original manuscript survives, but the play was first published in 1604; another version appeared in 1616. The tragedy Marlowe presented signaled a great departure from medieval morality plays in which an Everyman was tempted.

In 1593, perhaps because of comments attributed to him about discrepancies in the Bible, Marlowe fell under the suspicion of heresy. On May 18, 1593, he was arrested. He was quickly released on bail.

On May 30, 1593, the twenty-nine-year-old poet went to Dame Eleanore Bull's tavern in Deptford to have dinner with some of his beer-drinking friends: Ingram Frizer, Nicholas Skeres, and Robert Poley. Reports later said that there was a quarrel over the bill and that Marlowe slipped a dagger from his waistband sheath and stabbed at Frizer, who defended himself by driving that or his own dagger back into the young poet's eye. Marlowe fell to the floor in agony, blood spurting from the wound, which proved to be fatal.

John Lyly

John Lyly (1554–1606) had his greatest impact on evolving Renaissance prose literature and on the English language itself. He was educated at Magdalen College, Oxford, and went to London in 1576. He first gained recognition with the publication of two prose romances, *Euphues: The Anatomy of Wit* (1578), and *Euphues and His England* (1580). *Euphues* is a story told in letters in which Lyly added discussions on religion and love. His elaborate and flowery style became known as euphuism.

The finest of John Lyly's plays is considered to be *Endimion* (1588), which is still regarded as a literary masterpiece, though not suited to today's dramatic tastes.

FACT

Lyly's popularity waned with the rise of Thomas Kyd, Christopher Marlowe, and William Shakespeare, and his appeals to Queen Elizabeth for financial relief went unheeded. He had hoped to succeed Edmund Tilney in the court post of Master of the Revels, but Tilney outlived him.

Lyly's comedies marked an enormous advance in English drama. Their plots are drawn from classical mythology and legend. While his characters are often engaged in extremely poetic, euphemistic speeches filled with pedantry, the charm and wit of many dialogues, and the skillful construction of the romantic plots set standards that younger dramatists could not ignore.

Thomas Kyd

The details of Thomas Kyd's (1558–1594) life are obscure, though it's known that he shared a room with Christopher Marlowe for a while. He is best known for *The Spanish Tragedy* (1589), which began the tradition of English revenge tragedy. The son of a professional copyist or scrivener, Kyd was educated at the very fine Merchant Taylors School in London. There is no evidence that he attended a university before becoming a writer.

It is not known which company first played *The Spanish Tragedy* nor when, but Lord Strange's company played it sixteen times in 1592, and the Admiral's Men revived it in 1597, as did the Chamberlain's Men. The play became the most popular and influential tragedy of its day and was, early on, even more popular than Shakespeare's plays. It continued to be performed throughout the Elizabethan period. The character Hieronimo in *The Spanish Tragedy* is in many ways a model for Shakespeare's psychological study of *Hamlet*. By 1589, Kyd may even have written a now lost version of *Hamlet*, referred to now as the "*Ur*" or "original" *Hamlet*.

Other plays attributed to Kyd are *Soliman and Perseda* (1592) and *Cornelia* (1594), which was adapted from a French play by Robert Garnier. *Soliman and Perseda* is usually attributed to Kyd as well on the basis of style. Another play sometimes attributed to Kyd is *Arden of Feversham*, a dramatization of a crime that had been reported in 1551. If Kyd is the author of this play he can be considered the founder of middle-class tragedy as well as the revenge play.

Kyd denied the charge of atheism, claiming the offending evidence belonged to his roommate, Christopher Marlowe. He was nevertheless tortured and imprisoned.

Kyd was eventually released from prison but was a broken man who stopped writing plays. He died in poverty in December 1594, not yet thirty-six years old, his debt-ridden estate repudiated by his mother.

Ben Jonson

Ben Jonson (1572–1637) was sometimes Shakespeare's friend but always his rival. Or, rather, Jonson set Shakespeare up as his rival. History would remember him as "the next" greatest playwright of the English Renaissance. His Protestant father, who had been imprisoned and deprived of his estate during the Catholic reign of Mary Tudor, died when he was young. His step-father was a bricklayer. By good fortune, an unkown patron paid for the young Jonson to attend Westminster School. The scholar, Master Camden, recognized Jonson's exceptional literary ability and took the young man under his wing. Though Jonson never received a formal university education, because of Camden's instruction Jonson became one of the most learned men of Elizabethan and Jacobean times, and eventually received honorary degrees from Oxford and Cambridge universities.

His formal education ended early, and at first he followed his stepfather's trade as a bricklayer, then fought with some success with the Protestant English forces in the Netherlands. The Orange Men were defending their religious and political freedom against Catholicism and Spanish rule. The fiery young poet proved to be a formidable soldier. In one incident, he fought a Spaniard in a sword fight, killed him, and then stripped the corpse of its armor. One is reminded of a scene from Homer's *Odyssey*.

He returned to England in 1592, married a woman whom he would later describe as "a shrew, yet honest," and became an actor and playwright, though how good an actor was open to debate. (Good enough to play the leading role of Hieronimo in Kyd's *The Spanish Tragedy* it seems.) By 1597 he was writing plays for Philip Henslowe, London's leading impresario. With one exception (*The Case Is Altered*), these early plays are known only by their titles.

FACT

In 1596, his wife gave birth to a son whom Jonson called his "best piece of poetry." He was devastated when the boy died of the plague at age seven. Jonson plunged himself into the bohemian life of the city, drank a lot, and got into fights.

Rising Above

It was not until 1598 that he wrote *Every Man in His Humour*, a play that established him as a major playwright. Dedicated to Master Camden, *Every Man in His Humour* is a comedic masterpiece that paints a telling portrait of the Elizabethan age. Presented by the Lord Chamberlain's Men, legend has it that Shakespeare himself recommended his friend's play to them.

That same year Jonson got into a quarrel with the actor Gabriel Spencer and in a duel killed the man, though his blade was ten inches shorter than

Spencer's. He was imprisoned and escaped capital punishment by pleading "benefit of clergy"—the ability to read from the Latin Bible. He did not evade all discipline: he was branded on the thumb and his property confiscated.

FACT

In 1606, Jonson and his wife were brought before the consistory court in London to explain why they failed to go to church. He denied that his wife was guilty but admitted that his own religious opinions held him aloof from attendance. The matter was resolved by his agreeing to debate learned men, who might persuade him if they could, to conform to Anglican practices.

Jonson celebrated his release from jail by releasing his new play *Every Man Out of His Humour* (1599) to the stage. It was the longest play ever written for the Elizabethan public theater. The play proved a disaster, and Jonson had to look elsewhere for a theater to present his work. The obvious place was a private theater in which only young boys acted. Jonson added to his fame when he wrote *Cynthia's Revels* (1600) and *Poetaster* (1601).

Jonson made a mark second only to Shakespeare's in the public theater. His comedies *Volpone; or The Foxe* (1606) and *The Alchemist* (1610) were among the most popular and acclaimed plays of the period and are still performed today. Both plays are eloquent, compact, and satirical.

Collaborations

Although constantly quarreling with his fellow playwrights, Jonson collaborated with John Marston and George Chapman on *Eastward Ho!* (1605). Unfortunately, the play contained an unflattering reference to Scottish royalty and the new king, James I (who also ruled Scotland as James VI), took offense. Chapman and Marston were thrown into prison. Honor-bound, Jonson went to prison voluntarily, claiming he too had written the play and shared responsibility for it. In the end, they were spared—perhaps because of the newfound popularity Jonson was beginning to enjoy as a writer of masques for the court. Jonson also won royal attention with his

Entertainment at Althorpe, presented to King James' wife, Queen Anne, as she journeyed to England from Scotland in 1603.

FACT

The Restoration dramatists' (post-1660) use of type names for their characters came directly from what was called "Jonsonian humours." In the late Jacobean and Caroline years, Jonson, Shakespeare, and Francis Beaumont and John Fletcher provided all the models. But it was Jonson, and Jonson alone, who gave the essential impulse to dramatic characterization in comedy of the Restoration and also into the eighteenth and nineteenth centuries.

Jonson's career was coming to a close. In 1625 he wrote the *Twelfth Night* masque for the court but then had to wait five years before the court again asked for his services.

Jonson's Death

In 1628 he suffered what was apparently a stroke and, as a result, was confined to his room and chair, then ultimately to his bed. That same year he was made city chronologer and theoretically responsible for the city's pageants. In 1634 his salary for the post was made into a pension. Jonson died in 1637, just over twenty years after Shakespeare's death, and was buried in Westminster Abbey.

John Marston

John Marston (1575–1634), one of the first Elizabethan satirists, was a playwright who helped pave the way for Jonson's later success. A good definition of a satire is a play where human faults and vices are exposed and made ridiculous. Marston came from a good family and was a gentleman.

In 1605, *Eastward Ho!* got him a jail sentence for insulting the new king, James I. He wrote one other play in 1606, after which he seems to have retired from the theater. Later in Marston's life, he joined the Anglican

Church and took orders. Marston was a great satirist of his time and was in constant competition with Ben Jonson.

Beaumont and Fletcher

Francis Beaumont and John Fletcher worked together in English literature; they collaborated on many plays and they were both asked to append introductory poems to Jonson's *Volpone*.

According to John Aubrey, the notorious seventeenth-century gossip and diarist, the two playwrights "lived together on the Banke side, not far from the Play-house, both batchelors. They lay together . . . had one wench in the house between them . . . the same cloathes and cloake, &c., betweene them."

Of the fifty-four plays with which their names or the names of their other collaborators are associated, Beaumont alone wrote one or two and only nine or ten were Beaumont and Fletcher collaborations.

Scholars have had difficulty determining if either Beaumont or Fletcher had written a particular scene in the plays on which they collaborated, mostly because Beaumont many times revised Fletcher's scenes, and Fletcher edited much of Beaumont's work.

In the three masterpieces of the Beaumont and Fletcher collaboration, *The Maides Tragedy*, *Philaster*, and *A King and No King*, it is thought that Beaumont had the controlling hand, basing the analysis on a more solid structure than Fletcher's other collaborations.

John Fletcher

John Fletcher's (1579–1625) father, Richard Fletcher, was a successful clergyman who became the bishop successively of Bristol, Worcester, and London. He gained the dubious fame as a tormenting prosecutor in the trial of Mary, Queen of Scots, and as the chaplain sternly officiating at her execution.

When not quite twelve years old, Fletcher was accepted to Corpus Christi College, Cambridge, and two years later became a Bible clerk. From the time of his father's death (1596) until 1607 nothing is known of him, although the evidence of his later plays indicates that he did not inherit his father's religious bigotry. Fletcher also became Shakepeare's successor as principal playwright for the King's Men.

After 1613, Fletcher collaborated with or had his plays revised by Philip Massinger, who succeeded him in 1625 as chief playwright. Other collaborators included Nathan Field, William Rowley, and William Shakespeare, who worked with Fletcher on *Henry VIII*, *Two Noble Kinsmen* and, some argue, the lost *Cardenio*. Throughout his career he also wrote plays unaided. In 1625, while the plague raged in London, Fletcher made the mistake of staying in London to be measured for a suit of clothes. He died along with some 40,000 others.

Francis Beaumont

Francis Beaumont (1585–1616) was the son of Francis Beaumont, justice of common pleas in Charnwood Forest, Leicestershire. Beaumont entered Pembroke College, Oxford, in 1597, but on the sudden death of his father left the university without a degree. In November 1600 he entered London's Inner Temple with the intention of picking up his legal studies, but instead began to frequent the Mermaid Tavern.

In 1602 he published a poem, *Salmacis and Hermaphroditus*, a lush rewriting of a poem by Ovid. By 1607 Beaumont and Fletcher began collaborating on plays for the Children of the Queen's Revels and its successor, and then from 1609 until Beaumont's retirement in 1613, mainly for the King's Men at the Globe Theatre and the Blackfriars Theatre.

In 1613 Beaumont married an heiress, Ursula Isley of Sundridge in Kent, and retired from the theater. He died in London in 1616, a month before Shakespeare, and was buried in Westminster Abbey. As a playwright, Beaumont remains a shadowy figure.

John Ford

Because of his disdain for orthodoxy and his sympathetic treatment of unorthodox love, John Ford (1586–1639) is often considered the most modern of Elizabethan and Jacobean dramatists. He first appeared in print with *Fame's Memorial* (1606), a long elegy on the death of the Earl of Devonshire, followed by other occasional pieces before he finally concentrated on drama. His first attempt was likely the writing or revising of *A Bad Beginning Makes a Good Ending*, which was acted by the King's Men at court in 1612, and which was one of the four of Ford's unprinted plays that were accidentally destroyed.

His career as a playwright took off in 1621, when he coauthored *The Witch of Edmonton* with Thomas Dekker and William Rowley. He collaborated with Dekker on several other plays and with John Webster for at least one. After 1624 he worked alone, and his reputation rests chiefly upon his three tragedies of forbidden love, *'Tis Pity She's a Whore*, *The Broken Heart*, and *Love's Sacrifice*.

Thomas Middleton

While still in his teens, Thomas Middleton (1580–1627) published *The Wisdom of Solomon Paraphrased* (1597) and *Micro-Cynicon, Six Snarling Satires* (1599), but didn't graduate from Queen's College, Oxford, until 1598. There is no record of his connection with the theater until May 22, 1602, when producer Henslowe records in his diary a payment made to him together with Munday, Drayton, and Webster "in earnest of a book called *Caesar's Fall.*"

While he sometimes wrote alone, more often he wrote in collaboration with other well-known dramatists, notably Dekker and Rowley. He may have worked with Shakespeare on *Timon of Athens*. Two satirical tales, *The Black Book* and *Father Hubbard's Tale* (1604), show his early interest in the underside of London life, which he was to turn to good account in his comedies of manners written between 1604 and 1611.

The temporary amalgamation of the companies of Princess Elizabeth and Prince Charles in 1614 or so brought Middleton and Rowley together, and their period of collaboration began shortly thereafter. *The Changeling*, the best of Middleton and Rowley's joint efforts, written in 1622 and performed at Whitehall in 1624, was not published until 1653.

Middleton's one unaided tragedy, *Women, Beware Women*, written around 1612, was followed in 1613 by his first masque, *The Triumphs of*

Truth, and until his death he was in demand as a writer of this type of entertainment. Middleton possesses no great poetic gift, but his strengths were in his ability to structure drama and his well-honed dramatic sense.

John Webster

John Webster was the last of the great Jacobean playwrights. Like many of his contemporaries, little of certainty is known of him. He was probably born between 1580–1590 and died between 1525–1534. A John Webster was admitted to the Middle Temple on August 1, 1598, to study law. If this is the dramatist Webster it would explain the legal bent of many of his plays, including trial scenes in *The White Devil, The Devil's Law Case,* and *Appius and Virginia.*

The earliest known records of Webster's employment as a playwright are found in the diary of impresario Philip Henslowe, who noted in 1602 payments to Webster, Anthony Munday, Thomas Middleton, Michael Drayton, "and the rest" for a play titled *Caesar's Fall.* Over the next decade, Henslowe's records show Webster collaborating with Dekker and Heywood, writing a prologue to Marston's *Malcontent,* and composing two masterpieces, *The White Devil* and *The Duchess of Malfi.*

Webster's scope has been criticized as limited, as he wrote mostly about anguish and evil. But his poetry is of a high standard and holds its own with the best of Marlowe and Shakespeare.

T. S. Eliot described Webster as the poet who was "much possessed by death, and saw the skull beneath the skin."

After *The Duchess of Malfi,* Webster lapsed into mostly second-rate work. His death in 1625 marked the decline of the English theater. The stage was filled with mediocre writers such as Glapthorne, Brome, Markham, Suckling, and D'Avenant, reputed to be Shakespeare's illegitimate son. Then in 1642, the Puritans closed the public theaters, and there was darkness.

CHAPTER 4

How to Understand Elizabethan English

The thought of dealing with Shakespeare's work can seem quite daunting and about as accessible as Japanese No theater. More than likely the misperceptions about Shakespeare's language cause the hang-ups— all those old-time "thees" and "thous" and "prithees" and "folderols"—fol-de-what? Let's see if we can decipher the English language usage of the day.

4

Shakespeare's Language

Shakespeare was first a poet, and he quickly learned to use words not only to set up the plot but also to create images that told the playgoer what the characters' inner thoughts were. For example, in *King Richard III*, he writes:

Now is the winter of our discontent/Made glorious summer by this son of York.

Here, Shakespeare is describing the murderous bleakness of the War of the Roses—a civil war between the dukes of Lancaster and York, contenders for the throne of England—as *winter*. The word *discontent* shows the murderous bleakness of the War of the Roses. This long-lasting civil war between the dukes of Lancaster and York vying for the throne of England went on for decades. Thus the term, "winter." That one word conjures up cold, rain, snow, damp, bleakness, hardship, and so on. He then describes the winner of the war at the time of the play's beginning: the Duke of York, as a "son of York." His victory brought about a "glorious summer." The one word, "summer," offers images of warmth, peace, and prosperity, a far contrast of the "winter" it was about to replace.

What's really great about Shakespeare is that he does in two lines of only fifteen words what took several sentences to describe in the preceding paragraph! Reading Shakespeare does take effort, but as you become familiar with his language, you will be better able to make sense of what is being said in his plays.

The Context of Language

Most of us would agree that English has become the universal global language, despite the fact that statistically far more people speak Chinese. But have you stopped to think that the English you speak today would be hard for someone living in Wyoming in 1900 to follow? For instance:

I'm going to the mall to get new software for my computer. I'll pop into a cybercafé while I'm there and check my e-mail because I'm expecting my travel agent to confirm my red-eye flight to London tonight.

Language is all about context. And Shakespeare's language has a context you need to be familiar with in order to make sense of what's going on and why people say and do the things they do in the plays. That's why Shakespeare is sometimes done in modern dress or set in particular periods of modern history.

Shakespeare's English

Many people unfamiliar with the world of William Shakespeare think he wrote and spoke a form of Old English. Old English, however, is actually Anglo-Saxon. Readers now need to learn it as a new language. Chaucer wrote in "Middle English," which is somewhat recognizable but still quite different from our language. Shakespeare actually wrote in what linguists call "Early Modern English," which is remarkably close to the language we use today. In fact, he is credited with inventing words and phrases that are now part of our everyday speech, such as:

- Laughingstock
- Hot-blooded
- Ill-tempered
- Cold-blooded
- Puppy dog
- Eyesore
- Salad days
- Bated breath
- Bag and baggage

And this is to mention but a handful.

It is true that Shakespeare's syntax is not always the "subject-verb-object" sentence structure with which we are now familiar. Some of the words he used are now archaic, and some have changed their meaning.

The plays assume some sort of knowledge of Elizabethan events and history, and they are filled with references to Renaissance learning: Greek and Roman mythology, astrology, alchemy, and the theory of "humours."

Shakespeare was a writer who was aware of words and their meanings, but some of the subtleties of his language are difficult for modern audiences to appreciate because the words have changed meaning. For example, *naughty* now means "badly behaved," but in Shakespeare's time it had a harsher meaning: "wicked."

The Evolution of the English Language

The English language evolved from a combination of sources. Before 1066, Britain was invaded and colonized mainly by Angles, Saxons, and Jutes from Denmark and Germany who overran the Celtic-speaking natives, many of whom fled west to Wales and Ireland, or north to Scotland. Anglo-Saxon was a Germanic-sounding language, and perhaps the most important piece written in it was the epic poem *Beowulf*.

The most astounding change in the English language came when the Norman king, William the Conqueror, defeated King Harold at the battle of Hastings in 1066 and made himself king of England. Those who had lived in England all their lives continued to speak Anglo-Saxon. But the new lords spoke Norman French. Over 300 years later, by 1400, a blending of languages had taken place: thousands of French and Latin words had become absorbed into the Germanic Anglo-Saxon. This created a new language that came to be known as Middle English. Late in the Middle Ages, a linguistic change called "the great vowel shift" ushered in Modern English.

The major change was one of structure. The basis of all modern European romance tongues—French, Italian, and Spanish—is Latin. Word order is not very important in Latin (or Anglo-Saxon) because the words take their meaning from the differing endings or inflections they can have depending on the work they're supposed to do in a sentence.

Middle English became a language that more closely resembles our own in terms of sentence structure. The elements of a sentence (subject, verb, and object) became more dependent on word order than word form. One of the masterpieces of this period was Geoffrey Chaucer's *The Canterbury Tales*. Two hundred years later, by the time Shakespeare was born, English men and women were speaking Early Modern English. Later Modern English, which is essentially what we speak today, dates from about the middle of the seventeenth century. New concepts in grammar and spelling were categorized to make the language uniform. What we now know as "English" has changed little since that time.

QUESTION?

How many words did Shakespeare have in his vocabulary?
By Shakespeare's time, thousands of new words were entering the language from the publication of Greek and Latin texts, as well as from books in Italian, French, and Spanish. Of the approximately 25,000 different words that Shakespeare used in his plays, at least 2,000 of them were ones he either invented or recorded for the first time.

Elizabethan English

Perhaps because English was still in flux, Elizabethans were fascinated with language, even the unschooled, and they delighted in puns. In *Romeo and Juliet* for example, as Mercutio dies he says, "Ask for me tomorrow, and you shall find me a grave man." The pun, of course, is a play on grave, meaning "serious," and grave, meaning "dead." In *King Henry IV, Part II*, the Lord Chief Justice tells off the fat knight Sir John Falstaff, one-time drinking companion of Prince Harry, soon to be King Henry V:

Lord Chief Justice: Your means are very slender, and your waste is great. ("Waste" is a pun on the size of Falstaff's waist, that is, on his being fat. It is also a reference to the fact that he doesn't have much money because he's wasted it on drink, women, and gambling. Falstaff cleverly turns the wordplay around.) Sir John Falstaff: I would it were otherwise; I would my means were greater and my waist slenderer.

So what did Elizabethan English sound like? In Shakespeare's day English was not the Received English of the upper and middle classes that we hear now in many plays and movies, nor the clipped cockney accent of London. Surprisingly, it was probably closer to the accents of northern England, Scotland, and Ireland, and some dialects of the rural eastern and southern parts of the United States. Language experts say that the inhabitants of Ocracoke Island, part of the Outer Banks of North Carolina, which was originally founded by Elizabethan sailors and their families, speak the closest to Elizabethan English to this day.

The reason to recapture the original pronunciation as much as possible is that the lines sometimes make much more sense when spoken in the original dialect. For instance, if you can imagine an Irish accent speaking the following lines from *Julius Caesar* you would not hear Cassius say, "Upon what *meat* doth this our Caesar *feed*, that he hath grown so great." Instead, you might well hear, "Upon what *mate* doth this our Caesar *fade* . . ." and now we have a clever play on words (*mate*, also meaning "friend"; *fade* meaning "of lessening importance").

Playing with Words

In Shakespeare's day, the syntax of the language and grammar itself were still evolving, so some lines need more careful reading than others do. Like many Elizabethans, Shakespeare loved to play with words. Often, reflecting the influence of Latin, his sentences grew long.

New Words, New Meanings

Because of the changes in the structure of language as English developed from Middle English to Modern English, writers were able to invent new uses for words. Shakespeare often used nouns as verbs or adjectives as nouns. But the massive flow of foreign words into the English language during the sixteenth century created a multitude of variations for nearly every word. Shakespeare used this expanded vocabulary to make his language both more precise and more evocative.

In *Love's Labour's Lost* Berowne's ingenious comment "Light, seeking light, doth light of light beguile" plays upon four different senses of *light*—meaning in order: intellect, wisdom, eyesight, and daylight—so the sentence can be interpreted as reading: Wisdom can be as enticing to intellectuals as daylight to a sighted person.

FACT

A lot of words have disappeared from use. For example, who says micher meaning "a petty thief," or slubber meaning "clumsy and messy"? In Chaucer's time nice meant "ignorant" or "licentious"; by Shakespeare's time it meant "precise," as in a "nice distinction." Today it means "pleasant."

Shakespearean Style

Shakespeare also wrote in blank verse, that is, the lines do not have to rhyme. When they do, it is usually to mark the end of a scene, because there were no curtains, and the rhyme itself gave the clue to the audience that they were about to experience a scene change. The plays' language did have a rhythm, commonly called *iambic pentameter*. This is a flashy way of saying that a typical line has five, two-syllable units, with the emphasis on the second syllable. It's considered one of the most successful ways to write poetry that has a natural spoken form.

But Shakespeare also wrote in prose, which he often ascribed to the lower classes and the lowborn, while his kings spoke verse. However, King Lear speaks in prose as he goes mad, and *The Merry Wives of Windsor* is mainly in prose.

Shakespeare also used a lot of metaphors and similes. Writers of the day drew on the Bible, using such phrases as "strong as Samson" or "wicked as Herod." Shakespeare also made comparisons to the widely known Robin Hood and King Arthur stories. Members of the upper-middle-class and nobles sprinkled their speech with references to the Greek and Roman classics, such as "beauteous as Venus" or "bright as Phoebus Apollo." Shakespeare also personified inanimate objects, saying that trees blushed, or seas were angry.

Elizabethan Pronunciation

Because pronunciation is tough, it's great to see and hear the plays before you read them, if you can. Perhaps the most obvious sound is that of the rolled R as in mother. Think of a drawn-out pirate arrgh. In general, try to think Irish, or southern United States. The following list of word pronunciations will give you a flavor of the language as it was spoken.

Father	the long a sounds like a in "favor": F-ay-th-u-rrr.
Want	the a here sounds like the a in "apple."
Make	the a sounds like mek.
Head	eh sounds like the speech of someone from the deep south of the United States, as in haid, or daid for "dead."

I	pronounced (like a 1950s doo-wop singer) in two vowels, as in the u in "cup" and the ee in "bee" (uh-ee). Die becomes "duh-ee," my becomes "muh-ee."
Down	another doo-wop sound, pronounced uh-oo with the oo as in "soon." Think Canadian, as in abuh-oot for "about."
Mercy	the ur sound is pronounced mayor-cy.
Neither	pronounced neigh-ther.
Lord	drawn out oo sound as in "lured."
Cup	a short and rounded o as in "coop."

Thee and *thou* were informal pronouns used to refer to anyone who was your equal and intimate. One is the subject, the other the object of the sentence. For example, "I prithee (a contraction of I pray thee) take a sip," and "thou hast a fair face."

If you're going to enjoy Shakespeare, it's important to see the plays or at least listen to audio tapes of them, not just read them on your own. Plays are tough things to read at the best of times, and while the poetry of Shakespeare will spring from the pages soon enough, it helps to have a visual aid.

Then you will muse, as Shakespeare might, "I have never heard so musical a discord, such sweet thunder."

Name-Calling and Words of Scorn

Name-calling was an art in Shakespeare's day and audiences relished hearing them on the stage, even if the insults were not said in jest. Some of his best lines come from family members insulting other family members. "Thou art a boil, a plague-sore!" Lear screams at his daughter Goneril:

Thou art a boil,
A plague-sore, or embossed carbuncle,
In my corrupted blood.

"Thou toad," the duchess of York yells at her son Richard III. Because of Richard's deformed and twisted body, audiences yelled in agreement, as they did at lines aimed at Falstaff's corpulent body. Instead of just calling Falstaff a fat liar, Prince Hal calls him "A huge hill of flesh," then goes on to say:

A trunk of humours,
that bolting-hutch of beastliness, that swollen parcel
of dropsies, that huge bombard of sack, that stuffed
cloak-bag of guts, that roasted Manningtree ox with the
pudding in his belly.

Just memorize that for your next confrontation with a fat uncle or friend. It would be difficult to respond to this lashing with words. But name-calling was not all that Shakespeare wrote, and one can almost see a smile on Shakespeare's lips as another "putdown" flowed through his pen.

Shakespeare's writing proclaims he was glib of tongue and sharp of wit, and he loved to play with words, even more because there were no rules on how to write English. He could use words to debase speech spoken by another character, such as this line from *Troilus and Cressida*:

If you spend a word with me,
I shall make you bankrupt.

Then there are these terse words of scorn from *The Two Gentlemen of Verona*:

Would the fountain of your mind were clear again,
that I might water an ass at it.

All said, it would be best not to debate with Shakespeare.

Sexual Ribaldry

What made an Elizabethan audience laugh? A tour of Shakespeare's anatomical humor would do the trick. This from *The Comedy of Errors*:

"She is spherical, like a globe. I could find countries in her."
"In what part of her body stand Ireland?"
"Sir, in her buttocks. I found it out by the bogs."
"Where stood Belgia, the Netherlands?"
"Oh, sir, I did not look so low."

Belgia is Shakespeare's pun on "belly," and *bogs* was slang for "buttocks." In *The Taming of the Shrew*, which has a plethora of sexual banter, we find these lines:

"Who knows where a wasp does wear his sting? In his tail?"
"In his tongue."
"Whose tongue?"
"Yours, if you talk of tails, and so farewell."
"What, with my tongue in your tail."

Even Shakespeare's name, William, had many sexual connotations. "Will" could mean sexual desire and was simultaneously a pun for male and female sexual organs as well as a reference to his own name. Obviously, "Will," was one of his favorite words.

Shakespeare could be bawdy, sometimes vulgar, many times pushing the bounds of good taste, as attested to by these locker-room words.

Arise	an erection
Die	to have a sexual orgasm
Cork	penis, but it also meant God
Cod	another word referring to the male organ
Thing	penis, as in this line from *As You Like It*: "Why then, can one desire too much of a good thing?"
Quaint	Female genitalia
Count	numbers or a pun on female genitalia
Nothing	female genitalia, as used in these lines from *Hamlet*: Hamlet: "That is fair thought to lie between a maid's legs." Ophelia: "What my Lord?" Hamlet: "Nothing."
Hell	also used as a term for female genitalia

Then there is this sexual innuendo from *Othello* when referring to the sex act: "A beast with two backs."

Shakespeare's Soliloquies

A soliloquy is a speech, somewhat like an aside, revealing a character's thoughts. These long speeches gave the character a chance to strut and fret his time upon the stage—and then be heard some more. Hamlet's "To be, or not to be" soliloquy is the most famous line in theater, followed by Juliet's mournful cry of, "O Romeo, Romeo! Wherefore art thou Romeo." Third is Macbeth's: "To-morrow, and to-morrow, and to-morrow . . ." Then there is Shylock's deeply penetrating soliloquy in *The Merchant of Venice*. Let's take a look Hamlet's showstopper soliloquy first:

> *To be, or not to be: that is the question:*
> *Whether 't is nobler in the mind to suffer*
> *The slings and arrows of outrageous fortune,*
> *Or to take arms against a sea of troubles,*
> *And by opposing end them? To die: to sleep:*
> *No more; and by a sleep to say we end*
> *The heartache and the thousand natural shocks*
> *That flesh is heir to,—'t is a consummation*
> *Devoutly to be wish'd. To die, to sleep;*
> *To sleep: perchance to dream: ay, there's the rub:*
> *For in that sleep of death what dreams may come,*
> *When we have shuffled off this mortal coil,*
> *Must give us pause: there's the respect*
> *That makes calamity of so long life;*
> *For who would bear the whips and scorns of time,*
> *The oppressor's wrong, the proud man's contumely,*
> *The pangs of despised love, the law's delay,*
> *The insolence of office and the spurns*
> *That patient merit of the unworthy takes,*
> *When he himself might his quietus make*
> *With a bare bodkin? who would fardels bear,*
> *To grunt and sweat under a weary life,*
> *But that the dread of something after death,*
> *The undiscover'd country from whose bourn*
> *No traveller returns, puzzles the will*

And makes us rather bear those ills we have
Than fly to others that we know not of?
Thus conscience does make cowards of us all;
And thus the native hue of resolution
Is sicklied o'er with the pale cast of thought,
And enterprises of great pith and moment
With this regard their currents turn awry,
And lose the name of action.

From *Macbeth* we find these famous lines; no doubt, the most memorized speech in Shakespeare:

To-morrow, and to-morrow, and to-morrow,
Creeps in this petty pace from day to day
To the last syllable of recorded time,
And all our yesterdays have lighted fools
The way to dusty death. Out, out, brief candle!
Life 's but a walking shadow, a poor player
That struts and frets his hour upon the stage
And then is heard no more: it is a tale
Told by an idiot, full of sound and fury,
Signifying nothing.

Shylock, a Jewish moneylender in Venice was a challenging character for Elizabethans. Shylock has some intriguing speeches in *The Merchant of Venice* about the way that he is mistreated. He has given us one of the great statements that define humanity:

Hath not a Jew eyes?
Hath not a Jew hands, organs, dimensions, senses,
affections, passions; fed with the same food, hurt with
the same weapons, subject to the same diseases,
healed by the same means, warmed and cooled by the
same winter and summer as a Christian is?
If you prick us do we not bleed?
If you tickle us do we not laugh? If you poison us do we not die?

Tragic Mirth

Shakespeare realized that tragedy could wear down an audience, so he would add a humorous scene to lighten up the heavy darkness. It's as if he said to himself, "It's time to give the audience a break." He created humorous scenes in most of his tragedies, such as the nurse's ribald comments in *Romeo and Juliet*, and the country bumpkin who breaks up the tension in *Antony and Cleopatra*. Then there is the "Alas, poor Yorick!" scene from *Hamlet* when Hamlet is in the graveyard with his friend, Horatio, and discovers a skull, holds it up, and contemplates it:

> *Alas, poor Yorick! I knew him, Horatio: a fellow of infinite jest, of*
> *most excellent fancy. He hath borne me on his back a thousand*
> *times; and now, how abhorred in my imagination it is! my gorge*
> *rises at it. Here hung those lips that I have kissed I know not how oft.*
> *Where be your gibes now; your gambols, your songs?*
> *your flashes of merriment, that were wont to set the table on a roar?*
> *Not one now, to mock your own grinning? Quite chap-fallen?*
> *Now get you to my lady's chamber, and tell her, let her paint an inch*
> *thick, to this favour she must come*

The most famous of Shakespeare's humorous scenes occurs in *Macbeth* after Macbeth has killed the king. There is a jarring knock on the castle door and a drunken Porter enters. After delivering a chillingly comic soliloquy, the Porter opens the door. His character's salty humor and sexual innuendoes lighten the tragic event that has just occurred.

> *MacDuff:* "*What three things does drink especially provoke?*"
> *Porter:* "*Marry, sir, nose-painting, sleep and urine.*
> *Lechery, sir, it provokes and unprovokes;*
> *It provokes the desire but it takes away the performance.*"

Elizabethan Vocabulary

It helps to be familiar with several vocabulary words when reading or listening to Shakespeare. The following is a list of some of the more common Elizabethan words and their definitions.

Anon	until later
Arise (as a pun)	stand up or to get an erection
Aroint	away
Aside	a short speech revealing the character's innermost thought, spoken directly to the audience
Aye/yea	yes
Banns	notice of intent to marry
Beef	meat or prostitute
Broadside	a sheet of paper printed on one side often used for proclamations and ballads
Certes!	certainly!
Cousin	friend
Dear	significant or expensive
E'en	evening
Enow	enough
Fare-thee-well	goodbye
Fie	a curse
Fond	foolish
Get	to create or bring into existence
Grammarcy	thank you
Green	inexperienced or a color or virility
Head	army or source
Hello!	not a greeting, but an exclamation of surprise
Jade	jewel or prostitute
Marry	a mild curse contracted from "by the Virgin Mary"
Mayhap/perchance/belike	maybe
Morrow	day
Nay	no
Ne'er	never
Nice	trifling or silly
Oft	often
Poppet	a doll or child
Prithee/pray	please
Privy, jakes, or ajax	bathroom or john
Rub	to strike against something or an obstacle
Sad	serious

Sonnet	a fourteen-line poem with an iambic pentameter
Stay	to wait
Still	always
Sweeting	a term of endearment
Ta'en	short form of taken or mistaken for
Tell	to count
Thane	a Scottish earl
Verily	very or truly
Wherefore	why

How to Curse in Shakespeare

Do you find yourself using curse words too often? Can't think of any alternatives? You're still stuck in Anglo-Saxon times. Be modern: Think Elizabethan English. To create your own curses, memorize some choice terms from the following list, two adjectives and a noun minimum per curse, please. Shakespeare must have had great fun blending these words. You can use the curses as written in each line or mix them up. For example, try "Thou bawdy bat-fowled barnacle," or to sound more modern, try "You surly sheep-biting puttock."

Combine words from each of the three columns below.

ADJECTIVE	ADJECTIVE	NOUN
artless	base-court	apple-john
bawdy	bat-fowling	baggage
beslubbering	beef-witted	barnacle
bootless	beetle-headed	bladder
churlish	boil-brained	boar-pig
clouted	clay-brained	bum-bailey
cockered	clapper-clawed	bugbear
craven	common-kissing	canker-blossom
currish	crook-pated	clack-dish
dankish	dismal-dreaming	clotpole
errant	dread-bolted	death-token
fawning	earth-vexing	dewberry
fobbing	elf-skinned	flap-dragon

frothy	fen-sucked	flirt-gill
froward	fat-kidneyed	flax-wench
gleeking	flap-mouthed	foot-licker
goatish	fly-bitten	fustilarian
gorbellied	folly-fallen	giglet
infectious	full-gorged	haggard
loggerheaded	half-faced	hedge-pig
lumpish	hasty-witted	horn-beast
mammering	hedge-born	hugger-mugger
mangled	hell-hated	joithead
mewling	idle-headed	lewdster
paunchy	ill-breeding	lout
pribbling	ill-nurtured	maggot-pie
puking	knotty-pated	malt-worm
puny	milk-livered	mammet
rank	onion-eyed	minnow
reeky	plume-plucked	miscreant
roguish	pottle-deep	moldwarp
ruttish	pox-marked	mumble-news
saucy	reeling-ripe	nut-hook
spleeny	rough-hewn	pigeon-egg
spongy	rude-growing	pignut
surly	rump-fed	pumpion
tottering	shard-borne	puttock
unmuzzled	sheep-biting	rascal
vain	spur-galled	ratsbane
venomed	swag-bellied	scut
villainous	tardy-gaited	skainsmate
warped	tickle-brained	strumpet
wayward	toad-spotted	varlot
whoreson	wart-necked	vassal
weedy	unchin-snouted	whey-face
yeasty	weather-bitten	wagtail

Need more? Look up Shakespearean insults on the Internet. Or you can always read Shakespeare's plays and then make them up.

CHAPTER 5

Scenes from Elizabethan Life

What follows are thumbnail sketches of everyday life in Shakespeare's England that offer you a better sense of what the world was like during his time. Knowing what coins were used, how beggars were treated, and so forth will provide a context in which to appreciate Shakespeare's brilliance in finding the timeless universal elements in what would have been familiar to contemporary audiences.

Servants and Masters

Each wealthy household had servants, butlers, and stewards as status symbols of their class standing and to provide comfort for the master and mistress of the house. Male servants were called serving men; women, serving maids. The term valet, or simply man, came into use about 1567. In *Romeo and Juliet* Benvolio refers to Romeo's personal servant as "his man." As the master of the house, it was undignified to do almost anything for oneself, even lighting your pipe (as long as the servant was nearby).

Servants used their wits to rise in the world, to create an even better place for them and their children. A kitchen helper might aspire to become a butler in a great house. Servants were generally not paid a weekly or monthly wage, but they expected *vails* (tips) or *douceurs* (sweeteners) for their services. A good master was paternalistic but stern. His superior station was God-given.

Rules of Working in a Great House

This list of "rules" comes from *A Book of Orders and Rules*, written by Sir Sibbald David Scott in 1595.

A servant must not be absent from morning or evening meals or prayers lest he be fined two pence for each time.

Any man waiting table without a trencher (small tray) in his hand, except for good excuse, will be fined one penny.

For each oath, a servant will be fined a penny.

Any man provoking another to strike or striking another will be liable to dismissal.

For a dirty shirt on Sunday or a missing button, the fine will be sixpence.

After 8:00 A.M. no bed must be found unmade and no fireplace or candle box left uncleaned, or the fine will be one penny.

The hall must be cleaned in an hour.

The whole house must be swept and dusted each Friday.

Any man leaving a door open that he found shut will be fined one penny unless he can show good cause.

Patronage

As we've seen previously, young men sought patrons for their advancement. Nobles drew gentlemen like honey attracts flies, creating a feudal relationship based on personal loyalty, gifts, and favors. Some of the gentry put their sons into great homes for their education and advancement.

Nobles, or lords, maintained retainers or personal attendants, some of whom acted as bodyguards. To see that they had work to do they were also given household positions, such as gentleman or yeoman.

A noblewoman drew her cortege from relatives and the daughters of the gentry. Her gentlewomen joined her in sewing, minding the children, dispensing charity in the neighborhood, and taking charge of her clothing and jewelry. If the noblewoman felt a young unmarried girl from a good family was worthy of her help, she would find a suitable marriage.

Military Life

It was known as "taking the Queen's shilling," the payment offered by a recruiting officer to entice a young man to enlist in the army. Newly recruited soldiers received this first payment—"the Queen's shilling"—not always from the recruiter's hand, but by tradition, sunk at the bottom of a tankard of ale. Once the recruit drank the ale, he was committed to serving and received a uniform (the cost of which was usually deducted from his pay), took an oath to the Queen, and then with little training went off to fight overseas. Life expectancy was short.

Lord Mountjoy, Queen Elizabeth's general in Ireland, in 1601 commented on the mortality rate of his soldiers: "It has ever been seen that more than three parts of the four of these [men] do never return."

Foreigners and Travel

During Elizabeth's reign, partly because of the frequent armed skirmishes taking place in Europe, England became wary of foreigners. As a result, unless they were in the armed forces, young people were discouraged from going abroad. The truth is, only the wealthy could afford to travel anyway. A poor person worked as a servant, or on the land, or became a bandit or beggar.

Yet, ironically, during the last twenty years of Elizabeth's reign, the number of soldiers engaged in military service meant that more Englishmen traveled overseas than ever before.

FACT

Italy, especially, was off limits—because the pope, a powerful political figure at this time, lived there and because Catholicism was considered to be heretically infectious. Young men could lose their inheritance and social standing and come under serious official scrutiny just for traveling to Italy.

Selected for Service

When recruits were urgently needed, men were conscripted, or "pressed," often against their will. In *King Henry IV, Part I*, Falstaff describes the tricks he used to get extra money from those he pressed:

> *I press me none but good householders, yeomen's sons, inquire me out*
> contracted bachelors, such as had been asked twice of the banns—such a
> commodity of warm slaves as had as lief hear the devil as a drum . . . and they
> have bought out their services.

In other words, he pressed only those who were willing to bribe him to let them go—ending up with the leftovers, a group of such "scarecrows" that he is ashamed to be seen with them.

All men between the ages of sixteen and sixty were eligible to serve and had to appear at musters in town squares, on village greens, and at other places, where unlucky individuals would be selected for service. Moreover, many of these men were used as "food for powder," as Falstaff put it (*King Henry IV, Part I*). Only about 20 percent of the army was trained. The rest were simply given equipment and had to learn how to be a soldier while in the field.

The Nature of Warfare

The medieval feudal system was breaking down, and the development of gunpowder ushered in a new era of warfare. The maces and lances of knights in armor and longbows and crossbows of archers gave way to the more accurate cannons and mortars and ranks of soldiers wielding fuse-lit muskets and small arms, which changed the nature of warfare.

Many experienced soldiers were reluctant to give up their bows, partly because the technology of gunpowder weaponry was still in its infancy. Guns often exploded after being fired a few times because of poor metal-working, and the stress and heat caused compressed explosions inside the breech. For good reason, many soldiers took to turning their heads away while firing, thus missing their targets. It was much easier to train musketeers than bowmen, although a bow could be more accurate in the hands of an expert.

Country Life

In Shakespeare's day, much of England was still an agrarian society, but the medieval feudal system had finally begun to fade away. The comic image in *Monty Python and the Holy Grail* of peasants spending their days grubbing about in the mud and dung heaps is an exaggeration of what it was like to be poor in Elizabethan times, but it makes a point worth remembering. Country life was a hard life. Technically, anyone who worked the land was a "peasant," but though many farmers lived off land they didn't own, by Shakespeare's day, many other peasants had become landowners themselves.

Those who worked the land for others were totally at the whim and mercy of their betters. They "knew their place" in the social order and were grateful for what they had. Peasants were given a scrawny piece of land on which to build their one- or two-room shacks and to scratch out a subsistence level of living from their own crops and animals.

In exchange for having a place of their own, a tenant farmer worked on the owner's land at least three days a week. An overseer made sure the farmer and his family did everything right. The rest of the time, the peasant worked on his own land, banding together with other families to cope with big jobs such as bringing in the harvest and hay making. Women and children helped, though they often worked indoors cooking, cleaning, and taking care of babies.

FACT

At harvest time, the owner received a portion of a tenant's crops. If the crops failed, everyone starved. If the peasant needed to grind his grain, he did it at the owner's mill, leaving behind a portion for the owner. If he needed to bake his bread, he could use the owner's ovens if he left behind a loaf or two of bread.

Those who worked the land for others were on the lower rung of the social ladder. Few, if any, were literate. They could not marry or travel without the landlord's permission, and they were expected to return home if they did travel. Of course, they could leave the estate for good whenever they wanted, but how could they make a living without land? Besides, travel was dangerous. There were few roads, particularly through the forests that still covered much of the countryside, and virtually no organized police force of any description, so if a thief stole from them or beat them, chances are nobody would help.

Except for Sundays and Holy Days, tenant farmers worked long and hard in the fields, regardless of the weather. At different times throughout the sixteenth century, members of such families often didn't have enough food to feed themselves, so it shouldn't be a surprise to learn that unlanded peasants typically lived only into their thirties. Diseases were many, and medicine was rudimentary and expensive. Babies and children often died.

Tenant farmers had only two legitimate ways to gain their independence: save enough money to buy their own piece of land or marry a property owner, but only with the landowner's permission, and there was no guarantee he would give it.

Town Life

In exchange for an annual tax, townsfolk received a royal charter that allowed them to govern themselves. Once chartered, they were able to make their own laws, form trade guilds, and raise taxes. In most towns the people elected a mayor or bailiff and a local council to govern them.

The streets of the town, which were often noisy, chaotic places during the day, were filled with bustle and business. Tradesmen cried their wares at markets as they wandered through the streets. Here are some examples of town life, recorded in *Street Cries* by composor Orlando Gibbons (1583–1625):

"Buy any ink, will you buy any pens, very fine writing ink, will you buy any ink?"

"I ha' ripe peascods, ripe. Ripe damsons, fine ripe damsons. Hard garlic, hard. Fine potatoes, fine."

"What is't ye lack? Fine wrought shirts or smocks. Perfumed waistcoats, fine bone lace or edgings, sweet gloves, silk garters, very fine silk garters, fine combs or glasses. Old doublets, ha' ye any old doublets?"

"Ha' ye any corns on your feet or toes? Will ye buy any starch for a clear complexion, mistress?"

"Ha' ye any rats or mice to kill?"

Merchants and Craftsmen

The growing middle class was composed of merchants and craftsmen who were freemen and generally had a more comfortable life than country peasants. Merchants tended to be either traders or factory owners (craftsmen). Merchants traded with other merchants both at home and abroad and often owned their own ships. Many hired mercenary soldiers to protect the goods that were being shipped.

It was particularly important that the craftsmen douse any fires they used during the day, because houses were made from wood and plaster and were so packed together in narrow streets that if a house caught fire it was almost guaranteed that large parts of the town would burn, too.

Craftsmen deliberately set up shop in towns so that they could take advantage of the population's needs. Their houses were usually fair sized, sometimes two to three stories, and craftsmen often worked at windows that opened onto the street, giving them the chance to show off their skills to passersby, as well as to get the best light to work by. Crafts included confectioner, blacksmith, shoemaker, button-maker, box-maker, and soap-boiler.

Markets were held once or twice a week in the town square. They were always crowded, busy, noisy, smelly, and dirty, with people shouting, pushing, and generally hustling "for a penny" among the wooden stalls and carts displaying wares. At sunset, town bells tolled a curfew. Everyone finished their business and went home.

Entertainment

There was little in the way of entertainment besides drinking in pubs and alehouses and gambling, often at bear-baiting or cockfights, or some other kind of blood sport. Town fairs were held once or twice a year and were filled with contests, sports, and games. Early in the sixteenth century, guilds sometimes staged plays. Peasants needed their master's permission to attend any of these entertainments.

Merchants and craftsmen came from far and wide to sell their goods at these fairs. Jugglers, dancers, acrobats, and minstrels would wander through the crowds or set up a booth. The minstrels, in particular, wandered from town to town strumming a guitar, lute, or a viol, singing ballads and telling stories such as the legend of Robin Hood, the outlaw of Sherwood Forest.

Towns also competed with each other on Sunday afternoons with games such as bladder ball (an early form of soccer), rounders (somewhat like baseball), archery, wrestling, and so forth. Nobles played real tennis, an indoor sport, and battledores and shuttlecocks (a game similar to badminton), and also engaged in fencing and horse riding.

Guilds

In medieval times, rather like farm workers during harvest in the countryside, town merchants and craftsmen decided they could improve their lot by working together rather than separately. They banded together, forming unions called guilds. If you were a member of a guild you were able to vote for the head of the guild, who would serve a limited term in office. Guilds were important in local economies, maintaining product quality and industry standards. They also formed the basis of political power, and potentially, a guild leader could abuse that power. The guild system had begun to fray by Shakespeare's day but survived the early days of English capitalism.

Guilds were divided into hierarchies with masters at the top, journeymen in the middle, and apprentices at the bottom. A boy in his early teens would often be apprenticed to a master, who would be paid by the boy's family to care for him and educate him in his trade.

After seven or eight years the young man would rise to the rank of journeyman and receive a wage. After a journeyman acquired sufficient experience, he would create a "masterpiece," the best work of his craft, which would be judged by other masters within his guild. If the piece won their approval, he joined the ranks of Guild Master.

Few guilds included women, although there was a guild of laundresses. In London, there was a law called the Widow's Law that stated if a guild member died, his widow could take his place as long as she employed a journeyman to do her husband's work and split the profits with him.

The Urban Poor

The number of urban poor had been increasing before Elizabeth's reign and kept increasing during it. The trend toward enclosure or private ownership of what was previously considered common farmland forced many country people to turn to begging for their livelihood.

By Shakespeare's time, a large shifting population of landless unemployed men and women lived in London. These "masterless men" threatened the stability of society. They had no place in the social order and were the most likely to commit crimes to survive. Soldiers fortunate enough to return home from fighting overseas, but unlucky enough to be injured and unable to work, invariably became beggars on crutches.

FACT

The rural poor consisted mainly of widows and children who did not have the means to support themselves, as well as landless laborers, often unemployed in the winter once the harvests were done. Passing vagrants were likely to be ignored or persecuted for fear that they might squander the charity of the community or commit crimes.

By the last decade of Elizabeth's reign, the booming English economy was in decline and crime and vagrancy worsened. Poor harvests, outbreaks of the plague, and other ills caused agricultural prices to rise while wages plummeted. Nearly 80 percent of the English population fell below the subsistence level. Church and government aid was meager. Laws criminalized poverty, and the poor were punished brutally for the often desperate acts they committed to stay alive.

In the towns, the poor were considered a public nuisance, a potential threat to public welfare, and a burden on the greater community. Local authorities often tried to curb the practice of begging and discouraged the establishment of tenements—houses divided into many small suites to be rented to poor individuals or families.

Coins and Money

The values of the many different types of coins changed depending on the value of the metal used to make them. When the coinage was "debased," that is, when the amount of gold or silver in the coin was reduced, the value of the coin itself was reduced.

Halfpennies (pronounced "hay-pennies") and farthings were made of brass, lead, and occasionally even leather. Some merchants issued tokens that were redeemable as payment for goods and services by themselves and other merchants, though certainly not by all.

Value of the Coins

The following are some Elizabethan denominations with approximate current U.S. dollar equivalents. The translation of money values is a tricky subject, and while we can think of a penny then as being close to a dollar today, in truth it varied dramatically. At different times it could be worth only fifty cents or as much as $5 or more, depending on the variations of precious metals used to cast the coin (combinations of either brass, copper, silver, or gold), economic ups and downs, and a proportional value defined by the cost of goods and services against wages earned. It is important to remember that even if we say that a penny would now equal more than a dollar-and-a-half, in Shakespeare's day that same penny was one-sixth of a journeyman's daily wage.

MONETARY UNIT	EQUIVALENT IN U.S. DOLLARS
Farthing	$.40
Halfpenny piece	$.80
Three farthing piece	$1.20
Penny	$1.66
Half groat	$3.30
Three penny piece	$5.00
Groat	$6.60
Sixpence	$10.00
Shilling	$20.00
Half Crown	$50.00
Crown	$100.00
Angel	$140.00 to $200.00
Noble	$140.00 to $200.00
Royal	$200.00 to $280.00
£1 (pound)	$400.00
Sovereign	$400.00

The Cost of Living

Here is a soldier's shopping list (based on a Tudor soldier's food allowance):

24 oz. wheat bread: 1 penny

2/3 gallon beer: 1 penny

2 lbs. beef or mutton (cod or herring on Fridays): two pence (tuppence)
1/2 lb. butter: one and a half pence (penny hay-penny)
1 lb. cheese: one and a half pence
Total: seven pence

Average wages:

- Skilled workers could earn sixpence a day (sometimes as much as a shilling).
- Actors were paid a skilled worker's wages.
- Some apprentices received food, drink, and lodging. If they did, they earned less.
- Farm workers got maybe thruppence (three pennies) a day; women were paid less.
- Permanent household servants were paid annually, with board and food included—often no more than six shillings a year, or sixpence a week.

QUESTION?

How much were playwrights paid?
Playwright/producer Philip Henslowe was paid £3 to £5 for a play; on a good day his gross gate for a performance of a new play would be more than £3. On November 28, 1595, he took in £4 6s for the first performance of *Harey the V—The Famous Victories of King Henry V.* Shakespeare was no doubt paid up to £5 for writing a play, plus his percentage as a sharer.

The Cost of the Theater

Fees for attendance at a theater were:

- The lords' room: one shilling (twelve pence)
- The gentlemen's rooms: six pence
- The galleries: two pence (with cushion)
- The pit (for the groundlings): one penny

The cheapest seats in the private theaters were usually six pence, thus effectively excluding all but relatively wealthy patrons.

Outsiders

In 1290, Edward I expelled the Jews from England. In 1492, the Jews were expelled from Spain. Even though Jews had long been barred from England, anti-Semitism was still alive during Shakespeare's time, a hundred years later. Some ethnic groups were also abused simply because of the color of their skin and their minority status. The following offers brief descriptions of two minority groups—Jews and blacks. It can be noted that these two groups were portrayed in Shakespeare's plays.

Jews

Even after Edward I expelled them from England, a few Jews remained, though they could not publicly practice their faith. Dr. Rodrigo Lopez, the personal physician to Queen Elizabeth, was such a "New Christian." Yet in 1593 he was condemned to death for treason. Queen Elizabeth did not believe that Lopez was guilty, but she did nothing to prevent the execution. Lopez's trial instigated a new wave of anti-Semitism.

Other great cities, such as Amsterdam and Venice, allowed openly practicing Jews to remain, though they were forced to live in ghettos. Because they were banned from almost all kind of work, and because the Christian churches banned their followers from charging interest on loans, they flourished as moneylenders.

The vagaries of rising capitalism made banning the practice impractical and in Shakepeare's day, charging interest became a common business practice.

Blacks

There were few blacks living in London before Shakespeare's time. Then slave ships passing through London en route to the new colonies of America or the Caribbean islands stopped to take aboard provisions for the long trip across the Atlantic. Many blacks were sold to rich homes in

London, to become "exotic" servants, or sold to work in the brothels. Because they were few, they did not arouse prejudice. Rather they were treated as a curiosity. But, because the color black was associated with ugliness, savagery, even sin, they were also portrayed that way as characters in the theater, like Aaron in *Titus Andronicus*.

In this gore-splashed revenge tragedy, however, Aaron is less brutal than the murderous characters around him. Shakespeare even makes him capable of affection, highlighting the feelings Aaron shows for his infant son.

In *Othello,* Shakespeare refers to Othello as a Moor, a mysterious Muslim people from Africa who also settled in Spain. Roderigo's description of Othello having "thick lips" points toward that African rather than Arab origin. The word *Moor* itself comes from the country "Mauritania" but was used by Elizabethans to describe those from North and West Africa, as well as any Muslim. In 1601, after traders from North Africa had begun dealing in England, Queen Elizabeth expelled all Moors from the country.

What is remarkable is that Shakespeare chose to make Othello, a black man, the protagonist of one of his great tragedies. The play treats him sympathetically even when he is goaded by Iago to kill his wife, the love of his life.

CHAPTER 6

Shakespeare in Stratford-upon-Avon

If William Shakespeare left Anne for London when he was twenty-three, she would have been thirty-one. Susanna, their first child, would have been five, the twins, Judith and Hamnet, only two. We know nothing about the affection William and Anne had for each other, although the difference in age must have concerned Anne. The young playwright certainly had the freedom for romantic liaisons in London. Shakespeare may have alluded to his marriage and feelings for Anne when he wrote in *A Midsummer Night's Dream*, "The course of true love never did run smooth; / But either it was different in blood . . . / Or else misgraffed in respect of years—"

Shakespeare's Greatest Period of Writing

In 1611 Shakespeare, after a flurry of writing, which has been termed his greatest period, left London. In that ten-year period from 1599 to 1609, he wrote *Twelfth Night, Troilus and Cressida, Hamlet, Othello, Measure for Measure, King Lear, Macbeth, Coriolanus,* and *Anthony and Cleopatra.* His last works, written between 1609 and 1613 were *Pericles, Cymbeline, The Winter's Tale,* and *The Tempest.* It was then, his fingers blackened over the years from continually dipping a quill pen in the inkpot, that Shakespeare retired from the theater.

Hamnet Shakespeare's Death

In 1596, fifteen years before Shakespeare left London, Hamnet Shakespeare died. He was eleven years old. The reason is unknown, but we can safely assume that Shakespeare grieved deeply for his only male heir. The lines spoken by Constance in *King John*, which the playwright wrote the following year, no doubt referred to Shakespeare's anguish at losing his only son:

> *Grief fills the room up of my absent child,*
> *Lies in his bed, walks up and down with me,*
> *Puts on his pretty looks, repeats his words,*
> *Remembers me of all his gracious parts,*
> *Stuffs out his vacant garments with his form;*
> *Then have I reason to be fond of grief.*
> *Fare you well. Had you such a loss as I,*
> *I could give better comfort than you do.*

Some critics have suggested that in the play *Hamlet*, when Hamlet talks to his father's ghost at the beginning of the play, it is a psychological inversion of Shakespeare talking to his son's ghost.

Coat of Arms

The same year as Hamnet's death, the College of Heralds granted Shakespeare's father a dream that had long been denied to him: the Elizabethan status symbol, a coat of arms. The petition was granted for "good and loyal service" rendered to the Crown. The rough draft of the petition has a drawing of the family crest featuring a falcon with a spear in its claw, and the family motto, *Non Sanz Droit* (Not Without Right). Shakespeare inherited the title in 1601, at his father's death. He could now write "gentleman" after his name.

Shakespeare as a Businessman

In 1597, a year after his son's death, Shakespeare bought New Place, a "grete" house, one of the finest homes in Stratford. It stood on an acre of ground next to the Guild Chapel, not far from the schoolhouse Shakespeare attended as a youth. It was an imposing building built of brick and timber with three floors and five gables. He purchased it for £60 (a princely sum at the time) to house his wife and two daughters. It was a home in which he could learn to forget the shadowy presence of his son, Hamnet. These new rooms would not be filled with the absent child.

New Place stayed in the Shakespeare family for more than 100 years. His wife, Anne, lived in the house for twenty-four years, near her granddaughter, Elizabeth.

Realizing the value of land in Stratford, Shakespeare bought 125 acres in 1602, and in 1605 purchased a share in the Stratford tithe farm (for £440), from which he could collect tithes of grain and hay for himself or his heirs for thirty-one years. Where did these sums of money come from? After all, he was without any funds when he arrived in London, yet twenty-five years later he was a wealthy man. Other than the money he made as an actor and playwright, he was part owner of the Globe Theatre and the Blackfriars Theatre in London. He also earned money from his poetry. It is said that his patron, the Earl of Southampton, to whom he dedicated his long poems, paid him £1,000 for his sonnets, *Venus and Adonis* and *The Rape of Lucrece*, an enormous sum in Elizabethan times.

Shakespeare in Retirement

Mr. Shakespeare became an important member of the local gentry, an admired playwright (although hardly anyone in Stratford had seen any of his plays), and a fine and wealthy "gentleman."

Although he did not return to London to write plays, he did find time to collaborate on *Henry VIII* with John Fletcher, an up-and-coming playwright who was working as a dramatist with the King's Men. (*King Henry VIII* was performed at the Globe in London in 1613.) In Stratford, Shakespeare and Fletcher also collaborated on *The Two Noble Kinsmen*. They probably collaborated on the lost play *Cardenio* and, perhaps, *King Edward III*, which has, since 1760, been attributed by scholars to Shakespeare on the basis of internal evidence alone.

Where Are the Manuscripts?

Forty plays, yet there is not one handwritten manuscript, not one fragment of a play written by Shakespeare. During the performance of *Henry VIII* at the Globe Theatre in London in 1613, a cannon was fired for sound effect in a shed on the roof and the thatching caught fire. Someone tried to douse it with a flagon of ale, which fueled the flames, and the Globe burned to the ground. No one was hurt except a man whose pants caught fire.

We can surmise that when the Globe burned to the ground all his autographed copies of plays went up in flames. But there is also another reason we do not have those papers: Shakespeare did not regard his plays as having monetary value. The theater was not considered a true literary genre. The manuscripts were as much a part of the theater's stock as the costumes, sets, and props.

There is one scene from one play, *Sir Thomas More*, that may have been written in Shakespeare's hand, although he did not create the play. Two mediocre playwrights, Anthony Munday and Henry Chettle, wrote the play. When it was submitted to the Master of Revels for approval, one scene showing Londoners rioting in the city and being pacified by Sir Thomas More was deemed too vapid in its presentation. The authors hired another playwright to rewrite a powerful scene of More calling for law and order. Even then, the play was not approved. The handwritten play was eventually discovered in the British Library in London.

Scholars noted that the three-page scene of the rioting was written in a different hand than the rest. The style was obviously superior, rich in imagery and smooth in the flow of words and in the intentness of More's speech.

Even the spelling was different from the other writing and more in tune with Shakespeare's spelling. Did Shakespeare write the scene? That question will haunt future scholars—unless another manuscript is discovered.

Shakespeare's Last Will and Testament

The major surviving document that Shakespeare left behind was his last will and testament. The will had been drawn up by a Stratford lawyer, Francis Collins, and the language, as one writer noted, was "stilted, smelling of dead law." Shakespeare obviously did not care for the original draft, as he made corrections, which would be entered in the revised will by the lawyer.

Although he wanted his daughter, Judith, now thirty-two and a spinster, married, Shakespeare was incensed with her choice of a mate, Thomas Quiney, a tavern keeper with a disreputable past. When Quiney failed to get the proper marriage license, he and Judith were hauled before consistory court and excommunicated. Then to make matters worse, it was recorded that one month after Quiney's wedded day to Judith, he confessed to having "carnal intercourse" with another woman.

Shakespeare decided that Quiney would not inherit one portion of his estate, not "one tuppence." On the draft of his will, he slashed out the words "sonne in L[aw]," and referred to his daughter as "Judith," not mentioning her married name.

Shakespeare's will began, "In the name of God! Amen! I William Shackspeare [sic], of Stratford upon Avon in the countie of Warr, gent, in perfect health and memorie . . ." The will continued with a series of errors and inkblots as Shakespeare made handwritten revisions:

Where it read, "Item, I gyve, will, bequeath and devise unto my daughter Susanna Hall," he penned a flurry of writing between the lines "for better enabling her to performe this my will, and towards the performans thereof." The line continued, "all that capitall messuage of tenementes with thappurtenauances, in Stratford aforesaied, called the Newe Place, wherein I now dwell."

There was one other correction Shakespeare scratched at the end of the will: "Item, I give unto my wife my second best bed with the furniture."

Why did Shakespeare bequeath his wife, Anne, the "second best bed?"

The "first best bed" was the one guests were offered when visiting. Anne had slept in the second best bed, spending most of her nights alone while her husband was away. According to Elizabethan law a wife was entitled to one-third of her husband's estate. Shakespeare did not feel the need to be more specific in the will. After her husband died, Anne lived in New Place with her elder daughter, Susanna Hall, who had inherited the bulk of her father's estate.

Satisfied with the revised version changes in his last will and testament and then rewritten and corrected by the lawyer, Shakespeare signed the first two pages, then on the last page he wrote:

By me, William Shakespeare

Although the will is still in existence it is in deplorable condition. It has faded and is smeared by too many fingers during the more than 100 years it was on accessible display. Not only was it touched by adoring fingers, but it was also kissed in reverence.

Shakespeare's Death

In 1616, a few months after his daughter Judith was married and the will completed, Shakespeare died at the age of fifty-three and was entombed in Holy Trinity Church, the same church in which he had been baptized. As owner of a part of the Stratford tithes, he had the privilege of burial inside the Stratford Parish Church. The place he selected was one of prominence, inside the chancel rail before the high altar. His money, not his reputation as a playwright, had bought this honored resting place.

Tradition has it that he died of a fever after an evening's drinking with Ben Jonson and Michael Drayton.

Fifty years after Shakespeare's death Reverend John Ward of Stratford wrote in his diary, "Shakespeare, Draton, and Ben Jonson, had a merry meeting, and it seems drank too hard, for Shakespeare died of a feavour there contacted."

The playwright was dead, and by coincidence, exactly fifty-three years to the day from his birth. His stone slab in Holy Trinity Church in Stratford, which does not bear his name or date, has an epitaph that is thought to be the last words he ever wrote:

Good frend for Jesus sake forebeare,
to digg the dust encloased heare,
Bleste be ye man yt spares thes stones,
And curst be he yt moves my bones.

Doubters decry the idea that the great playwright wrote this less-than-poetic drivel. Whether or not the writing has any quality, Shakespeare had reason for the curse. Burial sites always became overcrowded, and grave-diggers had to make room for new bodies by dumping the old bones in charnel houses. One must surmise that Shakespeare simply wanted to arrive intact at the Last Judgment.

The Tombs in Holy Trinity Church

Today limbs from a double line of trees arch over the wide gravel pathway that leads to the entrance of Holy Trinity Church. In the church's graveyard great stone slabs used as grave markers stand crookedly on the grass like jagged teeth. Blackened with dry rot, the inscriptions on the tombstones are almost impossible to read, but enough can be deciphered to see that most of the stones date from the early 1800s.

Inside the church, Shakespeare's body is entombed beneath a stained glass window with its depiction of Christ on the Cross. The chiseled letters of Shakespeare's curse are worn and chipped where people once trod upon the tomb. (The original stone has been replaced by the one now on the grave, but church records indicate that it is an exact replica of the original.) Because the inscription on the stone is upside down to the viewer, a sign has been erected at the foot of the tomb that repeats the curse.

There are five tombs. The next in line to Shakespeare's is the tomb of Thomas Nashe, first husband of Shakespeare's granddaughter, Elizabeth (who died in 1670 at age sixty-two and was buried in a private lot with her second husband, John Barnard, a baronet). Beside Thomas Nashe is the tomb of doctor John Hall and next to him is his wife Susanna (Anne and William's first daughter). The last in line is Anne's tomb, with a rather commonplace inscription:

Here lyeth the wife of William Shakespeare who departed this life the 6th day of August 1623 being at the age of 67 yeares.

There is one final tomb, an empty one with no inscription. There is no stone for Shakespeare's second daughter, Judith, or her twin, Hamnet. Nor has any gravestone been found to mark their resting place.

Shakespeare's Bust at the Chancel in Holy Trinity Church

Six feet above and to the left of the tombs as one faces the altar is a stone bust of Shakespeare, carved by Gerard Janssen in 1623. It shows the playwright in a stiff pose wearing a painted burgundy shirt and blue vest, a feathered quill in one hand, writing on a sheet of paper. One stone finger, the index finger, has been broken off. The playwright stares straight ahead with an empty gaze, the face showing no glimmer of genius or even intelligence, just a fat man scribbling, the quill point resting on a stone pillow next to the sheet of paper.

Mark Twain wrote this disparaging note: "The precious bust, the calm bust, the serene bust, the emotionless bust, with the dandy mustache and the putty face, unseamed with care—the face which looked passionlessly down upon the awed pilgrims for a hundred and fifty years and will still look down upon the awed pilgrims three hundred more, with the deep, deep, deep, subtle, subtle, subtle expression of a bladder."

Originally Shakespeare was shown holding a sack of grain. As his popularity increased, a quill pen and stone pillow replaced the sack. The feather on the quill is replaced annually, plucked from a swan on the River Avon. The monument has the following inscription:

Stay, Passenger, why goest thou so fast?
Read if thou canst whom envious Death that is placed
Within this monument: Shakespeare, with whom
Quick nature dies; whose name doth deck this tomb
Far more than cost; since all that he hath writ
Leaves living art but page to serve his with.

Anne Hathaway Likeness

There are no known portraits of Anne Hathaway. One drawing has been discovered of a slender woman with tufts of blonde hair dressed in an Elizabethan bonnet with a ruff around her neck, which may be of Anne. The face of the woman is similar to an oil painting of Shakespeare and Anne's granddaughter, Elizabeth, which hangs in Nashe House next to the site of New Place. In the portrait Elizabeth is shown sitting on a chair, while her husband, Thomas Nashe, stands beside her, one arm draped over her shoulder, his other hand delicately holding her fingers. Elizabeth wears a single-strand pearl necklace, which accents her slender face and wide eyes. Her blonde hair is set in curls that fall to her shoulders.

Is this portrait of her granddaughter similar to what Anne Hathaway looked like? Perhaps they did have the same striking features and coloring.

The First Folio

During the time that Shakespeare was in London, eighteen of his plays were published individually in quartos, or pamphlets. Some of the plays were in finished form, some with rough texts based on the actors' memories or notes rather than complete scripts.

In November 1623, seven years after Shakespeare's death, two actors in the King's Men, Robert Hemings and Henry Condell, released the first printed edition of Shakespeare's plays. That is, almost all of them. This First

Folio (*folio* means "leaf" in Latin) listed thirty-six of Shakespeare's plays, omitting the last four: *Pericles, Prince of Tyre, The Two Noble Kinsmen,* the "lost play"*Cardenio,* and one that was attributed to Shakespeare later, *King Edward III.* On the title page the printer noted: "The Workes of William Shakespeare, containing all his Comedies, Histories, and Tragedies: Truly set forth, according to their first Originall."

FACT

One thousand copies of the First Folio were printed and a little over 200 exist today. The original Folio sold for about £1, the equivalent of about $50 today, a princely sum at the time. Today the value of a First Folio in mint condition would sell for over $1 million.

Ben Jonson wrote a dedicatory verse for the First Folio, which read: "Thou art a Monument, without a tombe, / And art alive still, while thy booke doth live."

In Praise of Shakespeare

Praise for the literary value of Shakespeare's plays was slow in coming. After the revival of drama at the time of the Restoration (1660), a change in the tastes of theatergoers began to diminish Shakespeare's popularity. At the same time women replaced boys in women's parts, and many of Shakespeare's plays lacked leading roles for women. They were no longer right for the times.

Yet, even then, Shakespeare had powerful defenders. Sir John Suckling, a courtier, simply said, "I love Shakespeare."

In 1598 Clergyman Francis Meres in his critique of English authors in *Palladis Tamia Wits Treasury* wrote, "As Plautus and Seneca are accounted the best for comedy and tragedy among the Latines: so Shakespeare among [the] English is the most excellent in both kinds for the stage."

The glorification of Shakespeare finally came to fruition with the Shakespeare Jubilee.

The Shakespeare Jubilee 1769

The Shakespeare Jubilee, which director/actor David Garrick had planned for five years, was the first of its kind. By the time he was ready, it was five years after the two hundredth anniversary of Shakespeare's birth, and not in the playwright's birth month, April, but in September.

A special amphitheater had been built where guests would watch the plays, dance at a costume ball, and partake of a 327-pound turtle, which had been shipped on a schooner from South America. This festive occasion began well enough: cannons fired, Stratford's Guild Chapel bell rang for a full day, and musicians and singers paraded the dusty streets, calling, "This is a day, a holiday! A holiday! Drive spleen and rancor away!"

For the next three days, the townspeople were inundated with song, wooed with odes to Shakespeare's greatness, and left spellbound by the plays. At first the audiences were more bemused by the stage presentations than entertained by them. Most had never read any of the plays, and even less had seen them performed. They never thought of their own Mr. Shakespeare as a man who would be immortalized by his own writings. Yet, the quality of the plays, the passion of Garrick's actors, soon had the people clamoring for more. This flood of rejoicing changed on the fourth day when the true flood came: the weather turned against Garrick—and the Bard—as heavy gray clouds lumbered across the skies, releasing a torrent of rain.

The River Avon flooded into the streets, threatening homes as well as the lives of the townspeople. One cleric, his voice resounding in Holy Trinity Church, avowed: "It is the wrath of God! This idolatrous proceeding has not the place in our hearts and minds. Or in God's!"

Yet the last play, *Othello*, went on in the Rotunda. Those gathered to see the play numbered 2,000, packed tightly into Stratford's Rotunda, a building that was meant to hold half as many. They sat on benches trying to keep their feet clear out of the puddles that had come with three days of torrential rain.

At the end of the performance, as Othello and Desdemona took their curtain call to the enthusiastic applause of audience, Garrick strode center stage. With his hands held high, he asked for silence and announced that he had composed an ode to Shakespeare, a special reading for the Jubilee. He began:

This man we now call Shakespeare wrote for the masses,
This man never felt he was writing for posterity.
He was simply a London playwright.
Now the playwright is no longer a man.
He is a monolith.

After the Jubilee was over, one local called it the "Resurrection of Shakespeare." It was more than that; it was the beginning of an industry. Stratford-upon-Avon became the destination for travelers who worshiped Shakespeare.

George Bernard Shaw, who deplored the worship of Shakespeare, coined the term *Bardolatry*, saying that Shakespeare's ideas were "platitudinous fudge." He also stated, "Without the single exception of Homer, there is no eminent writer, not even Sir Walter Scott, whom I can despise entirely, as I despise Shakespear [sic] when I measure my mind against his."

Bardolatry

Today in Stratford-upon-Avon the center of activity begins at Shakespeare's Birthplace, a two-story, half-timbered building. The brown-and-white paneled house is just one of the similarly built structures that date back to Shakespeare's time and give Stratford-upon-Avon much of its character. It is said that 200 years ago, splinters of what was touted to be Shakespeare's writing chair were sold to tourists, yet the chair never seemed to diminish in size. On the window of the birth room, such famous writers as Sir Walter Scott and Thomas Carlyle had, in reverence, scratched their signatures.

To get inside the house, one must pass through the Shakespeare Centre, a strikingly modern brick structure that adjoins Shakespeare's Birthplace. The Centre houses a collection of Shakespearean memorabilia, including one of the rare copies of the First Folio. One has to pass through room after room of gift shops to get to the exit. On display are multicolored quills with feathery ostrich plumes, maps, postcards, Shakespeare coloring books, games and toys, and even velvet paintings of his likeness.

One wonders what Shakespeare might think of all this idolatry. Perhaps this line from *A Midsummer Night's Dream* will suffice to speak for him: "Lord, what fools these mortals be."

CHAPTER 7

Did Shakespeare Write Shakespeare?

Homer composed *The Iliad*. No one has ever doubted his authorship. Yet, to accept Shakespeare as the author of the most poetic masterpieces in the English language has caused endless, and many times furious and vindictive, debates. There are those who say that an uneducated man could no more write *Hamlet* than a Russian serf could have penned *War and Peace*. Yet, Henry Ford and Thomas Edison, who didn't have university degrees, were monoliths of their time, as was the self-taught Abraham Lincoln.

Much Ado about Shakespeare

What could be more exciting than solving a mystery? What happened to the crew of the *Marie Celeste*? Is there a Bermuda triangle? What really happened in the Kennedy assassination? Who wrote Shakespeare's plays? Such detective work appeals to even writers, lawyers, and businesspeople who like to pursue Shakespeare as a hobby.

Shakespeare scholar Charlton Ogburn wrote: "It is the greatest Detective story there ever was . . . It's the greatest story in literature."

Despite several hundred years of scholarship, doubts still remain among some that the Stratford man wrote "The Collected Works of William Shakespeare." Among the nonbelievers are Walt Whitman, Mark Twain, Sigmund Freud, Helen Keller, Orson Welles, Charlie Chaplin, Malcolm X, and Supreme Court Justice Harry Blackmun. Ralph Waldo Emerson said it simply: "I cannot marry the life to the work."

How Did the Controversy Begin?

In 1769, a little more than 150 years after Shakespeare's death, Herbert Lawrence wrote *The Life and Adventures of Common Sense*. In his book he suggested that Sir Francis Bacon wrote Shakespeare's plays. At the time no one believed his theory. Sixteen years later, in 1785, Reverend James Wilmot began to theorize that Sir Francis Bacon was the true author of the plays. Concerned about offending people with his radical hypothesis he decided not to publish it.

In 1848 a New York lawyer by the name of Colonel Joseph C. Hart published a book with the title *The Romance of Yachting*, in which he managed to slip in between the declarations of his love for nautical life references that Sir Francis Bacon was the author of Shakespeare's plays.

The first time a book title was published that referred to the developing Shakespeare controversy was W. H. Smith's, *Was Bacon the Author of Shakespeare's Plays?* (1856), which was followed by *Bacon and Shakespeare* (1857).

Then along came Delia Bacon (no relationship to Sir Francis) who devoted her entire adult life to desperately trying to solve the mystery of who wrote Shakespeare; instead she drove herself to madness. Strangely, the eminent American author Nathaniel Hawthorne became interested and helped publish her book, *The Philosophy of the Plays of Shakespeare Unfolded* (1857). Due to the tome's pedantic prose—"That sanguinary passion which the heat of conflict proves is but the incident: it is the natural principle of absorption"—hardly anyone read it.

It must be noted that none of these early advocates of the Bacon/Shakespeare theory was a trained Shakespearean scholar. There was passion but little research. They based their claim on the presumption that it was impossible for a "Stratford rustic" to write the great plays attributed to Shakespeare.

Debating the Authorship Question

Throughout the years since the Sir Francis Bacon proposal, at least fifty-eight persons have been proposed as the true author of Shakespeare's works. The most prominent is Edward de Vere, seventeenth Earl of Oxford, the first choice of the anti-Stratfordian group known as "the Oxfordians." Following the earl in popularity is Sir Francis Bacon, favorite of the Baconians. Adding to the confusion are the Marlovians, who insist that Christopher Marlowe wrote the plays.

The controversy goes on, and there seems no end to it. Opinions can become volatile. In the words of Henry James, "Shakespeare is the biggest and most successful fraud ever practiced on a patient world!"

Actor Mel Gibson, who played in a movie version of *Hamlet*, said, "I believe he was a genius."

Poet John Dryden (1631–1700) put it this way: "Genius must be born, and never can be taught. "

George Bernard Shaw countered with, "Believers use the term *genius* to explain how a glove maker's son, with no specialized education, no breeding, no background of travel, no association with courtly discipline, became the greatest playwright the world has ever seen."

On the reverse side of the debate is Leonora Eyre saying, "The thing about the anti-Stratfordians is that they would prefer any crackpot theory rather than the simple idea that Shakespeare really was Shakespeare."

Shakespeare on Trial

Who is right, who is wrong? In 1987 a mock trial was held in Washington D.C. After much deliberation, three justices on the Supreme Court offered the opinion, unanimously, that Shakespeare was the author of Shakespeare's plays. The following year, in London, a similar trial was held, presided over by three lords of appeal, which achieved the same result. The primary reason for their decision was to discount each person who has been proposed throughout the last 200 years as possible heirs to Shakespeare's literary throne, including two who did occupy the throne, Queen Elizabeth I and King James I.

Since the controversy rages on, let's take a look at the schools of the two major contenders, Sir Francis Bacon and Edward de Vere, the seventeenth Earl of Oxford.

The Baconian Stance

Francis Bacon (1561–1626) was classically educated and extremely intelligent, graduating from Cambridge at the astonishing age of twelve. He wrote on a variety of subjects, and many of his views were similar to Shakespeare's. In a series of writings called *The Promus of Formularies and Elegancies* he recorded lines that were amazingly similar to Shakespeare's, such as these two familiar lines:

"All is not gold that glistens." (Bacon)
"All that glisters is not gold." (Shakespeare, *The Merchant of Venice*)

Those who believe that Sir Francis Bacon was "Shakespeare" were the first to claim authorship. It all began with the champions of Francis

Bacon—"Baconians," they are called. The Baconians have been thought of as the Indiana Joneses of scholarship. Their adventures led them to graveyards, castles, monasteries, anywhere in hopes of finding a long-lost manuscript. None has been found.

Sam Schoenbaum, Shakespeare expert, wrote, "A past that has been buried for several hundred years will still yield its secrets for those who will burrow in it and look for them, and God knows what will be found in the future."

The basis for the belief in Sir Frances Bacon is not the similarity in writing, but in Baconian ciphers, cryptograms, and codes. Baconians say, "Bacon, who was a leader in early scientific thought, and who invented ciphers to insure that posterity would remember him as Shakespeare, inserted secret messages in to his plays."

The Baconians decoded Shakespeare's epitaph on his tombstone, deciphering the first four lines as "FRA BA WRT EAR AY," which they interpret as: "Francis Bacon wrote Shakespeare's Plays." Then the search was on for clues in Shakespeare's plays that would identify the author as Bacon, such as his use of words meaning honor.

What is the longest word in Shakespeare?
Honorificabilitudinitatibus is a word Shakespeare made up for *Love's Labour's Lost*, meaning "to be loaded with honor." The word sent the Baconians in a frenzy, searching for a meaning, and finally announcing that the word was the Latin anagram for Hi ludi, tuiti sibi Fr. Bacono nati. This was conjured up to mean, "These Bacon's offspring are preserved for the world."

These ciphers, cryptograms, and anagrams "proved" Bacon's authorship of the plays. But this argument also proved to be so absurd that it was soon dropped, even by the pro-Baconians. Sam Schoenbaum wrote in *Shakespeare Lives*, "Why would a super-subtle mind have resorted to the juvenile devise of incorporating hidden messages in his plays?"

One might ask, "If Bacon wrote Shakespeare, who wrote Bacon?"

The Oxfordian Stance

The Oxfordians claim that Edward de Vere (1550–1604), the seventeenth Earl of Oxford, wrote all of Shakespeare's plays and poems. The Oxfordians base their claim on de Vere's aristocratic background—he descended from a long line of earls that were close to the English monarchy—and his education, ability, and world experience. Unlike Shakespeare, his biography is well documented. He spent a lot of time in Italy, which gave him the knowledge to write about that country in the plays of Shakespeare. He was also interested in drama and was a patron of Blackfriars Theatre.

FACT

Thomas Looney's (an unfortunate name for a researcher—he pronounced it Lawney) book *Shakespeare Identified in Edward de Vere, 17th Earl of Oxford* was the first work to claim de Vere wrote Shakespeare's plays. Looney didn't start with de Vere; he first made a list of the qualities that Shakespeare should possess, then matched those qualifications to de Vere.

Writing under his own name, Edward de Vere was recognized as a poet. Yet, nobody thought of him as a great poet, let alone a playwright. He did stop writing poetry to be able to—his champions say—spend his creative time writing great plays, the plays of Shakespeare.

David Bevington, a noted Shakespeare scholar, writes, "If Edward de Vere was so eager that someone should 'Report me and my cause aright to the unsatisfied,' why did he leave such enigmatic clues? Was the stigma of being a playwright so huge that he could tell no one, not even write it down for his friends? Ultimately the case collapses on lack of motive as well as lack of evidence, for it presupposes a social history of how playwrights got to be playwrights that is simply not in keeping with historical reality."

QUESTION?

Why would de Vere hide the fact that he had written the plays?
According to the Oxfordians, it would be unimaginable for a well-known earl of England to write for the common theater: The Elizabethan social code would have been violated if an aristocrat wrote plays under his own name. Oxfordians also claim that, due to the dangerous political metaphors and moralizing in the plays, he would put himself and his name in jeopardy.

Oxfordians feel strongly about their claims and say that those who support Shakespeare are blinded to the evidence by a vested self-interest. More extreme Oxfordians claim that Stratfordians are engaged in an active conspiracy to suppress pro-Oxford evidence. The truth is far more mundane. Oxfordians are not taken seriously by the Shakespeare establishment because most Oxfordians do not follow basic standards of scholarship, and the "evidence" they present is either distorted, taken out of context, or flat-out false.

QUOTE

Sigmund Freud: "I am almost convinced that the assumed name [William Shakespeare] conceals the personality of Edward de Vere. The man of Stratford seems to have nothing at all to justify his claim, whereas Oxford has almost everything."

The Stratfordians maintain that one of the greatest difficulties with the theory that the Earl of Oxford wrote Shakespeare's plays is the fact that de Vere died in 1604, yet still managed to produce some of his greatest plays postmortem. These plays include *King Lear* (1605–6), *Macbeth* (1606–7), *Antony and Cleopatra* (1606–7), *Coriolanus* (1608), *Cymbeline* (1608–10), *The Winter's Tale* (1609–11), and *The Tempest* (1611).

Most Oxfordians concede that these plays postdate de Vere's death but argue that de Vere wrote the plays before he died and that they were brought out as needed for performance, sometimes with added contemporary references to events after 1604 in order to make them look timely.

The problem with this argument is that when you examine the body of Shakespeare's plays as a whole, it is possible to trace a definable stylistic development. As David Bevington, professor of English Language and Literature at the University of Chicago, said in a 1989 PBS *Frontline* documentary about this issue:

"The argument [that de Vere wrote Shakespeare] has to posit a conspiracy of staggering proportions. Shakespeare, according to this scenario, agreed to serve as a front man for Oxford because the writing of plays was below the dignity of a great man. Shakespeare's friends in the company agreed to serve up his plays in the years after Oxford's death, publicizing the plays as by Shakespeare. Persons who knew Shakespeare well, like Ben Jonson, went along with the fiction, writing economiastac verses for Shakespeare after his death in 1616. The acting company, especially Shakespeare's colleagues John Heminges and Henry Condell, supervised the publication of all of the plays (except *Pericles*, *Cardenio*, and *The Two Noble Kinsmen*, which are regarded as collaborations) in a handsome folio volume in 1616, essentially the first of its kind to recognize a dramatist. Many writers poured out their praise for England's great national poet and playwright, and some of them knew Shakespeare personally. All of these people had to be either deceived by the presumed cover-up or, in many cases, accessories to a hoax."

The contest, summed up by *Frontline* correspondent Al Austin, comes down to this: "Those who believe de Vere was Shakespeare must accept an improbable hoax as part of it, a conspiracy of silence involving among others, Queen Elizabeth herself. Those who side with the Stratford man must believe in miracles."

Or, it might be added, accept the nature of genius for what it is—a rarity of generational proportions.

Candidates for Shakespeare's Literary Crown

8

There are at least fifty-eight candidates who have been offered up as the "true" Shakespeare. We have discussed the claims of Edward de Vere, (seventeenth Earl of Oxford) and Sir Francis Bacon (Lord Verulam) in Chapter 7. Now add these illustrious figures: Christopher Marlowe and Ben Jonson, then add William Stanley (sixth Earl of Derby), Roger Manners (Earl of Rutland), and even Queen Elizabeth I.

The Shakespeare Mystery

Irvin Leigh Matus's *Shakespeare, In Fact* (1994) is a good examination of the authorship question. Charlton Ogburn's *The Mysterious William Shakespeare* is generally considered the most thorough exposition of the Oxfordian case. In 1997, Joseph Sobran's *Alias Shakespeare* introduced newcomers to the Shakespeare authorship question.

FACT

Bertram Fields, *Players: The Mysterious Identity of William Shakespeare* (2005), is a new look at the controversy, and claims that "Shakespeare" was an assumed name for a group of poets and playwrights.

The Popular Candidates

Here are biographies of the front-runners in the race for Shakespeare's crown.

Christopher Marlowe (1564–93)

There can be no doubt that Christopher Marlowe was one of the great playwrights of the Elizabethan era, a talent equal to Shakespeare. But was he Shakespeare?

Marlowe's literary achievements during the short period of time he was actively writing are remarkable. Before leaving Cambridge, he had written *Tamburlaine the Great, Parts I and II*, which brought him acclaim. That was followed by *Doctor Faustus, Edward II,* and *The Massacre at Paris*. His last play was probably *The Jew of Malta*. Then the twenty-nine-year-old poet/ playwright was killed in a tavern brawl at Dame Eleanore Bull's tavern in Deptford, reputedly over payment of a dinner bill. It seems there was a quarrel and Marlowe drew his dagger against his friend Ingram Frizer, who drove his own dagger into Marlowe's eye.

Marlowe's violent end came during the month of May 1593. The wealth of Shakespeare's great plays were written in the fifteen years *following* Marlowe 's untimely demise.

Today's champions of Marlowe, who call themselves Marlovians, profess that he didn't actually die, but rather that the death was a staged cover-up. The young playwright found it prudent to disappear *in name* to avoid execution on the charges of heresy and blasphemy. Marlowe had pleaded that the archbishop of Canterbury—who wrote a note saying there was need to "stop the mouth of so dangerous a member of Christian Society"—had falsely charged him.

QUESTION?

Was Christopher Marlowe really killed in a tavern brawl?
Why, yes, say the Marlovians—killed in the sense that he was dead to the world and now had the freedom from persecution to write as he liked. Only two weeks after he went to his grave, the first work signed "Shakespeare" appeared in print. That first work, the Marlovians insist, was by Marlowe's hand.

But the accusations were serious, and the Privy Council issued orders for Marlowe's arrest on charges of heresy. According to the informer Richard Baines, Marlowe had ranted that Moses was but a juggler, that Christ's miracles were naught, and that Christ was a sexual pervert who indulged in sodomy with the beloved disciple, John. Marlowe had also been charged for indulging in pederasty, saying that men were fools who did not like boys. Marlovians say their champion had no choice but to go into hiding and continue writing—as Shakespeare.

The mystery of Marlowe's death is covered in Calvin Hoffman's book, *The Murder of the Man Who Was "Shaklespeare,"* and is further discussed in Anthony Burgess's *A Dead Man in Deptford.*

Ben Jonson

Ben Jonson, in *To the Memory of My Beloved, the Author, Mr. William Shakespeare,* wrote these lines:

Soul of the age!
The applause, the delight, the wonder of our stage!

Mr Shakespeare rise.

Does Jonson's eulogy sound like the voice of a man who would usurp Shakespeare's literary crown? Ben Johnson (1572–1637) was a close associate of William Shakespeare. He also made a mark second only to Shakespeare in the public theater. His comedies *Valpone* or *The Foxe* and *The Alchemist* were among the most popular and acclaimed plays of the period. He certainly had no need to write under the name Shakespeare.

William Stanley, Sixth Earl of Derby

Stanley is a major contender, mostly because he was everything Shakespeare wasn't: He was a direct descendent (through his mother) to the Tudor king, Henry VII; educated at Oxford; studied law; and traveled to Italy, Spain, and France. He was also raised in the area where many of the scenes in Shakespeare's plays took place. He invited acting companies to perform in his home and there tried his skill as an actor. His followers say he wrote plays for the public theater, but no such works have been found inscribed with his name.

FACT

William Stanley was born in 1561 and died 1642. He outlived Shakespeare by twenty-six years, yet no plays were written after 1616. Interestingly, Lord Stanley was the son-in-law of Edward de Vere, the Earl of Oxford, having married the earl's daughter.

Roger Manners, Fifteenth Earl of Rutland

Manners, although less popular a candidate than William Stanley, was well educated, having studied at Cambridge for seven years. He also traveled in Europe for five years, where he attended the University of Padua. To write Shakespeare's plays he had to be a prodigy, as the poem *Venus and Adonis* was published when he was only sixteen. He died in 1612, four years before Shakespeare.

Queen Elizabeth I

The queen is a delightful candidate. She knew Greek and Latin, wrote poetry, and loved to attend plays or have them performed at her court. At a session of parliament she once used the term *swaying scepter,* which her followers have said is a slight variation of the name Shakespeare, the name Elizabeth took to write the plays. They say she even left clues by matching episodes in the plays that paralleled events that occurred in her reign and her private life.

In the Epilogue in *Henry VIII* there are these words: "Tis ten to one this play can never please?" At the time there were *ten* kings in Europe and the *one* queen. Believers use this as a clue to their claim.

FACT

According to Dr. Lillian Schwartz, an expert in matching faces on a computer, Queen Elizabeth and Shakespeare's faces are the same! The doctor took the Droeshout etching of Shakespeare on the cover of the First Folio and matched it with a painting of the queen. Except for the beard, and Elizabeth's curly hair, the face structure matched.

Yet, in *All's Well That Ends Well* there are unseemly remarks about the queen's virginity. It seems unlikely that Elizabeth would write a play that criticized her as the reigning monarch. The major impediment to Elizabeth's authorship is that many of the plays were presumably written after her death in 1603.

King James I

First, let's say King James looked nothing like Shakespeare or his predecessor, Queen Elizabeth. Except for the splendor of his silver-threaded attire, he was an ordinary-looking man with brown hair and a ruddy complexion. His appearance—as a court jester once noted during the king's reign—was "tolerable." An Italian visitor to the court once said he was "handsome, noble, jovial, a man happily formed, neither fat or thin, of full vitality." There was no mention of the king's idiosyncrasies. Like many Elizabethans of the time, he never bathed or washed, believing bathing to be unhealthy. The king would sometimes dip his fingertips in rosewater. Even though his odor was masked by perfume, courtiers were careful to hold their breath as he passed.

FACT

During King James's reign two of the greatest volumes in the English language were produced: the First Folio and the King James Bible. According to legend, Shakespeare provided his own version of Psalm 46; the forty-sixth word from the beginning is shake and the forty-sixth word from the end is spear.

King James, the son of Mary, Queen of Scots, had been James VI of Scotland before ascending to the English throne. He loved the theater and changed the name of the Lord Chamberlain's Men to the King's Men. His followers say he used the nom de plume "Shakespeare" so that he could govern England without being termed "That Playwright" by foreign envoys.

The Partners Theory

The most recent theory as to the authorship of Shakespeare's play is that it was a collaboration of more than one playwright, a series of "partners."

In his book *Players: The Mysterious Identity of William Shakespeare*, author Bertram Fields writes:

In the end there are thirty-six plays. Their vocabulary is extraordinary. After all, they contain not only the thoughts of [the Earl of] Oxford, but also the contributions of other creative men, at least five of which—Bacon, Stanley, Jonson, Middleton, and Fletcher—are intelligent and well read. Even the Stratford man, after years in the theatre, has suggested lines calculated to please the common theatre audience, as well as arcane rural jargon acquired in and around Stratford.

According to Fields the scenario works like this: William Stanley discovers, after his father-in-law's (Edward de Vere) death, several plays. Knowing the clandestine partnership arrangement between the Oxford and the

Stratford man, Stanley consults his lawyer Francis Bacon, "the wisest man he knows," who also knew of the arrangement, and agrees that it should be continued. With Shakespeare as an agreeing "partner," the collaboration continues.

Fields goes on to say: "I believe the Stratford man did play a significant part in the creation of the plays, but that someone else originally created them and wrote the poems as well. I believe the author was brilliant, highly educated and widely traveled. But there are aspects of the plays that suggest a contribution by someone with 'street smarts' and a shrewd nose for what would play in the public theatre."

And there, according to Fields, you have it: Shakespeare, the man from Stratford, dabbled in playwrighting but never wrote the plays. The "partners" created the manuscripts and agreed to put the name of the Stratford man, "Shakespeare," on them. It makes for a fascinating collaboration, if true.

The Bizarre Candidates

Of all the candidates proposed for writing Shakespeare's plays, some reach even further into the realm of fantasy. Such as:

Sir Walter Raleigh

Raleigh was a confidant of Christopher Marlowe. He led a group of free-thinking intellectuals called the "School of Night" who met and discussed religious subjects. He was also the author of *History of the World*, a grand undertaking of research, but hardly the quality of *Hamlet*. In his history Raleigh recorded that Marlowe was the first great English dramatist, the most important Elizabethan playwright *before* William Shakespeare. He further wrote that Marlowe's masterpiece, *The Tragical History of Doctor Faustus*, established verse as the predominant form in English drama. It further stated that each of Marlowe's plays had, as a central character, a passionate man doomed to destruction by an inordinate desire for power. That is what Raleigh wrote in his *History*, but did he write Shakespeare? Certainly his adventures in the New World brought him fame, but there is no evidence that he wrote plays.

Sir Fulke-Greville, First Baron of Brooke

Greville was a minor poet of philosophical poems, and as such is a weak contender to be chosen by his few followers to be Shakespeare. Greville's poetry was published after his death.

FACT

Greville came to a bad end when he had an argument with one of his manservants in the tower of the castle over the contents of Greville's will. Angered because he was left only a pittance, the servant drew a knife and stabbed his master. Realizing the enormity of his action, the servant then turned the blade on himself. After twenty-seven agonizing days, Greville died. (It is said that the poet's ghost still haunts the castle.)

At Warwick Castle a few miles out of Stratford, a large oil painting hangs on the wall in a hallway. It shows a slender man (who has a slight resemblance to Shakespeare) with a goatee dressed in a black outfit wearing a felt hat with a gold chain around its crown. King James had granted the castle to Sir Fulke-Greville, who was a prominent Elizabethan courtier.

Anne Hathaway Shakespeare

Among the more unlikely female candidates is Anne Hathaway. Shakespeare's wife, as most scholars agree, would most likely not even have been able to write.

Daniel Defoe

Defoe wrote *Life and Adventures of Robinson Crusoe*. He was born in 1660, almost forty years after Shakespeare's death. Obviously, it would have been impossible for him to write the plays.

Sheik Zubayr bin William

The most bizarre of all the pretenders is Muammar al-Qaddafi's choice, Sheik Zubayr bin William. Quaddafi came up with his champion in 1989 when Radio Tehran announced that Libya's "Great One" had declared that an Arab sheik named Zubayr bin William, who had been born in the sixteenth century, was Shakespeare.

The Case for Shakespeare

As a newly emerging Victorian middle class arose and a liberal university education became the distinguishing mark of a gentleman, it became important for people to reinforce the superiority of their own lifestyle by thinking that Shakespeare's plays and poems could only have been the work of a university-educated gentleman rather than the genius of a somewhat self-taught middle-class glover's son.

The point that many scholars miss is that writing is about observing and reflecting the human condition. It is also about reading, and a great deal was being printed for the first time in English around Shakespeare's time. What's more, if you examine the careers of great writers throughout history, their formal academic education was the least relevant aspect of their success as a writer.

FACT

Playwrights did not have to be courtiers themselves to accurately portray court life, just as journalists today can re-create and interpret what happens in the White House or Congress without being in the administration or elected officials.

Many writers have come primarily from social classes below those of the ruling class. For example, James Joyce, D. H. Lawrence, Harold Pinter, Sam Shepard, and John Arden, all came from the working classes or middle classes. In pre-nineteenth-century times, John Webster was the son of a merchant tailor; Edmund Spenser's father was a cloth maker; Christopher Marlowe's father was a shoemaker in Canterbury; Ben Jonson's stepfather was a bricklayer. While these promising young men were well educated at schools such as the Merchant Taylor's School in London and the Westminster School, not all went on to university.

Yet, these men had enough education to challenge the concept of "knowing their place" and to move to thinking "outside the box," (as we would say today) and beyond society's expectations of them. So, they became writers in London. There, the theater, among other opportunities, provided them both employment and intellectual stimulation, and drew them into a world of urbane events. They either observed or became peripheral participants in the goings-on of kings and nobles, and were able to write compelling pictures of courtly life in their plays.

Is Hard Evidence Needed?

The lack of manuscripts or handwriting samples, other than the six known signatures, is not a criteria for stating that Shakespeare didn't write the plays. Play scripts, like many movie scripts today, existed so that an acting company could stage a play. The wonder is that so many of Shakespeare's plays were published at all. We have no original manuscripts of plays by Marlowe or Jonson, even though some of their plays rival Shakespeare's in their literary and dramatic qualities, and their authorship is not generally questioned.

No one suggests that Marlowe wasn't written by Marlowe or Jonson by Jonson. So why is Shakespeare singled out? The answer lies mainly in his greatness. True geniuses are few and far between, and there are those, such as Einstein and Shakespeare, who defied their backgrounds as their genius flowered. Shakespeare is among the greatest of our thinkers and creators, and so he is the subject of intense speculation. To argue that an obscure Stratford boy could not have become the Shakespeare of literature is to ignore the mystery of genius.

To Be or Not to Be Shakespeare—That Is the Question

Imagine if you can that an enthusiastic amateur could show professional scholars that all of Western culture has been bamboozled over the centuries by a hoax, that Shakespeare is really the Earl of Oxford. Imagine that this Stratford man called Shakespeare is nothing more than a "rural bumpkin" who could barely scribble his own name, a poor actor who "struts and frets his hour upon the stage and is heard no more."

Let's, like the anti-Strafordians, take a "To Be or Not to Be Quiz" to determine if that Stratford man really is Shakespeare.

How did one man, writing with a pen and ink, compose forty plays, more than 150 sonnets, and two long narrative poems?

One possible answer: He had collaborators. Or, as Virginia Woolf once said, "He writes at the speed that is quicker than anybody's quickest." Ben Jonson commented that "players have often mentioned it as an honor to Shakespeare that in writing (whatsoever he penned) he never blotted out a line."

Did Shakespeare have coauthors?

If yes, this would answer a lot of questions put forth in question one, but this would *not* satisfy the Oxfordians, Baconians, and Marlovians, who stand solidly behind their champion as the sole author of the plays. Thus far there has been no solid evidence that someone like de Vere wrote the plays. Nothing disproves that Shakespeare was the man from Stratford. As Stanley Wells wrote, "The burden of proof falls on the anti-Stratfordians, and they have yet to meet it."

Is there any proof that Shakespeare wrote the plays attributed to him?

The publication of the First Folio seven years after his death by two acting friends, which includes a forward by Ben Jonson, is certainly irrefutable proof. Shakespeare was also a member of the Lord Chamberlain's Men, London's premiere acting company. A warrant for payment registers that Shakespeare was a full-fledged professional in the company, in which he served as both actor and playwright.

Why doesn't Shakespeare's last will and testament mention any literary property such as books or play manuscripts?

Shakespeare did state in his will that he was leaving "all the rest of my goodes chattels Leases plate Jewels & household stuffe whatsoever" to his daughter Susanna and his "sonne in Law John Hall." It wasn't necessary to list books or manuscripts. Both "goodes" and "chattels" would cover those items. There could also have been another reason—he didn't have them. Play manuscripts were not considered valuable, nor did they belong to the actor. They were the property of the acting company, such as the King's Men. When the Globe Theatre burned to the ground, the fire quite possibly destroyed all manuscripts kept within the wooden structure, including those of other playwrights, like Marlowe and Jonson.

Why are there no letters to his wife, Anne, his daughter Susanna, or to his friends and associates in Stratford? One would think that Susanna and his older daughter, Judith, would have cherished these letter and preserved them.

Elizabethans didn't keep records or save letters as we do today. After Susanna's death the Shakespeare line ended. Over a period of 400 years since Shakespeare's death they were no doubt lost or discarded.

Why didn't Shakespeare keep a diary? Why didn't someone, such as his friend Ben Jonson, write a biography during the life of such a famous playwright?

During Elizabethan times, biographies simply were not written, unless the person was of royalty. To keep a diary would be presumptuous and tedious to a playwright.

Shakespeare's signature was almost an ineligible scrawl and each of the six different known signatures ranged in spelling from "Willn Shaksp" to "Wm Shaksp" to "William Shaks pear." Yet, he wrote thousands of words in plays, perhaps laboriously. One London antiquarian, John Aubrey, wrote of Shakespeare in 1680 that, "If invited to writ, he was in paine."

How many unreadable signatures by today's famous have you seen? Most of them are also ineligible scrawls. Imagine the task of writing the thousands upon thousands of words in forty plays and how seldom he needed to sign his name.

Did Shakespeare attend school in Stratford?

There is no proof of this as school records are nonexistent. Stanley Schoenbaum, a leading modern biographer of Shakespeare, wrote, "We need not doubt that Shakespeare received a grammar school education and the only likely place for it was the King's New School of Stratford-upon-Avon." Besides, the Stratford Grammar School was considered as one of the best in England.

Queen Elizabeth I died in 1603. Shakespeare, who at the time was thirty-eight, made no comment about the queen's death, yet a shower of accolades was made by almost every poet, author, and political figure. Why not Shakespeare?

Why not indeed? Anti-Stratfordians reply that the real Shakespeare may have died by that time, or he simply didn't want to show up in court and reveal his identity as Shakespeare. Was Shakespeare afraid? After all, he did make unseemly remarks about the queen's virginity in *All's Well That Ends Well.*

William Shakespeare died in 1616. There is no record of a public tribute, no national mourning or eulogies, no outpouring of grief. Certainly a famous poet and playwright would have had some mention, yet not one writer or actor in the theater wrote of his passing. Nothing was said until seven years later when the First Folio was printed.

Perhaps it was as William Shakespeare wanted: He was only a retired actor and didn't think of himself as a great playwright. He was a "gent" and a businessman.

The Final Question

Did the Stratford man, William Shakespeare, write the plays that have been attributed to his name? The case for the contenders, such as the Earl of Oxford, Sir Francis Bacon, and Christopher Marlowe, have been presented in the previous chapters, as has the case for the man from Stratford-upon-Avon. The answer to this final question is unmistakable: Not one of the fifty-eight candidates wrote in a style remotely like Shakespeare. As Stanley Wells said. "Shakespeare's works are imaginative. His voice is unique."

CHAPTER 9

The Sonnets and Poems

Most readers and playgoers don't think of Shakespeare as a great philosopher. Yet, in his sonnets and poems he expressed profound thoughts and feelings in words of great beauty. They can be read with great joy, a marvelous record of the playwright's versatile talents.

Shakespeare as a Poet

Shakespeare had great technical skills as a dramatist, but his work as a poet is where we learn of his ability to capture the speech of common men and the language of philosophers. An extremely talented poet, he was able to distill words to create some of the finest poetry in the English language.

In his plays, Shakespeare used the unrhymed iambic pentameter called blank verse. Shakespeare wasn't the first to develop it into dramatic verse form—that was done by Thomas Sackville and Thomas Norton, translator of *The Aeneid* and the coauthor of *Gorboduc* (England's first "regular tragedy," 1565). But Shakespeare perfected it. Although there were other great poets who used or would use this verse line, Shakespeare helped make iambic pentameter the greatest meter in English.

QUESTION?

Are any of Shakespeare's poems well known?
One poem, Sonnet 18, is no doubt the best known of the 154 sonnets, mostly for the number of times its lines have been quoted. Sonnet 18 begins, "Shall I compare thee to a summer's day? / Thou art more lovely and more temperate: / Rough winds do shake the darling buds of May, / And Summer's lease hath all too short a date."

One might ask: If Shakespeare—who had become an established playwright by 1592—was so successful, why did he decide to put his playwrighting aside and begin creating poems? The answer lies in the outbreak of the bubonic plague that year. All the theaters were closed by the London authorities because of the risk of infection spreading throughout the audiences.

Poetry, considered far superior to mere public entertainment, allowed Shakespeare to win a patron. Moreover, poetry was considered the highest form of literature. Shakespeare knew that the profession of poet was not as well paid as a playwright, yet it would provide a modicum of income. Not only was nondramatic poetry considered a higher form of art, it also attracted social prestige. But to do this he needed sufficient sums of money and that required the patronage of a nobleman.

In an attempt to put a few coins in his pocket after his sudden loss of income, Shakespeare published *Venus and Adonis* in 1593. It had a strange, somewhat deferential dedication to Henry Wriothesley, Earl of Southampton, the Baron of Titchfield (1573–1624). The earl was nineteen years old at the time, but already a wealthy and influential patron of the arts. The poem described itself as "the first heir of my invention," while promising "some graver labour" to come.

Rising to Fame

Venus and Adonis, a funny and erotic narrative poem loosely based on Ovid's *Metamorphosis*, was published by Richard Field, a Stratford neighbor of Shakespeare's, probably a childhood friend, who was fast becoming one of London's leading booksellers/publishers.

A far more serious narrative poem, *The Rape of Lucrece*, was published in May 1594. This poem was also dedicated to the Earl of Southampton, but the formal tone of the first poem's dedication was altered with words of a certain warm familiarity. Some scholars have suggested that this "familiarity" constituted a homosexual relationship.

One of the ironies of Shakespeare's life is that in his day he was famous not as the creator of Lear, Othello, Prospero, or Hamlet, but as the playwright of *Titus Andronicus* and the author of *Venus and Adonis*. No doubt, to Shakespeare's joy, *The Rape of Lucrece* was reprinted at least nine times during his lifetime.

Both *Venus and Adonis* and *The Rape of Lucrece* are full of gorgeous imagery and pagan spirit, and they are obviously the work of an intense young man. The fame that these two poems brought to Shakespeare no doubt substantially raised his profile as a serious writer, and, when the theaters reopened in 1594, helped the by-now thirty-year-old actor/playwright join Richard Burbage's acting company, the Lord Chamberlain's Men.

Although Shakespeare was successful writing his sonnets, it is not known how he felt about playwrighting. Searching for clues about Shakespeare's theatrical ambitions, we must go to his poetry for clues. Sonnet 111 says:

O for my sake doe you wish fortune chide,
The guiltie goddesse of my harmfull deeds,
That did not better for my life provide,
Then publick means which publick manners breeds.
Thence comes it that my name receives a brand,
And almost thence my nature is subdu'd
To what it works in, like the Dyer's hand.

Scholars generally agree that Shakespeare was being both sarcastic and ironic. But most scholars also agree that "harmful deeds" refers to his success in the theater, and the reference to his name receiving a "brand" (in the sense we would talk about a brand name today) because of his theatrical associations is unmistakable. The American scholar Oscar James Campbell (*A Shakespeare Encyclopaedia*, 1966) said there was "little doubt for which achievement he wished to be remembered: the preservation of the plays is owed to the efforts of others [meaning the people who published the First Folio], the [two early narrative] poems Shakespeare seems to have seen through the press himself."

Venus and Adonis

In short, *Venus and Adonis* describes the unrequited infatuation of Venus, the Roman goddess of love and beauty, for Adonis, a somewhat self-absorbed golden boy. All he wants to do is get on with his hunt, but Venus pursues him regardless. She pulls him off his horse, kisses him all over, and aggressively chases him over hill and dale until the hunter has become the prey. "No, lady, no; my heart longs not to groan, / But soundly sleeps while now it sleeps alone," he says. He returns to his hunt and gets killed by a wild boar. In her grief, Venus cries out, placing a curse on love for all eternity:

Sorrow on love hereafter shall attend.
It shall be waited on with jealousy,
Find sweet beginning, but unsavoury end . . .
The strongest body shall it make most weak,
Strike the wise dumb, and teach the fool to speak . . .
It shall be raging-mad, and silly-mild;

Make the young old, the old become a child.
It shall suspect where is no cause of fear;
It shall not fear where it should most mistrust . . .
It shall be cause of war and dire events,
And set dissension 'twixt the son and sire . . .
Sith in his prime death doth my love destroy,
They that love best their loves shall not enjoy."

She turns Adonis into a purple and white flower and vows to wear this nosegay "day and night."

The Rape of Lucrece

The *Rape of Lucrece* is more serious. It tells the story of Lucretia, an aristocratic Roman matron who is raped by Tarquin, the son of the Roman king. He steals into her bedroom determined to have his way with her, and the first half of the poem is told from his point of view as she begs to be spared. Nothing moves him. He tells her:

This night I must enjoy thee.
If thou deny, then force must work my way
For in thy bed I purpose to destroy thee.

The last half of the poem is told from her point of view, and focuses on the terrible experience she has just endured. Despite her distress she proclaims, "I am the mistress of my fate," and she decides to tell everyone what has happened to her before she kills herself. She tells her husband, father, and his lords what has been done to her and demands vengeance. Then she stabs herself in the heart to allow her soul to escape, and her bloody corpse is paraded through the streets of Rome. Tarquin is banished, and according to legend, the political fallout of the rape ended the rule by kings and led to the establishment of the Roman Republic.

Lesser-Known Poems

In 1599, when Shakespeare was solidly entrenched as a playwright, a volume of poetry titled *The Passionate Pilgrim* was published. Although his name did not appear on it as the author, it had been attributed to Shakespeare. However, only five of the poems are now considered his. A love elegy, *The Phoenix and the Turtle*, was published in 1601, but because it was not considered worthy of his writing, it was ignored. This was also true of *A Lover's Complaint*, which was published along with the sonnets in 1609, mostly as an afterthought, used to fill out the pages of the volume.

A Lover's Complaint is a monologue delivered to an old shepherd by a distraught young woman whose lover has left her. This betrayal sounds like what has happened endless times throughout history to lovers: He was handsome and intelligent, but she realized by the number of illegitimate children he fathered that he was not the marrying kind. She should have known better, but she let him have his way with her anyway, and he dropped her for someone else soon after.

In the 1980s and 1990s many Elizabethan scholars concluded that *A Funeral Elegy*, a poem published in 1612 and signed "W. S." exhibits many Shakespearean characteristics, although recently some of those (like Donald Foster) who first thought the poem Shakespeare's have backed away from that claim.

The enigmatic lyric *The Phoenix and the Turtle* (published in *Love's Martyr*, 1601), leaves many scholars bewildered. Is it a joke, obscene, or deadly serious? What is the "bird of loudest lay"? There has been little agreement and relatively little commentary about it.

The Sonnets

Shakespeare's sonnets were first published in 1609, but there is no clear evidence of when they were written. Scholars generally date them from 1594 to about 1599 (though some say 1597). Francis Meres in *Palladis Tamia* (1598) mentions that "honytongued Shakespeare, witnes his Venus and Adonis, his Lucrece, his sugred Sonnets among his private frinds."

The sonnet uses a formal rhyme scheme where each line is in iambic pentameter—each line has ten syllables denoting different thoughts, moods, or emotions. The two main forms of the sonnet are the Petrarchan (Italian) and the Shakespearean (English).

Italian Sonnet

While the Italians had been using the form for almost 200 years prior to Shakespeare's time, Sir Thomas Wyatt and Henry Howard, Earl of Surrey introduced the sonnet into England. William Shakespeare's first few years in London were spent writing in the Italian style.

There's no easy way to explain this, but here goes: The Italian sonnet form has an eight-line stanza (or octave) followed by a six-line stanza (or sestet). The octave has two quatrains, rhyming ABBA, ABBA, but avoiding a couplet. The first quatrain gives the theme, and the second develops it. The sestet is built on two or three different rhymes; the first three lines reflect on the theme, and the last three lines bring the whole poem to an end. Got that?

English Sonnet

The English sonnet differs from the Italian in that it is divided into three quatrains, each rhymed differently, with an independently rhymed couplet at the end. The rhyme scheme of the English sonnet is ABAB, CDCD, EFEF, GG. Each quatrain takes a different appearance of the idea or develops a different image to express the theme. Except for a few early poems, all of Shakespeare's sonnets were in this form.

Are all these rhyme schemes confusing? Don't worry about it unless you're going to study poetry seriously. It's easy enough to enjoy the sonnets as they are without having to delve into the technicalities.

Personal Poetry

Sonnets were personal poetry and usually circulated among one's friends and close acquaintances. It was thought "bad form" to publish sonnets and undesirable to write them for the purpose of being published. They were private thoughts for a select few.

Copyright laws in sixteenth century England were nonexistent, so a printer named Thomas Thorpe copied the sonnets and published them without Shakespeare's knowledge. Some critics disagree; they suggest that for some unknown reason, Shakespeare may have decided to work with Thorpe.

Are the Sonnets Autobiographical?

Shakespeare wrote 154 sonnets. Not much is known about Shakespeare's private life, so scholars have searched his plays and the sonnets in particular for hints, without much success. They have attracted more attention than anything else he wrote except *Hamlet*. As poetry, they are superb. People are just as interested in them because they may tell a story.

The story is hinted at, rather than told, and concerns Shakespeare's feelings toward a young nobleman who wronged him by stealing the affections of a sweetheart and by transferring his friendship to another poet. (Some think it might have been Marlowe, though that is unlikely looking at the dates.) In the end the young nobleman is forgiven. Critics and scholars disagree about whether the sonnets are autobiographical.

The first 126 sonnets are addressed to a man with the initials W. H. Scholars conjecture that W. H. may be the inverted initials of Henry Wriothesley, third Earl of Southampton, to whom Shakespeare had dedicated his earlier poems, or they may stand for William Herbert, Earl of Pembroke, or for someone else entirely.

The remaining poems are addressed to the so-called "dark lady" of the sonnets, since it is made clear that she is dark in hair and complexion. Guesses have been made as to who she might be. Some think it was Mary Fitton, a maid of honor at court and mistress of William Herbert, but the supposition does not have enough evidence to prove it.

Recurring Themes

Only by analyzing the entire set of sonnets, some critics say, is it possible to fathom Shakespeare's intent. For example, a sonnet with a certain meaning may be followed immediately by a sonnet conveying the opposite message. The first cannot be discussed without the second because the contradiction between the two defines their nature. The sonnets build on, cancel out, and are formed by each other. The meanings of the sonnets are all relative, but in general they are marked by the recurring themes of beauty, youthful beauty ravaged by time, and the ability of love and art to transcend time and even death.

In the first twenty-seven sonnets, Shakespeare proposes one method to outwit the passage of time. He urges the young man to have children so that his beauty will be preserved in posterity and therefore time will not have won the battle. The first two lines of the first sonnet present this theme:

From fairest creatures we desire increase,
That thereby beauty's rose might never die.

In Sonnet 11, Shakespeare tells the young man that when he grows old he will be young in his children and that:

Herein lives wisdom, beauty and increase;
Without this, folly, age and cold decay.

The poet goes on to explain to the young man that nature has given him a gift of beauty so that he may reproduce it. The couplet sums it up:

She [Mother Nature] carved thee for her seal, and meant thereby
Thou shouldst print more, not let that copy die.

Shakespeare's suggestions to the young man sometimes turn into accusations that he is hoarding the beauty, which he was lent, and therefore abusing the lease. After Sonnet 17, when it becomes apparent the young man is unwilling to marry, Shakespeare presents another way in which to wage war against time.

He says that his poetry will always exist and be read and that through his poetry his love will be forever alive. In Sonnet 15, Shakespeare writes in the last four lines:

Where wasteful time debateth with decay
To change your [the young man's] day of youth into sullied night;
And all in war with time for love of you,
As he [time] takes from you, I engraft you new.

Homosexuality or Platonic Love?

In the last of the sonnets, Shakespeare writes of the love between the writer and the young man, and the poet and his mistress. They describe a number of circumstances in the poet's relationship with these people. The final opponent of time is presented in Sonnet 116:

Love is not love
Which alters when it alteration finds,
Or bends with the remover to remove.
O no, it is an ever fixed mark
That looks on tempests and is never shaken;
It is the star to every wand'ring barque,
Whose worth's unknown although his height be taken.
Love's not time's fool, though rosy lips and cheeks
Within his bending sickle's compass come;
Love alters not with his brief hours and weeks,
But bears it out even to the edge of doom.

Some scholars suggest that the sonnets betray homosexuality between Shakespeare and another. The word *homosexual* had not yet been invented and would not be invented until the early twentieth century. Elizabethan law, however, condemned any act of sodomy. Whether Shakespeare expresses or does not express same-sex love in the sonnets cannot be proven. Readers, however, should also take into account both the concept of platonic, nonphysical love between men prevalent in the Renaissance and the more permissive attitudes toward same-sex love held by Renaissance playwrights, despite sixteenth-century magistrates.

Hallet Smith, writing in *The Riverside Shakespeare*, commented that, "the attitude of the poet toward the friend [the handsome young man] is one of love and admiration, deference and possessiveness, but it is not at all a sexual passion. Sonnet 20 makes quite clear the difference between the platonic love of a man for a man, more often expressed in the sixteenth century than the twentieth, and any kind of homosexual attachment."

Regardless of the uncertainty about who, where, when, and why, when it comes to Shakespeare, scholars agree that several of these poems are among the most perfect ever written.

CHAPTER 10

An Introduction to the Plays

Since his death, Shakespeare's plays have been performed almost continually, in English as well as other languages, and he is quoted more than any other single author. The plays have constantly been examined by critics trying to explain their timeless appeal, each criticism a reflection of the era in which the critic lived.

Shakespeare and Elizabethan Theater

Far too often critics have faulted Shakespeare's discrepancies when writing of philosophy, religion, or ideology. In *A Midsummer Night's Dream* he writes of young love as a burlesque of the kind of tragic love that he treats idealistically in *Romeo and Juliet*. In *Troilus and Cressida* he writes of the same tragic love cynically.

Philosophy and ideology aside, one must look at Shakespeare's strength—his characters. Within the pages of Shakespeare's plays lies an abundance of complex characters and their eloquent, vivid, and lyrical speech. These characters are vivid, they are alive, and they almost rise from the page, crying out to be heard. But Shakespeare declined to make them all good or all bad. Like Hamlet or Macbeth or King Lear, they are flawed, struggling with an inconsistent nature. Hamlet fascinates us because of his mental turmoil over whether or not to avenge his father's death. Because of this we wonder if he is truly mad. Even in a comic character such as boisterous and cowardly Falstaff, we ultimately find him moving.

FACT

One thing about the Elizabethan theater worth remembering is that it is far removed from the theater of today. There were no special effects, no extravagant set designs, no dazzling lighting effects, and no stereophonic sound. Yes, the costumes were lavishly rich and colorful, but the Elizabethan stage was bare. Other than a few props, such as swords and some simple scenic backgrounds (perhaps a balcony for Juliet), the audience relied on the actors' acting ability to make the play come alive.

This allowed the audience to focus on the play, not its equipment. Because of the design of the stage, the actors were in close contact with the playgoers, whose arms could rest on the "apron" that thrust into the audience. They could smell the sweat from an actor, feel the spittle from a dramatic speech. An Elizabethan player was in such close contact with the spectators, he could almost reach out and knight them with a sword. The actor played almost from the audience, not just to it from above. Today, this effect can somewhat be achieved by staging plays "in the round," that is, with the audience sitting 360 degrees around the action of the play, not just viewing it from in front of a stage.

The Four Time Periods

Shakespeare's plays can broadly be divided into four time periods:

- Pre-1594 (*King Richard III, The Comedy of Errors,* etc.)
- 1594–1600 (*King Henry V, A Midsummer Night's Dream,* etc.)
- 1600–1608 (*Macbeth, King Lear,* etc.)
- Post-1608 (*Cymbeline, The Tempest,* etc.)

The first period (pre-1594) has its roots in Greek, Roman, and medieval English drama—the plays show a certain obviousness. It's possible that Shakespeare was influenced by Christopher Marlowe—now considered Shakespeare's greatest literary rival—whose writing was gaining recognition as Shakespeare's playwrighting career began.

The second period (1594–1600) shows a clearly maturing author, and the plays are less labored and predictable. The histories of this period portray royalty in human terms rather than as ciphers to move along a plot. He experiments with blending comedy and tragedy, considered a trademark of Shakespeare's that would become a stylistic signature.

The third period (1600–1608) marks the great tragedies. At this point he wrote the plays that would earn him his place in history. Lear, Hamlet, Macbeth, and Othello are classic tragic protagonists in the best dramatic sense. The comedies, meanwhile, grow moody and ambiguous.

FACT

Scholars still debate whether these last plays show Shakespeare writing in a form of dramatic shorthand, or whether the plays reflect an evolving theatrical trend from Elizabethan tastes to Jacobean as James I's reign took hold.

The last period is one of cynical plays followed by plays of deep symbolism. At the end of his career, and facing middle age, Shakespeare seemed preoccupied with stories of redemption. The "Romances" show Shakespeare at his most symbolic.

Chronological Order of Plays

Despite the above, dating and grouping Shakespeare's plays is problematic. In 1598 commentator Francis Meres created a kind of literary marker when he wrote that Shakespeare was "the greatest English playwright," and listed his plays to date. This list has helped scholars distinguish the earlier plays from the later ones.

Meres also lists a play named *Love's Labour's Won*, which may have been revised and turned into *All's Well That Ends Well*. A reasonable approximation of the order of the plays has been deduced from dates of publication, references in writings of the same time, allusions in the plays to then-current events, thematic relationships, and stylistic comparisons.

The Early Plays (Pre-1594)

What play came first? The order in which Shakespeare's plays has been written has caused speculation, arguments, and near fisticuffs among scholars. Some are adamant that the first plays are the three parts of *King Henry VI*. But it is not clear if *Part I* was written before or after Parts *II* and *III*. *King Richard III*, because if its "kingly" title is related to these plays. Richard is hardly a soul mate of Henry, but that is where he has been placed as the final part of a first quartet of historical plays since his reign falls into that chronological order. Still others think *The Comedy of Errors* was Shakespeare's first play. Some evidence suggests it might have been *King Edward III*, a new play now being considered by many critics as part of the canon.

After the early Henrys, it's believed that what came next were *The Comedy of Errors*, *Titus Andronicus*, *The Taming of the Shrew*, *The Two Gentlemen of Verona*, *Love's Labour's Lost*, and *Romeo and Juliet*. The two tragedies, *Titus Andronicus* and *Romeo and Juliet*, were performed successfully in Shakespeare's lifetime to the joy of audiences who loved a little blood and gore on the stage.

After these early plays, and before his great tragedies, Shakespeare wrote *King Richard II, A Midsummer Night's Dream, King John, The Merchant of Venice, King Henry IV Parts I* and *II, Much Ado About Nothing, King Henry V, Julius Caesar, As You Like It,* and *Twelfth Night. King Richard II,* each part of *King Henry IV,* and *King Henry V* form a second quartet of historical plays, although each can stand alone. *King Henry IV* introduces the fat knight Falstaff, one of Shakespeare's classic creations who has enjoyed immense popularity from the beginning.

The Great Tragedies (1600–1608)

Shakespeare's great tragedies and the "problem plays" (meaning they are hard to categorize and critique) date from 1600 with *Hamlet.* Following this are *The Merry Wives of Windsor* (written on the request of Queen Elizabeth I, who wanted to see a play featuring Falstaff), *Troilus and Cressida, All's Well That Ends Well, Measure for Measure, Othello, King Lear, Macbeth, Antony and Cleopatra, Coriolanus,* and *Timon of Athens.*

FACT

Othello, King Lear, and *Macbeth* deal with the conflict of order and chaos, good and evil, and spirituality and hedonism. *Pericles, Cymbeline, The Winter's Tale* and *The Tempest* are grouped as "romances" and are considered tragicomedies. The main characters seem to encompass a tragic potential to rival Lear or Othello, but the plays can be considered comedies because they end happily, often through magical ends.

Appreciating Shakespeare's Greatness

As with any exceptionally popular author, Shakespeare's work was appreciated differently over time. In his own day, for example, according to Ben Jonson, *Titus Andronicus,* a bloodthirsty revenge melodrama regarded as one of Shakespeare's least interesting plays until the release of Julie Taymor's movie version, was particularly enjoyed. The poet John Dryden (1631–1700) in *Essay on Dramatic Poesy,* preferred *King Richard II;* and Samuel Johnson (1709–84), in his *Preface to Shakespeare* admired the comedies.

What Was Popular in Elizabethan Times?

It makes sense that *Titus Andronicus* would have pleased the crowd in an age where bloody executions were popular spectacles. Yet Shakespeare was criticized for mixing comedy, romance, and tragedy, blending them into one. Certainly *Romeo and Juliet* is a love story with a tragic ending. Critics of the time, such as John Dryden and Samuel Johnson, accused Shakespeare of corrupting the language with false wit, puns, and ambiguity. Modern critics certainly didn't share that view and have praised the language for adding depth and resonance of meaning. Ben Jonson, Shakespeare's rival, promoted Shakespeare's genius, even though many of his contemporaries disagreed with him.

Beginning with A. C. Bradley's seminal text *Shakespearean Tragedy*, published in 1904, the twentieth century has been the most prolific in appreciating and commenting on Shakespeare's greatness. George Wilson Knight (*The Imperial Theme* and *The Crown of Life*), Harley Granville-Barker (*Preface to Shakespeare*), and others have contributed to our understanding of the plays and poetry.

The first collected edition of Shakespeare is the First Folio, published in 1623. It includes all the plays except *Pericles, Prince of Tyre, King Edward III, The Two Noble Kinsmen*, and the lost play *Cardenio*. Eighteen of the plays exist in earlier quarto editions, eight of which are extremely corrupt, probably reconstructed from an actor's memory. In 1709, Nicholas Rowe was the first to publish Shakespeare's plays divided into acts and scenes and with exits and entrances marked. Other important early editions include Alexander Pope's (1725), Lewis Theobald's (1733), and Samuel Johnson's (1765).

Among Shakespeare's most important sources, Raphael Holinshed's *Chronicles of England, Scotland, and Ireland* (1587) is significant for the English history plays. For his Roman tragedies he used Sir Thomas North's translation (1579) of *Plutarch's Lives*. Since plagiarism was not a problem, nor were ideas copyrighted, Shakespeare revised old plays and turned English prose romances into drama (*As You Like It* and *The Winter's Tale*). He also freely used the works of his contemporaries in Europe.

The following table, following genre and alphabet, shows how Shakespeare's plays are usually grouped:

COMEDY	HISTORY	TRAGEDY
All's Well That Ends Well	King Edward III	Antony and Cleopatra
As You Like It	King Henry IV, Part I	Cardenio
The Comedy of Errors	King Henry IV, Part II	Coriolanus
Cymbeline	King Henry V	Hamlet, Prince of Denmark
Love's Labour's Lost	King Henry VI, Part I	Julius Caesar
Measure for Measure	King Henry VI, Part II	King Lear
The Merchant of Venice	King Henry VI, Part III	Macbeth
The Merry Wives of Windsor	King Henry VIII	Othello, Moor of Venice
A Midsummer Night's Dream	King John	Romeo and Juliet
Much Ado About Nothing	King Richard II	Timon of Athens
Pericles, Prince of Tyre	King Richard III	Titus Andronicus
The Taming of the Shrew		
The Tempest		
Troilus and Cressida		
Twelfth Night		
The Two Gentlemen of Verona		
The Two Noble Kinsmen		
The Winter's Tale		

Shakespearean Comedy

Comedy, in its simplest terms, is a play with a light touch and a happy ending, usually signaled by a wedding. The audience is at the theater to laugh and to enjoy themselves. Yet Shakespeare carries the genre further with his tragic comedies, such as *The Tempest*, and several problem plays like *All's Well That Ends Well*. He invites his audiences to enjoy a temporary perfection not found in the real world. Outside the magic circle of the theater, lost children are not returned, wicked brothers rarely repent, statues do not come to life, and if we leave a Shakespearean comedy with a tear in our eyes, it is only an acknowledgment that the enchantment of the theater has staved off this "mortal coil" for an hour or two, but now we must return to the bitterness that life can bring us.

Shakespearean History

With the exceptions of *King John* and *King Henry VIII* (coauthored with John Fletcher), the histories or historical plays cover the Wars of the Roses, a series of violent civil wars fought over the English Crown. (*King John* stands as an odd man out, but it is a play more about character than plot.)

The Tudor Dynasty

The history starts with Edward III, whose army defeated the French at the Battle of Crécy in 1346, establishing England as a great military power, and picks up the story again in 1398, two years before Richard II is deposed. It then moves to 1485, when Henry VII defeated Richard III at the Battle of Bosworth and established the Tudor dynasty.

Henry VII was Elizabeth I's grandfather, and he went to considerable effort to legitimize his right to the throne of England by force of arms. *King Henry VIII* is about the birth of Queen Elizabeth as a result of divorce.

The plays cleave quite rigidly to the Tudor party line. Shakespeare was certainly no fool and was not about to upset his patron queen or suggest that she was somehow not the legitimate heir to the throne, regardless of historical truth.

The Lancaster Dynasty

As has been stated before, plays about kings and dynasties were not written in chronological order. The *King Henry VI* trilogy and *King Richard III* were written close together near the start of Shakespeare's career (around 1589–1593). They cover the fall of the Lancaster dynasty—that is, events in English history between 1422 and 1485. Then, about three years later (around 1595–1599), came *King Richard II*, and after another couple of years *King Henry IV, Parts I* and *II*, and then finally *King Henry V*. This second series, written at the height of Shakespeare's powers, moves back in time to examine the rise of the Lancastrians, covering English history from 1398 to 1420.

QUESTION?

How could an Elizabethan audience keep track of the lineage of the royalty of England?
Although Shakespeare's audiences were not well educated, the historical events he wrote about had only recently been recorded by Hall and Holinshed, which gave the stories new currency, as did books like *A Mirror For Magistrates*. Having been a very "ora-aural" nation until Shakespeare's time, it is also probable that many versions of historical events had entered into popular legend. The battles among houses of royalty and the rise and fall of kings were woven into the fabric of English culture and are part of the country's patriotic national mythology.

Sources of Historical Material

Shakespeare was not reluctant to use a number of different sources in writing his history plays. His primary source for historical material is generally agreed to be Raphael Holinshed's massive work, *The Chronicles of England, Scotland, and Ireland*, published in 1586–1587. Holinshed's accounts read more like an encyclopedia, yet his well-researched book provided the chronology of events that allowed Shakespeare to reproduce, or change, history to suit his dramatic purpose. Shakespeare wasn't the only one to use Holinshed's work. Other playwrights found within the covers of the book a wealth of material. Nor was Holinshed the only historical chronicler who was popular during Shakespeare's time.

As he matured as a playwright, Shakespeare focused more on building character and less on plot or historical events. He realized that a fictious Falstaff and an imagined Boar's Head tavern where Fat Jack drank with Prince Hal were worth more dramatically than a phony re-creation of battle.

One of the principal questions that preoccupy the characters in the history plays is the divine right of kings, that is, whether or not the king of England is appointed by God. This linchpin philosophy of social order was not challenged until the overthrow of Charles I during the English Civil War in 1642. If a king is divinely appointed, the theory goes, then his overthrow or murder will come to haunt the king who gains the throne through such blasphemous means.

This ghost manifests itself in *Hamlet*, *Macbeth*, *Julius Caesar*, and *King Richard III*, and it hovers over *King Richard II* and its sequels. The murder of the former King Richard II will haunt King Henry IV for the rest of his life, and only his son Henry V can redeem the curse.

When Shakespeare next returned to history, it was not to Holinshed's England, but to the Rome of Plutarch and Ovid for *Julius Caesar* and *Antony and Cleopatra*. Rightly, they are considered tragedies rather than histories because they so firmly focus on character.

The Wars of the Roses

To best follow the eight Shakespeare plays that trace the Wars of the Roses it's helpful to understand the historical events they re-create. For over 100 years, England's royal family was split into two struggling factions: the Lancaster family, symbolized by a red rose, and the York family, symbolized by a white rose.

The problems began in the late fourteenth century, with the death of King Edward III. Edward had seven sons, and the third and fourth sons became dynastic heads: John of Gaunt, Duke of Lancaster, and his younger brother Edmund, Duke of York.

Edward III was succeeded by Richard II, who was descended from Edward's oldest son, and was neither a Yorkist nor a Lancastrian. Richard ruled for several years before he was overthrown by his cousin, Henry Bolingbroke, the son of John of Gaunt. Bolingbroke became Henry IV and founded the Lancastrian dynasty. Henry IV was in turn succeeded by his son, Henry V, who was succeeded by his son, Henry VI.

In the late fifteenth century, fighting broke out again, this time between Lancastrians and Yorkists. After a bloody struggle, the Yorkists Edward, Clarence, and their younger brother Richard murdered Henry VI (along with his son and destined heir, Edward, Prince of Wales).

The oldest of the York brothers took the throne as King Edward IV. After he died, his younger brother Richard III took the throne, and he remained there until he was defeated in battle by Henry, Duke of Richmond, who became Henry VII and established peace and the Tudor dynasty.

Thus reads the entangled lives and chaotic history of English royalty.

Shakespearean Tragedy

While Holinshed's history of England proved a source for many early plays, what did Shakespeare use for Roman history? North's translation of Plutarch's *Lives of the Noble Greeks and Romans* no doubt exerted a greater influence over Shakespeare than any other classical source. For example, many scholars consider *Julius Caesar* to be the play that bridges the history and tragedy genres, with Brutus the first of Shakespeare's tragic heroes.

Though there are others, the four most famous Shakespearean tragedies are *King Lear*, *Hamlet*, *Othello*, and *Macbeth*. *Hamlet* is about an emotionally scarred young man trying to come to terms with his urge to avenge the murder of his father, the King, and his awareness of the resultant perdition should he follow that urge. Othello, a Moor and feted general in the army of Venice, is victimized as a result of his love for Desdemona, the daughter of a Venetian statesman. The villain of the play is Iago, Othello's trusted advisor, who plots revenge against Othello, Desdemona, and Cassio because Othello has promoted Cassio to a position Iago feels should be his. Macbeth is a noble warrior driven by his ambition and that of his ruthless wife to murder to attain power. *King Lear* is a tragic story of hubris—of an old man who makes a foolish mistake and pays for it with a descent into madness as his children betray and abandon him, and his world crumbles around him.

CHAPTER 11

Shakespeare's Comedies

As previously noted, what defines a Shakespearean comedy is a light touch, a happy ending, and a wedding, though these plays also contain farce and slapstick. To Shakespeare, comedy meant that foolish humans were able to triumph over adversity, which implies a positive reading of human experience. Comedy to some experts means looking to the future, past the wedding that concludes the action onstage, to the offstage sexual union that ensures life goes on. The end of the comedy is an occasion for jokes, smiles, and nudges with an elbow.

A Midsummer Night's Dream

Main Characters

Theseus—the Duke of Athens; he represents tradition, authority, and wisdom. He is about to marry Hippolyta

Hippolyta—an Amazon queen; Theseus won her as a bride by defeating her in a sword fight

Egeus—Hermia's father

Philostrate—Master of Revels

Hermia—daughter of Egeus

Lysander—a young man in love with Hermia

Helena—Hermia's friend, who is in love with Demetrius

Demetrius—another young man in love with Hermia

Oberon—king of the fairies

Titania—queen of the fairies

Puck—otherwise known as Robin Goodfellow

Peaseblossom, Cobweb, Moth, and Mustardseed—fairy attendants to Titania

Bottom, Peter Quince, Francis Flute, Tom Snout, Snug, Robin Starveling— Athenian tradesmen

Introduction

A Midsummer Night's Dream is one of Shakespeare's early comedies, probably written in 1595. It is also one of the few totally original plays he wrote, stemming, we must assume, from his fertile imagination. Scholars believe that he wrote the play as a confection of entertainment for the marriage celebration of Elizabeth Carey, granddaughter of a patron of the Lord Chamberlain's Men. Shakespeare was a member of this theatrical troupe. Not burdened by historical references, it must have been a joy for him to write. The influence of the Latin writer Ovid is also evident.

The Play

The tangled love gets confusing in *A Midsummer Night's Dream*, sometimes reading like a comedy television sitcom: Helena loves Demetrius; Demetrius once was engaged to Helena, but now loves her friend, Hermia; Hermia loves Lysander; Lysander returns her love. To add to this confusion of comedy, Egeus, Hermia's father, gets Theseus, the Duke of Athens, to insist that Hermia marry Demetrius. Athenian law decrees that Hermia follow her father's will; Theseus gives her till morning to choose between Demetrius, a life in a nunnery, or a death sentence. Hermia flees with Lysander into the surrounding forest and the comedy of this comely couple ends happily.

In *A Midsummer Night's Dream*, Shakespeare offers a plethora of characters, a mix of situations and a forest setting. There we find Oberon and Titania, king and queen of fairies, arguing over a boy Titania has adopted. Oberon wants the boy as one of his retinue. Oberon instructs his servant Puck to sprinkle love drops in the queen's eyes while she sleeps, telling Puck that when Titania awakens she will fall in love with the first living thing she sees.

Meanwhile four other characters become involved in the comedy: Helena and Demetrius, who chase after Lysander and Hermia. Oberon, overhearing Demetrius reject the lovesick Helena, takes pity on her and tells Puck to use the love drops on Demetrius as well, so that Demetrius will fall for Helena. Puck, not the smartest of the king's servants, gets confused and puts the drops in Lysander's eyes instead. He wakes up to see Helena. Now the drugged Lysander wants Helena and rejects a stunned Hermia.

To add to this comedy mixture, a group of Athenian craftsmen, ignorant of all these comings and goings and knowing nothing about the love drops or the lovers, are rehearsing a production of a play, *Pyramus and Thisbe*, to be acted at the duke's wedding. Puck casts a spell on one of them, Bottom, giving him the head of a donkey. Using all of his mental power, he organizes things so that Bottom is the first creature Titania sees when she awakes.

The puzzling story line continues: Bottom is unaware of his new head. Although he doesn't understand why, he ends up being kept lavishly by the fairy queen. Oberon enjoys Titania's humiliation but is not happy that Puck has botched the attempt to reunite Demetrius and Helena. Now to add to the plot, Oberon himself puts the love potion in Demetrius's eyes and makes sure Helena is the first person he sees. Helena is confused, but unconvinced, and thinks both Demetrius and Lysander are mocking her because both now profess love for her.

Oberon, seeing all the perplexed personages, decides it's time to sort things out. He puts the four lovers to sleep and gives Lysander the antidote for the love potion so that he will love Hermia again when they all wake up. Next, Oberon gives Titania the antidote, and the king and queen reconcile.

No, the story's not finished yet. Theseus and Hippolyta discover Lysander, Hermia, Helena, and Demetrius asleep in the forest. Shaking their heads in wonder, they return to Athens to make sense of what they think is a strange dream. Bottom, believing that he dreamt he had the head of an ass, returns to his players, and they perform *Pyramus and Thisbe* at the wedding feast, which becomes the weddings of three couples. Curtain.

Commentary

A Midsummer Night's Dream is full of paradoxes. The play can be analyzed thusly: First, it's all about imagination versus reality. The play is not only the poet's dream but also the audience's. It blends imaginative fancy with the stately traditions of Athenian aristocracy. The conflicts between youthful rebellion and authoritarianism and between the magical and the everyday lend the play a timeless quality. It blurs the distinction between reality and imagination for both the characters—and the audience, joyfully so.

The play has been an interesting indicator of the eras in which it has been produced. Modern interpretations, for example, have cast the fairy world as a Freudian repository of repressions and erotic desires. It is a testament to Shakespeare's genius that the play can be reinvented in so many different ways; the universal concerns of the nature of love, reality, sexuality, imagination, and the status quo social order give the play a timeless appeal. It's worth recalling that unlike other forms of literature, plays have live audiences—not passive readers—that are active participants in the theatrical experience.

Famous Lines

"For aught that I could ever read,
Could ever hear by tale or history,
The course of true love never did run smooth" (Act I, Scene I).

"Love looks not with the eyes, but with the mind;
And therefore is winged Cupid painted blind" (Act I, Scene I).

"That would hang us, every mother's son" (Act I, Scene II).

"I'll put a girdle round about the earth
In forty minutes" (Act II, Scene I).

"I know a bank where the wild thyme blows,
Where oxlips and the nodding violet grows,
Quite over-canopied with luscious woodbine,
With sweet musk-roses and with eglantine"(Act II, Scene I).

"Lord, what fools these mortals be!" (Act III, Scene II).

"I have had a dream, past the wit of man to say what dream it was" (Act IV, Scene I).

"The best in this kind are but shadows" (Act V, Scene I).

As You Like It

Main Characters

Duke Senior—father of Rosalind; forced to live in exile in the Forest of Arden after his kingdom was usurped by his brother Duke Frederick

Rosalind (Ganymede)—daughter of Duke Senior; forced to flee to the Forest of Arden disguised as a young man called Ganymede; in love with Orlando

Lord Amiens—a faithful lord of Duke Senior in exile in the forest; an optimist

Lord Jaques—a faithful lord of Duke Senior in exile in the forest; a pessimist

Duke Frederick—Duke Senior's brother and usurper of Senior's throne; Celia's father

Celia (Aliena)—Duke Frederick's daughter, Rosalind's cousin, and Rosalind's best friend; she falls in love with Oliver at first sight

Charles—a champion wrestler

Touchstone—a court clown who accompanies Rosalind and Celia; he falls in love with Audrey, a goatherd

Oliver—oldest son of Sir Rowland De Bois, and Orlando's older brother; for some reason, unknown even to himself, Oliver hates Orlando

Orlando—younger brother of Oliver; fearing for his life, he flees to the Forest of Arden; he's in love with Rosalind

Adam—an old retainer of Sir Rowland De Bois

Silvius—a young shepherd, in love with Phebe

Phebe—a young shepherdess who falls in love with Ganymede (Rosalind)

Corin—a friend of Silvius

Audrey—a goatherd, in love with Touchstone

William—a young country boy in love with Audrey

Introduction

As You Like It was most likely written between the years 1598 and 1600. It belongs to a literary tradition known as pastoral, which began in the literature of ancient Greece, flourished through Roman times, most particularly in the work of Virgil, and continued into Shakespeare's time.

Typically, a pastoral story involves exiles from urban life who arrive in the countryside and try to live as common folk. Though also the basis of great and conservative court entertainments known as *masques*, pastoral comedy became a forum for social commentary at a time when such open criticism could be problematic for a writer, not to mention dangerous on occasion.

The Play

As the play opens, Duke Senior has taken refuge in the Forest of Arden with a band of loyal followers, while his daughter, Rosalind, stays behind at the court of Duke Frederick, who has usurped his brother's throne.

We meet another set of brothers at odds with each other; Orlando and Oliver hate each other. Since their father's death, Oliver has long mistreated his younger brother, Orlando. When Orlando enters a wrestling match sponsored by Duke Frederick, Oliver tells Orlando's opponent, Charles—a champion wrestler—to break Orlando's neck if he can. To everyone's surprise, Orlando wins the match and attracts Rosalind's attention.

Duke Frederick decides to banish Rosalind to Arden as he did her father, Duke Senior. Celia, Frederick's daughter and Rosalind's best friend, decides to travel with her. Rosalind disguises herself as a boy called Ganymede, and Celia becomes Ganymede's sister, Aliena. The clown Touchstone accompanies them.

FACT

As You Like It delights in the ridiculousness of humans, constantly punching holes in the beliefs of one character through the analysis of other characters who are equally blind to the absurdity of their own value systems. This technique raises the play from simple entertainment to one that offers a social critique and stresses the complexity of things—the simultaneous pleasures and pains of being human.

Orlando wanders the forest, leaving love poems on the branches of trees for Rosalind. She, meanwhile, sets out to lead a pastoral life. Before long, however, disguised as Ganymede, Rosalind promises to help Orlando win his love's affection. Pretending to be Ganymede, she tells Orlando she will "play" Rosalind and help him woo her.

Still disguised as Ganymede, Rosalind tries to make a match between Silvius and Phebe, which goes awry; Phebe falls for Ganymede instead. Touchstone courts a country girl named Audrey, adding to the multiple romances.

Oliver enters the forest after Orlando. Orlando saves him from a lion, and the two brothers reconcile. Oliver then falls in love with Celia; Duke Senior promises to marry them the next day. Rosalind makes Phebe promise to marry Silvius if she can't have Ganymede, then tells Orlando that Rosalind will marry him that day as well.

When all have gathered for the wedding, Rosalind reveals herself as the erstwhile Ganymede. She and Orlando are happily reunited, and Phebe agrees to marry Silvius. Touchstone also marries Audrey. In a final resolution, we learn that Duke Frederick has seen the error of his ways and opted for a monastic life, restoring Duke Senior's throne.

Commentary

As You Like It is considered one of Shakespeare's best comedies. It pokes fun at the conventions of romantic love and explores the evils of primogeniture, a common English practice during Shakespeare's time in which the oldest son inherited everything, leaving younger siblings at their older brother's mercy.

The play manipulates the typical conventions of a pastoral in order to explore other issues. For instance, it was common in a pastoral for people to wear disguises. In *As You Like It*, Rosalind dresses as a man in order to make her journey into exile less dangerous. But Shakespeare pushes the tradition by having Rosalind, in disguise, encounter Orlando, and then role-play herself in order to teach Orlando how to woo her. In effect, the play raises questions about gender roles.

Famous Lines

"One out of suits with fortune" (Act I, Scene II).

"My pride fell with my fortunes" (Act I, Scene II).

"Beauty provoketh thieves sooner than gold" (Act I, Scene III).

"True is it that we have seen better days" (Act II, Scene VII).

"All the world's a stage,
And all the men and women merely players.
They have their exits and their entrances;
And one man in his time plays many parts,
His acts being seven ages. At first the infant,
Mewling and puking in the nurse's arms.
And then the whining school-boy, with his satchel
And shining morning face, creeping like snail
Unwillingly to school. And then the lover,
Sighing like furnace, with a woful ballad
Made to his mistress' eyebrow. Then a soldier,
Full of strange oaths and bearded like the pard;
Jealous in honour, sudden and quick in quarrel,
Seeking the bubble reputation
Even in the cannon's mouth. And then the justice,
In fair round belly with good capon lined,
With eyes severe and beard of formal cut,
Full of wise saws and modern instances;
And so he plays his part. The sixth age shifts
Into the lean and slipper'd pantaloon,
With spectacles on nose and pouch on side;
His youthful hose, well saved, a world too wide
For his shrunk shank; and his big manly voice,
Turning again toward childish treble, pipes
And whistles in his sound. Last scene of all,
That ends this strange eventful history,

Is second childishness and mere oblivion,
Sans teeth, sans eyes, sans taste, sans everything" (Act II, Scene VII).

"Blow, blow, thou winter wind!
Thou art not so unkind
As man's ingratitude" (Act II, Scene VII).

"He that wants money, means, and content is without three good friends"
(Act III, Scene II).

"With bag and baggage" (Act III, Scene II).

"Neither rhyme nor reason" (Act III, Scene II).

"I had rather have a fool to make me merry than experience to make me
sad" (Act IV, Scene I).

"Can one desire too much of a good thing?" (Act IV, Scene I).

"For ever and a day" (Act IV, Scene I).

"It is meat and drink to me" (Act V, Scene I).

"The fool doth think he is wise, but the wise man knows himself to be a
fool" (Act V, Scene I).

"How bitter a thing it is to look into happiness through another man's eyes!"
(Act V, Scene II).

"An ill-favoured thing, sir, but mine own" (Act V, Scene IV).

Love's Labour's Lost

Main Characters

Ferdinand—king of Navarre; a scholar

Berowne, Longaville, and Dumaine—three lords who have joined the king in his oath of scholarship; they fall in love with Rosaline, Maria, and Katherine, respectively

Princess of France—a visitor to the king

Rosaline, Maria, and Katherine—three ladies attending the princess who catch the fancy of the king's lords

Boyet—a lord attending the princess

Don Armado—described as "a fantastical Spaniard"; he catches Costard and Jaquenetta in the forest and falls in love with Jaquenetta

Moth—Don Armado's page

Costard—a clown

Jaquenetta—a country girl

Sir Nathaniel—a curate

Holofernes—a schoolmaster

Dull—a constable

Introduction

Love's Labour's Lost is an early play, published in 1598 and probably written about 1595. It was included as a comedy in Shakespeare's First Folio and is a meditation on love, though without a marriage at the end, which is untypical of a Shakespearean comedy. This is one of the few plays where the source of the play is unknown, though some scholars guess it may have come from *L'Académie Françoise* (1577), by Pierre de la Primaudaye, about a society of scholars.

Love's Labour's Lost was probably first performed in December of 1597, most likely as a Christmas entertainment for Queen Elizabeth I, and repeated about the same time of year for King James I in 1604.

The Play

Ferdinand, king of Navarre, declares that for a year his court will, in effect, become a school, and to keep distractions to a minimum, no women will be allowed during that time. His nobles, Berowne, Longaville, and Dumaine, agree to cloister themselves with the king, although Berowne has his reservations about how successful they will be. Berowne also points out that the king has forgotten that an embassy will arrive that very day with the princess of France. Rather than receive her at court, the Navarrese set out to meet the princess. Meanwhile, Costard, the king's fool, is about to be punished for dallying with a country girl, Jaquenetta.

The princess and her entourage are not happy when Ferdinand denies them entrance into the court. In protest, she camps in front of the court, and she and her ladies make plans to get even with Ferdinand and his courtiers.

Armado, who is in love with Jaquenetta, tells Costard he can go free if Costard delivers a letter to Jaquenetta. Next, Berowne asks him to take a letter to Rosaline. Totally confused, Costard delivers the letter intended for Jaquenetta to the princess of France and gives Rosaline's letter to Jaquenetta.

Shakespeare is famous for his puns, and this play has more than 200 of them. It is something of a parody of Elizabethan manners and personality types, and so it tends to go over the head of modern audiences. While the play might seem a dour, dreary affair, in the right hands it can actually be funny.

Ferdinand and his men eavesdrop on one another and overhear each other professing love for the princess and her gentlewomen. When the lords pay a visit to the ladies in disguise, however, the women are forewarned, disguise themselves, and make fun of the men. The men return as themselves, but the women continue to bait them, delighting in the men's confusion.

When things are finally being sorted out, and they are to be entertained by a play performed by some amateur actors, the princess learns that her father has died, and she must leave immediately. She tells Ferdinand that if he spends a year cloistered in a remote hermitage for breaking his own oath, she will marry him. With their mistress leaving, and knowing not what else to do, each of her ladies-in-waiting obtain similar promises from the king's lords vowing that they will return to Navarre the following year and marry if their loves have proven true.

Commentary

The play examines the idea that despite efforts to avoid passion, as human beings we can't get away from our emotions. At the end, we are reminded of this truth when, in the middle of blooming love, the pain of loss intrudes. Shakespeare seems to be suggesting that we often don't treasure what we have until we no longer have it, suggesting that is it best to appreciate the happiness of the moment.

Famous Lines

"Light seeking light doth light of light beguile" (Act I, Scene I).

"Affliction may one day smile again; and till then, sit thee down, sorrow!" (Act I, Scene I).

"To sell a bargain well is as cunning as fast and loose" (Act III, Scene I).

"They have been at a great feast of languages, and stolen the scraps" (Act V, Scene I).

"A jest's prosperity lies in the ear
Of him that hears it, never in the tongue
Of him that makes it" (Act V, Scene II).

Much Ado About Nothing

Main Characters

Leonato—the father of Hero and the uncle of Beatrice

Don Pedro—sometimes called "the Prince"; a longtime friend of Leonato

Don John—sometimes called "the Bastard"; the illegitimate brother of Don Pedro

Claudio—a young soldier who falls in love with Hero

Hero—the beautiful young daughter of Leonato and the cousin of Beatrice

Benedick—a friend and soldier of Don Pedro

Beatrice—Leonato's niece and Hero's cousin

Margaret—Hero's maid

Ursula—one of Hero's serving women

Borachio—Don John's servant and Margaret's lover

Conrade—one of Don John's servants

Dogberry—the constable of Messina

Verges—Dogberry's assistant

Antonio—Leonato's older brother and uncle to Hero and Beatrice

Friar Francis—a monk

Introduction

Much Ado About Nothing is generally considered one of Shakespeare's best comedies. It was probably written around 1598–99, as Shakespeare was approaching the middle of his career. Like *A Midsummer Night's Dream, As You Like It*, and *Twelfth Night*, it has few dark elements and provides a happy ending with no deaths.

The verbal sparring between Beatrice and Benedick may have been inspired by the fictional debates between a man and a woman created by the Italian writer Baldassare Castiglione in *The Book of the Courtier* (1528). Critics think the Hero-Claudio plot is based on *Orlando Furioso* (1532), an Italian epic poem by Ludovico Ariosto. Shakespeare may have read a translation by Sir John Harrington published in 1591. The character of Dogberry, the comic policeman or constable, is reminiscent of Constable Dull in *Love's Labour's Lost* and is an original creation by Shakespeare.

The Play

Don Pedro, the prince of Arragon, and two of his officers, Benedick and Claudio, visit Don Pedro's old friend Leonato, the governor of Messina. Claudio quickly falls in love with Leonato's daughter, Hero. Benedick continues a battle of wits with Beatrice, the governor's niece.

Don Pedro, with Leonato, Claudio, and Hero's help, decides it's time Benedick and Beatrice stopped tormenting each other verbally and admit that they are in love. To that end, Benedick and Beatrice are each made to think the other has secretly professed a great love for the other.

Don John despises Claudio, and when he learns about his impending marriage to Hero, he decides to ruin it. He tells Claudio that Pedro wants Hero for himself. Then he gets his servant Borachio and Hero's maid Margaret to stage an episode that will make it seem as though Hero is a loose woman.

FACT

The play has been popular since it was first staged and it is a contemporary favorite. In 1862, Hector Berlioz used it as the basis for his opera *Beatrice and Benedict*. *What To Do About Nothing*, a 1998 play by Judy Sheehan, retells the story, using gossip and eavesdropping as key elements, and setting it against the backdrop of the McCarthy "red scare" during the early 1950s in America.

Claudio is so upset that he denounces Hero at the altar. Friar Francis hides her away and with Beatrice's help announces that Hero has died of grief. Borachio drunkenly boasts of his part in the plan—and the 1,000 ducats Don John paid him—and is arrested by Dogberry and the watch.

Hero is exonerated and Claudio is grief-stricken at what he has done, still thinking Hero dead. Leonato demands a public apology from Claudio, then tells him that he must marry one of his nieces in Hero's place. The niece turns out to be Hero, of course, miraculously brought back to life. Claudio and Hero are reunited, and Benedick and Beatrice realize they love each other and get married at the same time. The bastard Don John is apprehended and will be brought to justice for his mischief making.

Commentary

Although *Much Ado About Nothing* is a light comedy, some critics are troubled by the anger, betrayal, hatred, grief, and despair that are at the center of the play. Like other Shakespearean comedies, for part of the time *Much Ado About Nothing* threatens to become a tragedy. The plot is an elaborate network of schemes and tricks, and it shares elements with *Romeo and Juliet*, *The Taming of the Shrew*, and even *Othello*, reminding us that comedy and tragedy are opposite ends of the same line.

Beatrice and Benedick's mature love affair can be compared in some ways to Antony and Cleopatra's, but is much happier and healthier. They are one of Shakespeare's most mature and nuanced couples.

While Hero and Claudio are the engine of the plot, it is actually the courtship of the older and wiser Benedick and Beatrice that makes this play such fun. Their journey from an emotional defensiveness and withdrawal brought about by their ages, which they defend with great wit, to deep affection is developed with a rich humor and compassion.

Famous Lines

"He wears his faith but as the fashion of his hat" (Act I, Scene I).

"What, my dear Lady Disdain! are you yet living?" (Act I, Scene I).

"Shall I never see a bachelor of threescore again?" (Act I, Scene I).

"As merry as the day is long" (Act II, Scene I).

"Speak low if you speak love" (Act II, Scene I).

"Friendship is constant in all other things
Save in the office and affairs of love:
Therefore all hearts in love use their own tongues;
Let every eye negotiate for itself
And trust no agent" (Act II, Scene I).

"Some Cupid kills with arrows, some with traps" (Act III, Scene I).

"Every one can master a grief but he that has it" (Act III, Scene II).

"Are you good men and true?" (Act III, Scene III).

"O, what men dare do! what men may do! what men daily do, not knowing
what they do!" (Act IV, Scene I).

"For it so falls out
That what we have we prize not to the worth
Whiles we enjoy it, but being lack'd and lost,
Why, then we rack the value; then we find
The virtue that possession would not show us
Whiles it was ours" (Act IV, Scene I).

"Condemned into everlasting redemption" (Act IV, Scene II).

"For there was never yet philosopher
That could endure the toothache patiently" (Act V, Scene I).

"Done to death by slanderous tongues" (Act V, Scene III).

The Comedy of Errors

Main Characters

Antipholus of Syracuse—the twin brother of Antipholus of Ephesus and
the son of Egeon
Antipholus of Ephesus—the twin brother of Antipholus of Syracuse and
the son of Egeon; a well-respected merchant in Ephesus and Adriana's
husband
Dromio of Syracuse—the slave of Antipholus of Syracuse and the twin
brother of Dromio of Ephesus
Dromio of Ephesus—the slave of Antipholus of Ephesus and the twin
brother of Dromio of Syracuse

Adriana—the wife of Antipholus of Ephesus

Luciana—Adriana's unmarried sister

Solinus—the Duke of Ephesus

Egeon—husband of the Abbess (Emilia); father of the two Antipholuses; he is searching for the missing half of his family

Abbess—Emilia, the long-lost wife of Egeon and the mother of both the Antipholuses

Balthasar—a merchant in Syracuse

Angelo—a goldsmith in Syracuse

Merchant—a friend of Antipholus of Syracuse

Second Merchant—a tradesman to whom Angelo is in debt

Doctor Pinch—a schoolteacher and would-be exorcist

Luce/Nell—Dromio of Ephesus's wife

Courtesan—an expensive prostitute

Introduction

The Comedy of Errors is an early play (some scholars think Shakespeare's first) with an emphasis on slapstick. It was first performed on December 28, 1594, at the Gray's Inn Christmas Revels, to an audience largely composed of lawyers and law students.

Shakespeare drew on the Roman comedy *Menaechmi* by Plautus (*c.* 254–184 B.C.E.) for his plot. Shakespeare had a grammar school education, and possibly was a schoolteacher prior to moving to London, so he may well have read the play in its original Latin. In 1594 an English translation was printed, though it had probably been floating around in manuscript form for some time before that.

FACT

As usual, Shakespeare made a number of changes to the original story: a second set of identical twins (the Dromios), the expansion of Adriana's character, a new character Luciana, and the subplot of Egeon and Emilia. The style of the comedy is modeled on the *commedia dell'arte* that developed in northern Italy from about 1550 onward.

The Comedy of Errors is driven by coincidence and slapstick, its events confined within a single day. Characters are mistaken for one another, but do not pretend to be other than who they are—there are no disguises here.

Typical of Shakespeare, there are also hints of tragedy—the story hinges on a threat of execution and includes broken families, troubled marriages, slavery, beatings, and a beheading.

The Play

The play is concerned with the separation and ultimate reunion of Egeon and his wife Emilia, and their twin sons, Antipholus of Ephesus (Antipholus E.) and Antipholus of Syracuse (Antipholus S.). The family is separated at sea during a storm, thirty-three years before the action of the play.

Egeon, Antipholus S., and Dromio S. survive the shipwreck together and grow up in Syracuse. Seven years before the action starts they decide to search, separately, for their lost family. Emilia survives with Antipholus E. and Dromio E., only to have a "rude" fisherman steal the boys from her. In sorrow, she becomes a nun. Eventually, Antipholus E. and Dromio E. move to Ephesus, though they don't know their mother Emilia is living there as well. Antipholus E. marries Adriana.

Ignoring a law that strangers can be put to death, Egeon comes to the city looking for Antipholus E. and his servant Dromio E. He is arrested and sentenced to death for entering enemy territory. Soon after, Antipholus S. and his servant, Dromio S., enter the city on business. The identical twins are easily confused by the citizens of Ephesus who think the Antipholus and Dromio they know have gone mad. Doctor Pinch, a schoolmaster, even tries to exorcise the devil from Antipholus E.

As Egeon's execution draws near, Egeon recognizes his son Antipholus E., though Antipholus E. doesn't recognize his father. Simultaneously, Emilia appears from the convent with Antipholus S. and Dromio S., who have taken refuge there, and the family reunites. Solinus pardons Egeon for entering the city, Antipholus S. begins to court Luciana (Adriana's sister), and Emilia holds a feast to celebrate the family's reunion.

Commentary

The Comedy of Errors is a comedy, so all the characters' confusion is cleared up at the end. The darker issues of imminent execution, cuckoldry, and a broken marriage are easily resolved. Duke Solinus begins the play as almost a tyrant, but ends it as a forgiving father figure. The broken halves of Egeon's family, separated for more than thirty years, get put back together, and husband and wife reconcile as if time were unimportant. Even the poor abused slaves, the Dromios, quickly forget their beatings and embrace, emphasizing the play's main theme: Love will triumph over all.

Famous Lines

"The pleasing punishment that women bear" (Act I, Scene I).

"A wretched soul, bruised with adversity" (Act III, Scene I).

"Every why hath a wherefore" (Act II, Scene II).

"Let's go hand in hand, not one before another" (Act V, Scene I).

The Merchant of Venice

Main Characters

Portia—a wealthy heiress from Belmont
Shylock—a Jewish moneylender in Venice
Antonio—a merchant and friend to Bassanio
Bassanio—Antonio's friend, a gentleman of Venice
Gratiano—a friend of Bassanio who is in fiercely anti-Semitic
Lorenzo—a friend of Bassanio and Antonio. In love with Jessica
Jessica—Shylock's daughter, who is in love with Lorenzo
Nerissa—Portia's lady-in-waiting
Salerio and Solanio—Venetian gentlemen
Launcelot Gobbo—Shylock's servant

Old Gobbo—Launcelot's father
The Prince of Morocco—one of Portia's suitors
The Prince of Arragon—one of Portia's suitors
Tubal—a Jew, one of Shylock's friends

Introduction

Many people forget that *The Merchant of Venice* is a comedy because the character of Shylock and the theme of anti-Semitism are so serious, and somewhat treated as such in the play. It was written around 1596.

FACT

The Merchant of Venice weaves together two ancient folktales, one involving a vengeful, greedy creditor trying to exact a pound of flesh, and the other involving a suitor's choice among three chests to thereby win his mate.

The characters of the merchant, the suitor, the lady, and the villainous Jew can be found in several contemporary Italian story collections. The cross-dressing heroine and the Italian location make *The Merchant of Venice* similar to earlier comedies. Portia is considered by many scholars to be Shakespeare's first great heroine, and Shylock's complex and not altogether unsympathetic villain make the play one of Shakespeare's best.

While Shylock is clearly a stereotypical caricature of a money-obsessed, vicious medieval Jew, a case can be made that Shakespeare wanted to make anti-Semites peer into a mirror and see their own reflection. By merging the two stories, Shakespeare makes one a metaphor for the other.

Shylock is one of the most interesting Shakespearean characters for modern audiences. England had excluded communities of Jews for centuries, so all the moneylenders in London would have been Christians. Anti-Semitism was common in the sixteenth century throughout most of Europe, where Catholics and Protestants were busy finding excuses to slaughter one another; Jews were often comic villains in Elizabethan theater.

The Play

Antonio, a wealthy merchant, is feeling depressed, while his friend, Bassanio, needs his financial help so that he can court a wealthy woman, Portia, and win her hand in marriage. Antonio agrees to help Bassanio.

Portia complains to her servant, Nerissa, about the provisions of her father's will. The suitor who correctly chooses one of three chests (gold, silver, and lead) may marry Portia and get her money. If they fail, they must never marry. Portia doesn't like any of her suitors, except Bassanio, and prays that he chooses in time and correctly.

Back in Venice, Bassanio convinces Shylock the Jew to lend him 3,000 ducats. Antonio becomes his guarantor, putting up "a pound of flesh" as the bond. Shylock hates Antonio, and he lends the money hoping Antonio will default on the loan. Antonio is certain one of his ships will arrive before the three-month deadline is up.

Shylock's servant, Launcelot Gobbo, tells his father, old Gobbo, that he wants to leave Shylock and work for Bassanio. Shylock's daughter, Jessica, meanwhile, has fallen in love with Antonio's friend Lorenzo and intends to convert to Christianity in order to marry him.

Gratiano, Salerio, and Lorenzo help Jessica elope with Lorenzo. They all head off to meet Bassanio. Solanio and Salerio gossip about Antonio's ship sinking and make fun of Shylock's losing his daughter.

Bassanio correctly chooses the lead casket and wins Portia's hand and fortune in marriage. To seal the deal, Portia gives Bassanio a ring, warning him never to lose it, or he'll risk losing her love. Gratiano then announces his intention to wed Nerissa.

Salerio, Lorenzo, and Jessica arrive and tell Bassanio that Antonio has lost his ships. What's more, Shylock is determined Antonio should forfeit his bond. Bassanio immediately leaves for Venice to repay the loan. Meanwhile, Shylock has Antonio arrested for failure to repay the loan in time. Portia and Nerissa decide to disguise themselves as a lawyer and his clerk and follow Bassiano to Venice.

Shylock's Petition

The duke presides over Shylock's petition to cut "a pound of flesh from Antonio's breast" since that was the terms of the bond, even though Bassanio offers him 6,000 ducats (rather than the 3,000 he originally lent) for repayment. Nerissa and Portia, disguised as a court clerk and doctor of civil law, arrive at the court and join Gratiano, Bassanio, and the duke, in trying to dissuade Shylock, to no avail. He will have his bond, no more and no less; that is what the law allows. Shylock seems to be victorious.

QUESTION?

Is Shylock a hero or villain?
First and foremost, Shylock is an anti-Semitic creation for an Elizabethan audience accustomed to seeing Jews as comic foils for Christian heroes. Yet Shylock's eloquence is so great that modern productions elevate him to the level of tragic hero. But the play is ultimately a comedy; Shylock's elimination at the end of Act IV thus allows for the happy ending in Act V.

Then Portia points out that he's correct in that the law does indeed let him collect his pound of flesh, but he must be careful: no blood must be shed and exactly one pound must be taken. Shylock realizes this is impossible. He tries to change his mind and take the money instead. Portia pounds home another nail: Shylock is himself guilty of conspiring to kill Antonio, a fellow citizen. As punishment, the duke and Antonio decide that Shylock must give half his possessions to the court and promise to give the rest to his daughter and new son-in-law (Lorenzo) upon his death. What's more, he must become a Christian. Defeated, Shylock is forced to agree.

A Happy Ending

Still disguised as the lawyer, Portia asks Bassanio for his wedding ring. Despite his vow, and after some prodding by Antonio, Bassiano reluctantly hands it over. Nerissa (disguised as Portia's clerk) gets her husband (Gratiano) to do the same thing with his wedding ring.

Back at Portia's house, Bassanio and Portia, and Gratiano and Nerissa reunite. After quarreling over the loss of rings, the women admit their ruse and return the rings to their husbands. Antonio also discovers that three of his ships have come to port full of merchandise, and Jessica and Lorenzo learn they will get Shylock's possessions on his death.

Commentary

The play is really two fairy tales that come together at the trial scene. Until this point, Shylock's story takes center stage and Portia's courtships are something of a subplot. By the trial, Shylock has had enough. He has become a vengeful figure, blinded to humanity and compassion by the chance to finally exact revenge against those who have wronged him: "I'll have my bond," he gloats, ignoring pleas for mercy from all around him.

Portia sets up Shylock, offering him a chance to escape with the money. If he is merciful it is a win-win situation for everyone. When Shylock refuses, she is justified in crushing him. But he threatens to turn the play into something other than it is, and he must be gotten rid of once and for all so that the happy ending can take place.

Shylock seems almost too vivid for the rest of the characters in *The Merchant of Venice*. His determination to extract his pound of flesh at any cost is clearly the work of a comic villain whose downfall we will applaud. The good-humored intrigue of the rings that ends the play is something of an anticlimax: love, mercy, and compassion have conquered all.

Famous Lines

"I hold the world but as the world, Gratiano,—
A stage, where every man must play a part;
And mine a sad one" (Act I, Scene I).

"In my school-days, when I had lost one shaft,
I shot his fellow of the selfsame flight
The selfsame way, with more advised watch,
To find the other forth; and by adventuring both,
I oft found both" (Act I, Scene I).

"God made him, and therefore let him pass for a man" (Act I, Scene II).

"I will buy with you, sell with you, talk with you, walk with you, and so following; but I will not eat with you, drink with you, nor pray with you. What news on the Rialto?" (Act I, Scene III).

"The devil can cite Scripture for his purpose" (Act I, Scene III).

"You call me misbeliever, cut-throat dog,
And spit upon my Jewish gaberdine" (Act I, Scene III).

"Mislike me not for my complexion,
The shadow'd livery of the burnish'd sun" (Act II, Scene I).

"It is a wise father that knows his own child" (Act II, Scene II).

"Truth will come to sight; murder cannot be hid long" (Act II, Scene II).

"In the twinkling of an eye" (Act II, Scene II).
"But love is blind, and lovers cannot see
The pretty follies that themselves commit" (Act II, Scene VI).

"All that glisters is not gold" (Act II, Scene VI).

"I am a Jew. Hath not a Jew eyes? Hath not a Jew hands, organs, dimensions, senses, affections, passions?" (Act III, Scene I).

"The villany you teach me I will execute, and it shall go hard, but I will better the instruction" (Act III, Scene I).

"Tell me where is fancy bred,
Or in the heart or in the head?
How begot, how nourished?
Reply, reply" (Act III, Scene II).

"There is no vice so simple but assumes
Some mark of virtue in his outward parts" (Act III, Scene II).

"You take my house when you do take the prop
That doth sustain my house; you take my life
When you do take the means whereby I live" (Act IV, Scene I).

The Merry Wives of Windsor

Main Characters

Mistress Ford—married to Ford and a friend of Mistress Page

Mistress Page—a friend of Mistress Ford; she and her husband disagree
about who should marry their daughter, Anne

Falstaff—a knight and a scoundrel

Ford—husband of Mistress Ford; calls himself Brooke

Page—husband of Mistress Page

Sir Hugh Evans—the local clergyman; he is Welsh

Caius—the local doctor; he is French

Anne Page—daughter of Page and Mistress Page

Fenton—a suitor for Anne Page's hand

Slender—a suitor for Anne Page's hand

Shallow—a figure of the law, who is foolish

Mistress Quickly—Caius's servant

Bardolph, Pistol, and Nim—Falstaff's men

Host—host of the Garter Inn

William Page—Anne's brother and Page's son

Simple—Slender's servant

Introduction

The Merry Wives of Windsor was probably written around 1597. It is Shakespeare's most middle-class play in setting, subject matter, and outlook. It's also one of his most farcical, using physical gags and linguistic jokes to establish a comic tone that influences the play's ultimate spirit of reconciliation. It is concerned with phenomena of an emerging merchant/guild middle class filling the gap between agrarian peasant and landed gentry.

According to theatrical legend, Elizabeth I saw *King Henry IV, Part I* and liked the character of Falstaff so much she asked Shakespeare to write another play about him, allegedly giving him only fourteen days. It was once thought that Shakespeare put aside *King Henry IV, Part II* to complete *The Merry Wives of Windsor*, and he included several characters who appear in both plays, including Pistol, Nim, Bardolph, Mistress Quickly, and Shallow.

Falstaff and his entourage were supposedly good friends with Prince Hal, later Henry V, which lends a royal flavor to the archetypal suburban events of *The Merry Wives of Windsor*. Windsor, its castle still used as a residence by royalty today, has always been considered a royal town.

FACT

The Merry Wives of Windsor captures life in an English provincial town in the late sixteenth century and refers to other, older plays. The main plot closely resembles *Il Pecorone*, a 1558 Italian play by Ser Giovanni Fiorentino, which in turn draws on ancient Roman comedy.

Scholars concur that the first performance was on April 23, 1597, at a feast of the Order of the Garter, which Queen Elizabeth I attended. There are two different versions: the First Quarto (1602) and the First Folio (1623). The Quarto is most likely a reconstruction from memory by actors and others. It is half the length of the Folio version, and is likely poorly remembered, or trimmed for provincial performances. The Folio version is printed from a manuscript that was based on either a playhouse promptbook or an authorial manuscript, and has a close connection with the first performance of the play.

The Play

Sir John Falstaff, a rogue who is "financially challenged," hatches a scheme to raise funds by seducing Mistresses Ford and Page at the same time in an attempt to get at their husbands' money. Falstaff, however, has overestimated his charm and his ingenuity. The two women are friends, and discovering his plot, decide to make him suffer for his impertinence. They send him letters encouraging his advances.

Mistresses Ford and Page enjoy their fun. Falstaff is in danger of being discovered and hides in a basket of dirty laundry, which is then tossed into the River Thames. He is later dressed as a woman and beaten. Finally, the women tell their husbands what's going on, and all plot one final humiliation for the old knight.

Meanwhile, Page's daughter, Anne, is being courted by two suitors favored by her parents, but she is in love with Fenton. It is decided that Sir Hugh Evans will lead Anne and the town's children dressed as fairies in a late-night attack on the knight as he waits in the woods for Mistresses Page and Ford. Anne's father, Page, tells Slender, one of Anne's suitors, that he should elope with his daughter after the prank. Mistress Page pulls her favorite suitor, Doctor Caius, aside and tells him the same thing. Because she will be in disguise, the two men will recognize Anne by the color of her dress. Anne, meanwhile, makes plans of her own to elope with Fenton.

FACT

The Merry Wives of Windsor was a great favorite of Friedrich Engels, coauthor with Karl Marx of the *Communist Manifesto*. No doubt he enjoyed the way Shakespeare made fun of the emerging bourgeoisie. With the exception of *The Comedy of Errors*, it is probably Shakespeare's most overtly farcical play.

Falstaff is convinced to dress up as the god Herne (complete with antlers). While he waits in anticipation for the women to come to him, he is suddenly set upon and tormented by Anne and the children, dressed as fairies. The wives and husbands eventually reveal themselves to Falstaff, who is forgiven his roguish ways.

Slender and Doctor Caius reappear, chagrined. Both men erred on the color of Anne's dress (Slender thought it was white; Caius thought it was green) and ran off with boys instead of Anne. Fenton arrives with Anne. The two of them are married and Anne's parents begrudgingly accept the fact.

Commentary

Mistresses Page and Ford determine that wives can lead boisterous, vivid lives (i.e., be merry) without having to betray their husbands. Page understands this, but Ford takes some convincing. The romance of Fenton and Anne Page affirms the idea of romantic love as a means of transcending class.

The Merry Wives of Windsor also emphasizes the provincial mindset, by making fun of a community that in turn makes fun of outsiders. Slender's pretensions make him look like a fool. Justice Shallow, whose authority derives from the Crown, ends up much the same. Sir Hugh Evans, the Welsh clergyman, is mocked for his foreign accent, as is Dr. Caius. Slender and Mistress Quickly depend on cliché, while Quickly hears sexual double entendres in Latin conjugations and declensions. The hostility of the rising merchant class to the aristocracy is clearly seen in Page's rejection of Fenton's request for Anne's hand and the continued abuse of the impoverished knight, Falstaff.

While the play celebrates the mistresses' autonomy (due in part to their husbands' wealth and social positions), the only woman who is "liberated" is Anne, who avoids a marriage chosen for her by her parents in favor of a partnership of her own choosing against their will.

Famous Lines

"If there be no great love in the beginning, yet heaven may decrease it upon better acquaintance, when we are married and have more occasion to know one another: I hope, upon familiarity will grow more contempt" (Act I, Scene I).

"This is the short and the long of it" (Act II, Scene II).

"This is the third time; I hope good luck lies in odd numbers. . . . There is divinity in odd numbers, either in nativity, chance, or death" (Act V, Scene I).

The Taming of the Shrew

Main Characters

Katherina—the shrew of the title, also called Kate
Petruchio—a gentleman from Verona
Bianca—Kate's younger sister

Baptista Minola—one of the wealthiest men in Padua; father of the two
    girls
Lucentio—a young student from Pisa who is in love with Bianca
Tranio—Lucentio's servant
Gremio and Hortensio—Bianca's suitors
Grumio—Petruchio's servant

Introduction

The Taming of the Shrew is an early comedy, loosely termed "romantic" along with *Much Ado About Nothing* and *A Midsummer Night's Dream*. Such plays are lighthearted and often slapstick in style, filled with disguises and deception, and end happily. This is in sharp contrast to the later comedies that are much darker and filled with cynicism and a sometimes bitter irony. (The "Romances," on the other hand, are called such because they use material from old adventure stories and often invoke magic.)

The Taming of the Shrew is clearly a young playwright's work and focuses more squarely on marriage than almost any other of the early comedies. While the other plays end with a marriage, *The Taming of the Shrew* takes this almost as a starting point, following the early days of married life.

Elizabethan Marriages

The average sixteenth-century playgoer was interested in discussions about marriage, in part because Henry VIII's separation from the Catholic Church in 1536 was brought about by wrangling over a divorce. (Shakespeare dealt with this subject more directly in his play *King Henry VIII*. Henry named himself "Defender of the Faith," a title still held by British monarchs, and formed the Church of England.) When the Pope refused to annul Henry's marriage to Catherine of Aragon, Henry took matters into his own hands. He declared himself head of the church in England and had his marriage nullified in order to clear the way for his second marriage to Anne Boleyn. Henry VIII is often remembered for his six wives. He divorced two and beheaded two; one died after giving birth, and one survived him.

FACT

The plot was familiar to Elizabethan audiences, being drawn from popular ballads and folktales such as "A Merry Jest of a Shrewde Curste Wyfe" published in 1550. In the ballad the woman is thrashed to a bloody pulp and then wrapped in the salted skin of an old horse.

This recent history would be very much on the minds of an Elizabethan audience. Great pain, death, and turmoil had resulted from the break with Rome. Unless you were a determined king of England willing to suffer excommunication, the late sixteenth and early seventeenth centuries offered few ways out of an unhappy marriage, so the resolution of marital disputes was a hot topic in the popular literature of the era.

Elizabethan marriages were still being made along medieval lines— they were far more often made for money, land, or power than for love. A woman had few options for survival when set adrift from the rule and support of a man, either her father or her husband, and less often, her brother. The fact that Queen Elizabeth I never married was cause for great concern to Elizabethans because of its potential to undermine the power structure of society.

The Shrew

Of particular worry among men, were "shrews" or "scolds," that is, cantankerous or gossipy women who resisted or undermined the natural authority of their husbands or fathers. A large number of sermons, plays, and pamphlets of the time address related topics: the taming of shrews by their husbands or the public punishment of scolds (by repeated dunking in a river, for example). Some of this literature is diplomatic, and some is clearly misogynistic. It's difficult to sometimes tell (perhaps deliberately so) what is meant as parody and what is being presented as an ideal. This is also true for *The Taming of the Shrew*. Shakespeare's own marriage, at least at first, is thought not to have been the greatest, and he spent many years of it living apart from his family in London, while they stayed on in Stratford.

Viewing from a Distance

The main part of *The Taming of the Shrew* is set in Padua, a city in northern Italy. To Elizabethan England, Italy was a beautiful country of rich food, loose women, and generally materialistic and pleasurable living. It became a favorite setting of Shakespeare and his contemporaries for plays involving deceit, money, beautiful women, cross-dressing, or anything worth taking a little sinful pleasure in—but at a safe distance from England.

This idea of "viewing from a distance" is particularly true of *The Taming of the Shrew*, because it has an "outer" and an "inner" play. The frame, or outer play, is actually set in the English countryside and consists of only the first two scenes, called the Induction, where a group of English actors prepare to present the inner play, the story of Kate and Petruchio.

The Outer Play

Outside an alehouse somewhere in England, a beggar named Christopher Sly is arguing with the hostess of the alehouse. The hostess leaves to fetch the local authorities, and Sly passes out, drunk.

A passing lord decides to have some fun with the sleeping beggar. The lord decides to see if, with the right surroundings, he can convince a common man that he is really of high birth. So he orders his servants to take Sly back to his house and treat him as if he were a lord.

At the house, the servants place Sly in the lord's bed with fine clothes and jewelry, and the Lord disguises himself as one of the serving men. When Sly awakes, they present him with good wine and food and tell him that he is their master. He protests that he remembers being a poor tinker (a mender of pots). They tell him this memory is the result of a madness he has been in for fifteen years. They put on quite a show, pleading and wailing in feigned distress at his continued illness, but Sly is still skeptical.

When his "wife" is brought in—a male page dressed up as a woman—he is finally convinced. The servants are overjoyed that his "memory" has returned, and they wish to entertain him. As luck would have it, a group of players happen to be in town, and they prepare to put on a play for the enjoyment of Sly and his wife.

The "play within a play" forms the main action of *The Taming of the Shrew*. The text only returns to Sly briefly after this Induction, and it never concludes his story.

The Play within a Play

Lucentio arrives in Padua with his manservant Tranio to study at the university. Baptista, a wealthy merchant of Padua, has two daughters, Katherina and Bianca. Lucentio falls in love with Bianca, the younger and kinder daughter, and becomes one of several suitors who vie for her hand. Lucentio and Tranio (his servant) switch clothes, and thus disguised, Lucentio offers his services as a tutor for Bianca in order to get closer to her.

Because of her older sister Katherina's shrewish disposition, Bianca's father has declared that no one will marry Bianca until Katherina has a husband. The suitors are beside themselves. Enter Petruchio, in Padua to visit his friend Hortensio (one of Bianca's suitors). Petruchio is attracted to Katherina's large dowry, and Hortensio sees a potential solution to his problem, which will put him in good stead with Baptista.

Despite all the warnings he gets about the fiery Kate, Petruchio claims that he finds her charming and pleasant. The marriage is arranged, and Petruchio immediately sets out to tame Kate—who prefers to be called "Katherine." He shows up late to his own wedding, constantly contradicts whatever she says, calling the sun the moon, refuses to give her food until she agrees with him, and so on. Finally, an exhausted Kate is "tamed" into docility.

The matches of Kate and Petruchio and Lucentio and Bianca become contrasting versions of marriage. It is interesting to compare the concept of love and partnership in more mature men and women in *The Taming of the Shrew* with Benedick and Beatrice in *Much Ado About Nothing*.

Lucentio wins Bianca's heart and Hortensio happily marries a rich widow in Padua. Petruchio and Kate return for Bianca's wedding. During the wedding feast, Petruchio makes a bet with the other two new husbands that he has the most obedient wife. Knowing her previous behavior the men take the bet, only to discover that Petruchio really has "tamed" his wife. In a complete turnabout, Kate gives Bianca a lecture on how to be a good and loving and obedient wife.

Commentary

When you watch *The Taming of the Shrew*, it's important to remember the context of the play. In Elizabethan times marriages were made to secure and increase property far more often than because the potential bride and groom loved each other. People were married without ever having courted. Spouses hoped to learn to love their partner once they were wed. There's no guarantee that love at first sight brings greater happiness in marriage than the slowly developed, consistent love of a couple who learn to live with and for each other.

The fatal, overpowering passions of *Romeo and Juliet* are not the best basis for a marriage, Shakespeare suggests. Petruchio and Kate end up being well matched. Only a happy-go-lucky, persistent, self-assured man like Petruchio could break through Kate's defenses. Few, including her father, have been able to say no to her, but Petruchio enjoys it.

She is shocked when Petruchio is late for their wedding, and her reaction is not anger at being stood up, but fear she will die a lonely old maid. She wants a relationship of mutual respect. But to get there she must rethink her whole attitude toward men. Petruchio's attempts to stifle and humiliate her are meant only to force her to stop blindly lashing out. She must see him for who he is and what he can give her.

The result is that Kate can enjoy her married life and find an equal partner. She finally reveals near the end of the play that she can love her husband in married life without feeling she has somehow lost her earlier independence that brought her only anger and distress. It is this revelation that she tries to teach her younger sister at the end of the play.

Famous Lines

"I'll not budge an inch" (Induction, Scene I).

"And thereby hangs a tale" (Act IV, Scene I).

"Such duty as the subject owes the prince,
Even such a woman oweth to her husband" (Act V, Scene II).

"Who wooed in haste, and means to wed at leisure" (Act III, Scene II).

The Two Gentlemen of Verona

Main Characters

Proteus—Valentine's supposed best friend and one of the title gentlemen of Verona

Valentine—the other title gentleman of Verona

Julia—Proteus' beloved, and mistress to Lucetta

Silvia—daughter to the Duke of Milan and beloved of Valentine

Duke of Milan—Silvia's father

Lucetta—Julia's servant

Launce—Proteus's servant

Speed—Valentine's page

Thurio—a rival for Silvia's hand

Sir Eglamour—the gentleman who helps Silvia escape the Duke of Milan's court

Antonio—father to Proteus and master to Panthino

Host—houses Julia

Crab—Launce's dog

Panthino—Antonio's servant

Introduction

Critics are not certain exactly when *The Two Gentlemen of Verona* was written, though it was not published until 1634. For much of this century, scholars believed *The Two Gentlemen of Verona* might be Shakespeare's first play, attributing any perceived weakness to the work of a young writer. The dominant view today is that the play is late and was coauthored with John Fletcher. Collaboration may also explain some inconsistencies in the text. Authors such as Geoffrey Chaucer, Francis Bacon, John Lyly, and George Peele had undertaken similar debates between romantic love and male friendship prior to Shakespeare's attempt to tackle the subject in *The Two Gentlemen of Verona*. Chaucer's *Knight's Tale* provides the most direct source for the main plot.

While the date of the play's composition may be uncertain, its literary ancestors are not. After Chaucer, the most significant source for the play is the story of Felix and Felismena, from Portuguese writer Jorge de Montemayor's work *Diana*. Shakespeare may have either read *Diana* in a French translation or seen a version of it performed at court in 1585. In the original play, Silvia's equivalent is killed off and Valentine does not exist. As was often his way, Shakespeare changed the original story to create a happier, more symmetrical ending.

The Play

Valentine's father sends him to take up a position in the Duke of Milan's court, and his friend Proteus reluctantly goes with him, not wanting to leave his beloved Julia. Once in Milan, Valentine falls for the Duke's daughter, Silvia. However, Silvia is betrothed to Thurio, a wealthy courtier, although she clearly prefers Valentine. The two decide to elope, and Valentine confides in Proteus.

Proteus, however, also falls for Silvia, and in order to get Valentine out of the way and get in her father's good graces, Proteus betrays his friend's plan to the Duke. Valentine is banished, Silvia is imprisoned, and Proteus becomes a confidant of the Duke.

Valentine comes across a band of outlaws and is elected their leader. Meanwhile, Julia, disguised as a boy page, enters Milan looking for Proteus, who is trying unsuccessfully to court Silvia. Silvia still loves Valentine. Julia, in disguise, becomes a page to Proteus, and ends up being an intermediary between Proteus and Silvia. Silvia finally seizes an opportunity to escape and goes in search of Valentine. In the forest, Valentine's outlaws capture her.

The Duke, Proteus, and Thurio set off to rescue Silvia, and Proteus recovers Silvia before the outlaws can take her to Valentine. As Proteus makes one last attempt to convince Silvia to love him, he and Valentine meet up again.

The two men eventually make peace with each other, and in a gesture of reconciliation, Valentine offers Silvia to Proteus, which causes Julia (who is still disguised as a page) to faint. Proteus finally recognizes her, much to his shame. The Duke and Thurio now arrive on the scene. Thurio backs off his claim to Silvia when challenged by Valentine, and Valentine gets Silvia with the Duke's approval. Proteus and Julia are reconciled, and the Duke grants a pardon to the outlaws.

Commentary

The Two Gentlemen of Verona is about the conflict of loyalty and passion. While the play eventually decides that friendship is more important (that is, the love of friends is purer than romantic love), the twists and turns that each character takes in order to reach that conclusion involve a number of other issues.

FACT

Proteus is more concerned with social position and money than romance. The servants Launce, Speed, and Lucetta act as foils to their respective masters Proteus, Valentine, and Julia. The servants give us clues about their masters. Launce's pragmatic reasoning about love, for example, shows us that Proteus is more concerned with social position and money than romance.

The forest (and countryside in general) plays an important role in Shakespeare's plays. From the fairy-filled forest of Athens to the magic of Prospero's deserted island in *A Midsummer Night's Dream*, social status there becomes irrelevant. People are judged on their merits, not on their parentage. Such a breakdown encourages a rebellion that can include cross-dressing and even same-sex romance. When, for example, Proteus realizes he can't have Silvia, suddenly "Sebastian" (Julia) is attractive to him. Valentine's friendship with Proteus, and how they eventually resolve the contentious issue of Silvia, further reinforces the idea of gender-bending, and skirts the issue of homosexuality.

Famous Lines

"That man that hath a tongue, I say, is no man,
If with his tongue he cannot win a woman" (Act III, Scene I).

"Is she not passing fair?" (Act IV, Scene IV).

"Come not within the measure of my wrath" (Act V, Scene IV).

Twelfth Night

Main Characters

Viola (Cesario)—a young woman
Duke Orsino—a powerful nobleman in the coastal country of Illyria
Olivia—a wealthy countess
Sebastian—Viola's lost twin brother
Malvolio—Lady Olivia's straitlaced steward
Feste—a clown; in the service of Olivia
Sir Toby Belch—Olivia's uncle
Sir Andrew Aguecheek—a friend of Sir Toby
Maria—Olivia's witty, clever, serving woman
Antonio—a gentleman who rescues young Sebastian

Introduction

Twelfth Night was written in 1601 around the middle of Shakespeare's career. Many critics consider it one of his great comedies, along with *As You Like It*, *Much Ado About Nothing*, and *A Midsummer Night's Dream*.

QUESTION?

What does "twelfth night" refer to?
Twelfth night refers to the last night of Christmas celebrations that were popular in Elizabethan times—usually January 6—which is also known in the church calendar as Epiphany, the Feast of the Magi (the "Wise Men" who visited the newly born Jesus). That holy day, however, covers over a Pagan mid-winter holiday, Saturnalia, which became the medieval "Feast of Fools," a day given to madcap fun, disguises, and pranks.

Twelfth Night is about illusion, deception, disguises, madness, and perhaps same-sex love. It is certainly concerned with the extraordinary things we'll do in the name of love. It's a fun, entertaining play. One of the most accessible of the several movie adaptations is, arguably, Trevor Nunn's 1996 version starring Helena Bonham Carter. Music has been written for and about the play, including an opera composed by Smetana, and works by Brahms, Schubert, and Sibelius.

The Play

Viola and her twin brother Sebastian are shipwrecked in a violent storm off the coast of Illyria and lose contact, with each thinking the other is dead. Viola disguises herself as a boy named Cesario and becomes a page in the service of Duke Orsino.

Lost in Love

Olivia is in mourning for her father and brother and not interested in being courted. Orsino, however, is determined to woo her. He sends Cesario to Olivia with love letters. Cesario insists on being allowed to see Olivia. Olivia finally agrees, and on meeting the boy messenger takes a fancy to Cesario.

She sends her steward, Malvolio, after Cesario with a ring she purports Cesario left behind by mistake. Viola finds herself in a bind: She realizes to her dismay that Olivia has fallen for Cesario—and Viola herself has a stirring of affection for Orsino, who is still besotted with Olivia.

Sebastian (Viola's twin) is rescued by Antonio and they become fast friends. At some risk to himself, because he ran afoul of Duke Orsino, Antonio helps Sebastian.

Back in Olivia's house, Sir Toby Belch (her uncle, who has shades of Falstaff about him) has hoodwinked a foppish wealthy friend, Sir Andrew Aguecheek, into supporting him by convincing him that Olivia might be interested in marrying him. Malvolio is a pompous and bossy steward who has a running feud with Sir Toby. With the help of Maria, Olivia's maid, and Feste, a clown, Sir Toby plots to bring Malvolio down a peg or two.

Maria writes a love letter to Malvolio that makes him think Olivia has fallen for him. Malvolio's self-importance makes him fall for the trick, which eventually leads to his being locked up as a madman.

Confusion Abounds

Meanwhile, Sir Toby is egging Sir Andrew into a duel with Cesario. Olivia is now in love with Cesario, even though Cesario continues to press Orsino's cause. As Cesario and Sir Andrew prepare for a duel that neither wants, Antonio happens upon the scene. Believing Viola to be Sebastian, he intervenes and is arrested. Viola, of course, does not recognize Antonio, who now thinks his newfound friend has abandoned and betrayed him.

Sir Andrew encounters Sebastian, thinking he is Cesario. This time Cesario doesn't back down when Aguecheek challenges him, and resoundingly beats him. Olivia intervenes just in time, and mistakes Sebastian for Cesario and continues to press her suit for him. A bemused Sebastian agrees to marry her.

Antonio is brought before Orsino for questioning, and Viola relates the events of the duel. Pointing to Cesario, Antonio tells everyone how he dragged "this man" from the surf, saving his life. Olivia now enters, searching for her new husband whom she mistakes for Cesario. Adding to this confusion, Sir Toby and Sir Andrew enter, claiming that Cesario has violently assaulted them.

In the middle of Viola's denials, Sebastian appears. The brother and sister recognize one another and are reunited. Sebastian helps to clear the confusion as to who fought and married whom. At the end, Orsino and Viola pledge their love, Olivia and Sebastian remain happily married, and Olivia rebukes Sir Toby and Maria for their abuse of Malvolio, who vows his revenge upon the whole lot. Sir Toby agrees to marry Maria to make up for getting her in trouble, and all, except the disgruntled Malvolio, live happily ever after.

Commentary

Twelfth Night is one of Shakespeare's "transvestite comedies," a category that also includes *As You Like It* and, to a lesser degree, *The Merchant of Ven-*

ice. These plays feature female protagonists who, for one reason or another, have to disguise themselves as young men.

FACT

It's worth remembering that in Shakespeare's day, all the parts were played by men, so Viola would actually have been a boy pretending to be a girl pretending to be a boy. Some contemporary critics have also found a great deal of interest in the homoerotic implications of these comedies,

Many scholars think the play was first performed on January 6, 1601, at the Whitehall for an Italian nobleman, Duke Orsino of Bracciano. Others think it was first performed on February 2, 1602.

Twelfth Night is only one of two Shakespearean plays to have an "alternative" title: *Twelfth Night; or, What You Will*, although critics are not quite sure what the play's two titles mean. (*King Henry VIII* is also *All is True.*) *Twelfth Night* itself serves as a double reference to the twelfth night of the Christmas celebration and the underlying "Feast of Fools," a holiday celebrated as a festival in which everything was turned upside down—much like the topsy-turvy world of Illyria.

Famous Lines

"If music be the food of love, play on;
Give me excess of it, that, surfeiting,
The appetite may sicken, and so die.
That strain again! it had a dying fall:
O, it came o'er my ear like the sweet sound
That breathes upon a bank of violets,
Stealing and giving odor!" (Act I, Scene I).

"We will draw the curtain and show you the picture" (Act I, Scene V).

"He does it with a better grace, but I do it more natural" (Act II, Scene III).

"Is there no respect of place, persons, nor time in you?" (Act II, Scene III).

"My purpose is, indeed, a horse of that color" (Act II, Scene III).

"She never told her love,
But let concealment, like a worm i' the bud,
Feed on her damask cheek: she pined in thought,
And with a green and yellow melancholy
She sat like patience on a monument,
Smiling at grief" (Act II, Scene IV).

"I am all the daughters of my father's house,
And all the brothers too" (Act II, Scene IV).

"Some are born great, some achieve greatness, and some have greatness
thrust upon 'em" (Act II, Scene V).

"Love sought is good, but given unsought is better" (Act III, Scene I).

"Still you keep o' the windy side of the law" (Act III, Scene IV).

"Out of the jaws of death" (Act III, Scene IV).

"For the rain it raineth every day" (Act V, Scene I).

CHAPTER 12

Shakespeare's Problem Comedies

All's Well That Ends Well is grouped with *Troilus and Cressida* and *Measure for Measure* in what are typically referred to as Shakespeare's "problem comedies." All three share a bitter humor and a cynical view of human relations that contrast sharply with earlier, sunnier comedies such as *Twelfth Night* and *As You Like It*. Even the title of *All's Well That Ends Well* is ironic.

All's Well That Ends Well

Main Characters

Helena—the daughter of a great doctor, now the ward of the Countess of Rosillion; she loves the Countess's son, Bertram, though he does not return her affections

Bertram—the Count of Rossillion; handsome and well-liked, he is an excellent soldier, but a jerk in his relationship with Helena, whom he marries unwillingly and then abandons

Countess of Rossillion—Bertram's mother and Helena's guardian

King of France—deathly ill when the play begins, he is miraculously cured by Helena, who uses one of her father's medicines; as a reward for saving his life, he makes Bertram marry Helena

Parolles—a liar and a braggart

Lafew—an old French nobleman

Dumaine, First Lord—a genial French nobleman

Dumaine, Second Lord—the First Lord Dumaine's brother

Diana—a young Florentine Bertram tries to seduce; she helps Helena trick Bertram

Widow—Diana's mother

Mariana—a woman of Florence

Duke of Florence—the ruler of Florence

Clown—an old servant of the Countess who serves as a messenger

Steward—another servant of the Countess

Introduction

The earliest copy of *All's Well That Ends Well* appears in the Folio of 1623, seven years after Shakespeare died. Some critics date it from 1598 or earlier and associate it with a "lost play" called *Love's Labour's Won*, which is listed in a 1598 catalogue of Shakespeare's plays. Some critics think that *All's Well That Ends Well* is a reworked version that Shakespeare published at a later date. The most common dating puts it between 1601 and 1606.

Throughout his career, Shakespeare explored the paradox of the evil in good people and goodness in bad people. The only truly unsympathetic figure in *All's Well That Ends Well* is Parolles, who is less a villain than a comically amoral rogue.

The source of the story is Boccaccio's *Decameron*, a classic of early Renaissance literature, written between 1348 and 1358. The *Decameron* (essentially a short-story collection with a framework somewhat like *Canterbury Tales* or *1001 Arabian Nights*), was translated into English in the mid-sixteenth century by William Painter as *The Palace of Pleasure*, and it was this version that Shakespeare probably drew upon.

Shakespeare, of course, altered and reshaped the original story, adding characters such as Lafew, the Countess, and Parolles, but kept the basic elements—the bed trick and the war in Florence.

The Play

When his father dies, Bertram becomes Count of Rosillion. Helena is the orphaned daughter of a great doctor and has lived in the Rosillion household under the guardianship of Bertram's mother, the Countess.

Helena follows Bertram to Paris, where the King of France has been taken deathly ill. Helena bears one of her father's prescriptions and when she cures the King, in gratitude he tells her she can have her pick of the bachelors at his court. Over the years, Helena has developed a secret love for Bertram. Now she can act on this love.

She picks Bertram, who is distressed by the prospect, feeling that Helena is beneath him. Under protest, Bertram agrees to the marriage. Helena returns to Rosillion and the Countess, at first assuming that Bertram will be along directly. Bertram, however, slips off to fight in Tuscany with his cowardly friend, Parolles.

When it becomes apparent that Bertram is not returning home, Bertram sends word that Helena can't call him husband until she wears his ring (which he always wears) and bears his child. This is not a simple task considering that Bertram is in Italy and has no intention of ever sleeping with her.

Helena now sets out for Florence. She winds up lodging with a widow whose daughter Diana, ironically, is the object of Bertram's affections. With Diana's help, Helena designs a trap for Bertram.

FACT

Audiences and critics are almost always divided on how they feel about Helena ending up with Bertram. As a result of this confusion in the ending, *All's Well That Ends Well* is not performed often in today's theater.

Diana makes Bertram give her his ring before they share a bed. Helena then takes Diana's place in the dark. She exchanges rings with him, giving him one that the King had given her for Bertram.

She next spreads a rumor that she has died, and Bertram figures that he is in the clear. Back in France, the King recognizes the ring Bertram bears as the one he gave Helena. When Bertram is caught in a series of lies, the King has him arrested (supposing that Bertram has murdered her). Diana and her widowed mother arrive demanding justice, and when Helena finally turns up bearing Bertram's ring, carrying his child, and revealing the truth to all, Bertram repents the error of his ways and swears his love for Helena.

Commentary

All's Well That Ends Well is often described as a problem play, distinguished from the earlier, more cheerful comedies by a sophisticated bitterness toward human relations. These plays' happy endings are really nothing of the sort. It's hard for a modern audience to imagine Bertram and Helena enjoying a happy marriage.

For a play about love, *All's Well That Ends Well* is remarkably cynical. Helena's low opinion of men seems well founded. The successful central deception is the bedroom switch that enables Helena to become pregnant by Bertram, who had avoided marrying her, to trick him into living with her. It works, Shakespeare suggests, because in the dark all women look alike to men.

For modern audiences, the idea of great women picking men who are unworthy of them is disquieting. It's particularly tough with *All's Well That Ends Well* because Bertram turns out to be such a jerk. He abandons Helena, tries to seduce an innocent woman, and only repents because he has no choice. It's either marriage or jail.

QUESTION?

Was Shakespeare commenting on what it meant to be a woman alone, with few prospects of earning a living in a male-dominated world?
Given the cynicism of the story, one can't help but wonder if unrecognized desperation plays some small part in Helena's determination to "nail" Bertram.

The resourceful Helena, meanwhile, while loved by everyone (except Bertram), also gives us pause for thought. She seems to be a classic example of "why good women make bad choices." Why does she so relentlessly pursue a man who is so demonstratively unworthy of her? Nothing stands in Helena's way as she "gets her man." While we may admire her, by the time she's triumphant, our opinion of her good taste is all but gone.

Famous Lines

"All the learned and authentic fellows" (Act II, Scene III).

"A young man married is a man that's marr'd" (Act II, Scene III).

"Praising what is lost makes the remembrance dear" (Act V, Scene III).

Measure for Measure

Main Characters

Isabella—a virtuous young woman; sister to Claudio

Vincentio—the Duke of Vienna; he spends most of his time disguised as a friar

Claudio—Isabella's brother; sentenced to death for impregnating an unmarried woman

Lord Angelo—a hypocrite who rules strictly and without mercy

Escalus—a wise lord who advises Angelo

Lucio—a flamboyant bachelor

Mariana—Angelo's fiancée

Mistress Overdone—a madam

Pompey—a clown who works for Mistress Overdone

Provost—the jailer

Elbow—a dimwitted constable

Barnadine—a prisoner in the jail

Juliet—Claudio's lover

Introduction

Measure for Measure takes its title from the Gospel of Matthew: "with what measure ye mete, it shall be measured to you again" (Matthew 7:2), a passage from the Sermon on the Mount, one of Jesus' most famous sermons.

While some documents indicate it was first performed at court at Whitehall on St. Stephen's Night (December 26) 1604, others suggest that it was written and first performed earlier that year. Lucio's allusion to a hoped-for peace may well refer to King James I's attempts in 1604 to negotiate a peace agreement with Spain; the proclamation to tear down the brothels may refer to King James's edict in 1603 to tear down houses affected by the plague (the plague and venereal disease were often related in Renaissance literature). A number of critics have noted similarities between Duke Vincentio's and King James's dislike of crowds, his use of disguise, and his aversion to slander.

FACT

Giovanni Battista Giraldi (also known as Cinthio), an Italian writer and philosopher, first wrote this story as a 1565 novella called *Hecatommithi*, then as a play called *Epita* in 1583. Another dramatist, George Whetstone, wrote the story as a play in 1578 called *Promos and Cassandra*, and in 1581 Thomas Lupton wrote a play called *Too Good to Be True*.

The earliest, and thus most authoritative, text for the play is the First Folio, which was printed in 1623. The lack of stage directions suggests it is a prompt copy. Shakespeare took the source of the play from a real case in Italy. In 1547, a judge promised a murderer he would not be sentenced to death if the murderer's wife had sex with him. After he had enjoyed himself, the judge went back on his word and executed the man anyway.

The Play

Vincentio, the Duke of Vienna, is concerned about what his people think of his ruling ability. To discover the truth, he appoints his deputy, Angelo, to rule in his place, saying he is taking a sabbatical. He empowers Angelo to enforce unpopular morality laws, mostly because he wants to maintain a good and fair image with his people and doesn't want to accept the unpopular task of being strict. Angelo, a zealot, is perfect for the task. Vincentio puts on a show of leaving, but he remains in town disguised as a monk.

Claudio's Death Sentence

Angelo's harshness upsets a lot of people, particularly when Claudio is arrested for getting his fiancée, Juliet, pregnant before they are married. Angelo condemns him to death. While agreeing with his moral stance, Claudio's sister, Isabella, nevertheless pleads with Angelo for her brother's life.

Angelo won't budge at first. Gradually, Isabella's beauty and chaste virtue excite him. He propositions her: He will pardon Claudio if she sleeps with him. Isabella turns him down, vowing that her chastity and honor are her life.

When she tells Claudio what happened, he at first goes along, but soon tries to talk his sister into trading her virtue for his life. Vincentio (in disguise) overhears their conversation and sets into motion a plot to save both Claudio and Isabella from their predicament.

The Duke Steps In

Duke Vincentio knows Angelo was once engaged to Mariana, who still loves him. He persuades Isabella to feign acceptance of Angelo's offer and when the moment comes, Mariana will switch places in the dark with Isabella (the bed trick of *All's Well That Ends Well*). Mariana agrees, and events go as planned except that after getting his way, Angelo orders Claudio's execution anyway.

Luckily, Duke Vincentio hears about this and persuades the jailer to substitute another condemned man for Claudio and to carry out the execution "as planned." Isabella is led to believe that Claudio has died, that Angelo has betrayed her, and that she should seek justice from the Vincentio, who is expected to return soon.

Isabel and Mariana make their accusations against Angelo to Duke Vincentio, who appears as himself. Angelo first says Isabella is lying and blames the "monk" for putting her up to this. When Vincentio reveals himself as the monk, Angelo is forced to throw himself on the mercy of Vincentio and Isabella. Claudio is revealed to be alive, Mariana pleads for Angelo's life, and Vincentio orders that Angelo should marry Mariana and Claudio should marry Juliet. Vincentio then tells Isabella he will marry her. She, however, never says another word.

Commentary

Measure for Measure has been faulted for not tying up the ending in a neat, satisfying bow. It's like leaving the heroine hanging from a tree over the edge of a cliff. Questions have to be asked: Why does Isabella agree to Vincentio's plan? The bed switch still makes Mariana commit the same crime for which Claudio is condemned. Isabella still condemns her brother's actions. She agrees with Angelo, but not about the punishment he intends to mete out. Perhaps Shakespeare simply got tired of the play and didn't untangle the plot twists and tie up the loose ends. Perhaps he wanted his audience to think about how much more true such tangles are to life than are neat endings.

At the beginning of the play Isabella was about to become a nun. At no time during the play does she profess love for Vincentio, or he for her. He's disguised as a monk for most of it anyway. Yet we are left with the distinct impression she will become his bride.

Although *Measure for Measure* explores themes of sexual harassment and women's rights (ideas that had rarely been explored at the time), it is not a play about women's liberation. Yes, it touches on issues of sexuality and the independence of women. But the female characters in *Measure for Measure* are quite different from the feisty women of earlier comedies. Here, however, no male disguise protects the heroines.

The play certainly raises important moral issues. Its structure revolves around secret identities: Vincentio disguises himself as a monk, and most of the problems are resolved when he reveals his identity. Vincentio solves Claudio and Isabella's problem with a plan involving mistaken identity. Mariana takes Isabella's place, and the head of a dead pirate is used to deceive Angelo.

Duke Vincentio, in effect, functions as a kind of puppetmaster. He may have placed a proxy ruler in power during his absence, but he is still pulling the strings. He is an interesting paradox: a character who is wise but unable to maintain order.

Measure for Measure is also a problem play because it does not follow through with the moral questions it raises. No one reconsiders his or her beliefs about freedom, justice, sexual relationships, or morality, and Isabella in particular never really has to deal with the consequences of having to commit a sin in order to save her brother.

Famous Lines

"Our doubts are traitors,
And make us lose the good we oft might win
By fearing to attempt" (Act I, Scene IV).

"Some rise by sin, and some by virtue fall" (Act II, Scene I).

"Condemn the fault, and not the actor of it?" (Act II, Scene II).

"O, it is excellent
To have a giant's strength; but it is tyrannous
To use it like a giant" (Act II, Scene II).

"The miserable have no other medicine,
But only hope" (Act III, Scene I).

"O, what may man within him hide,
Though angel on the outward side!" (Act III, Scene II).

"They say, best men are moulded out of faults,
And, for the most, become much more the better
For being a little bad" (Act V, Scene I).

"What's mine is yours, and what is yours is mine" (Act V, Scene I).

Troilus and Cressida

Main Characters

Troilus—a prince of Troy; the younger brother of Hector and Paris
Cressida—a beautiful young Trojan woman
Hector—a prince of Troy
Ulysses—one of the Greek commanders
Pandarus—Cressida's uncle
Thersites—a deformed slave serving Ajax
Achilles—the greatest of the Greek warriors
Ajax—a Greek warrior
Agamemnon—a Greek general; brother of Menelaus
Diomedes—a Greek commander
Paris—a prince of Troy
Menelaus—a Greek commander
Helen—Menelaus's wife

Calchas—a Trojan priest, and Cressida's father

Aeneas—a Trojan commander

Nestor—the oldest of the Greek commanders

Cassandra—a Trojan princess and prophetess; she is considered mad

Patroclus—a Greek warrior; Achilles's best friend, and maybe his lover

Priam—the king of Troy, and the father of Hector, Paris, and Troilus, among
others

Antenor—a Trojan commander

Helenus—a prince of Troy

Andromache—Hector's wife

Introduction

Troilus and Cressida is one of Shakespeare's later plays, assumed to have been written shortly after *Hamlet*. It was probably performed in the winter of 1602–1603, but no record of the performance survives. The genre classification of *Troilus and Cressida* has created a difficult problem for scholars. Is it a history? It was labeled as one in an early folio. Is it a tragedy? Not really. To confuse matters further, it is sometimes grouped with the so-called "problem comedies," such as *Measure for Measure* and *All's Well That Ends Well*. One thing that can be agreed on is that all three share a dark, bitter wit and a pessimistic view of human relations.

FACT

It's important to remember the popularity of Greek and Roman mythology in Shakespeare's time. The story of Troy was a well-known one and the events of the play, including the denouement, would have been expected from the beginning—Cressida's treachery and Hector's death would have been as predictable as the ending of a B movie today.

Sources for the play include classical mythology and Homer's *Iliad*, which contains the Achilles-Hector story. The romance of *Troilus and Cressida* is principally derived from Chaucer's great fourteenth-century epic,

Troilus and Criseyde. Typically, Shakespeare took only the bare bones of this story, which he combined with other medieval retellings of the tale.

The Play

The Trojan War is in its seventh year. The Greeks besieging Troy are bickering among themselves. When Hector, a Trojan hero, issues a challenge to fight any Greek in one-on-one combat, Ulysses arranges for Ajax to be the Greek champion. Ulysses hopes to spur Achilles out of his lethargy, and thus reinvigorate the Greek armies.

Calchas deserts Troy for the Greek encampment. In exchange for intelligence about the Trojan forces, Calchas asks the Greeks to exchange a Trojan prisoner for Cressida. Agamemnon, commander of the Greek army, agrees to this, and Cressida is soon parted from Troilus, who is devastated.

Once inside the Greek encampment, Cressida meets—and flirts with—all the Greek generals. Hector and Ajax battle each other to a standstill and eventually call a truce. The Trojan and Greek generals dine together at a feast.

Diomedes has been courting Cressida since her arrival in the Greek camp. While accompanying Ulysses, the heartbroken Troilus sees Cressida give Diomedes the love token Troilus gave her when she left Troy. He vows to kill Diomedes in battle.

During the battle next day, Hector slays Achilles's friend (and perhaps lover) Patroclus. When Achilles meets Hector on the field of battle the next day he is so incensed he has his men kill Hector while he is unarmed and resting. Troy has suffered a grave defeat, and an enraged Troilus hurls curses at Achilles and Pandarus alike from the city walls.

Commentary

Troilus and Cressida is one of Shakespeare's more difficult plays. It's a romance set against the backdrop of an interminable war that is draining the humanity out of all who are engaged in it.

The play has a cast of generally unsympathetic characters but as in any great tragedy, it tackles the broad theme of conflict between an individual's interests and those of the state. In this case, the conflict is between the romance of the title characters and the wartime politics that put Cressida in the Greek camp where she is forced to make the best of her situation.

The play's general pessimism is matched only by that in *Timon of Athens*. Heroes such as Achilles and Ajax are presented as self-absorbed thugs, and the central romance of *Troilus and Cressida* is reduced to a roll in the grass that passes for love amid boredom and bloodshed. In the words of the archcynic Thersites, "All the argument is a whore and a cuckold," which rather sums up the Trojan War.

Structurally, the play feels disjointed. Shakespeare uses anticlimax throughout the play, so scenes we think will be critical turn out to be letdowns. This is especially true in the duel between Hector and Ajax, which ends in a draw, and again in the final battle, in which the events we expect do not transpire: Troilus is not avenged for the loss of his beloved, and Hector does not have a climactic duel with his great adversary, Achilles, but is ambushed and killed while he's unarmed.

FACT

Some critics have suggested that this play was performed only once, or not at all—possibly because some of the characters in the Greek and Trojan armies were thinly disguised caricatures of contemporaries, either of other playwrights or of members of King James I's court.

The play is almost defiantly philosophical. The argument between Hector and Troilus over the value of fighting to keep Helen in Troy is rich in insight, while Ulysses, one of the play's most interesting characters, discusses the role of order in society. Thersites is another interesting character. For all his abusiveness to the people around him, he ends up being the only moralist, even if that morality is delivered in bitter language about a futile situation made worse by uncaring, scheming heroes.

Famous Lines

"The common curse of mankind—folly and ignorance" (Act II, Scene III).

"All lovers swear more performance than they are able, and yet reserve an
ability that they never perform; vowing more than the perfection of ten,
and discharging less than the tenth part of one" (Act III, Scene II).

"The end crowns all,
And that old common arbitrator, Time,
Will one day end it" (Act IV, Scene V).

CHAPTER 13

Shakespeare's Tragic Comedies

As he developed as a writer, Shakespeare seemed to deliberately shun categorization, writing comedies that could be farcical, bitter, magical, and sometimes tragic all at the same time. Yet the more complicated and sophisticated the comedy, the more likely the triumphant ending will be undermined by melancholy. The paradox of difficult characters in the comedies, such as Shylock or Malvolio, and the potentially tragic events that seem to be averted at the eleventh hour, suggest that Shakespeare was deliberately calling attention to the theatricality of the occasion.

Cymbeline

Main Characters

Cymbeline—the king of Britain and Imogen's father

Imogen—Cymbeline's daughter; she is in love with lowborn Posthumus rather than Cymbeline's stepson Cloten

Posthumus—Cymbeline's protégé; he marries Imogen in secret, against her father's wishes

Queen—Cymbeline's wife; a villainous woman

Cloten—the queen's son; an arrogant idiot

Iachimo—a scheming Frenchman living in Italy

Pisanio—Posthumus's loyal servant

Belarius—a British nobleman, unjustly banished by Cymbeline; he kidnapped Cymbeline's infant sons to revenge himself on the king, and disguised as a shepherd, raised them as his own

Guiderius—Cymbeline's eldest son, raised by Belarius as Polydore

Arviragus—Cymbeline's younger son, raised by Belarius as Cadwal

Philario—an Italian gentleman

Caius Lucius—the Roman ambassador to Britain

Cornelius—a doctor

Philarmonus—a Roman soothsayer

Jupiter—the king of Olympus in Roman mythology

Introduction

Cymbeline is one of Shakespeare's last plays and was written and performed around 1609–1610, probably on the indoor Blackfriars' stage rather than at the Globe. It joins *The Winter's Tale* and *The Tempest* in a short list of "Romances" that are considered tragicomedies. Death and despair, while never victorious in the end, loom as ever-present shadows.

The Play

At times it seems that Cymbeline's host of characters are running around like dogs chasing their tails. Cymbeline, the king of Britain, lost his two boys,

Guiderius and Arviragus, twenty years earlier. The two boys were kidnapped by Belarius, who took them as revenge for Cymbeline's unfairly banishing him. Cymbeline is left with one heir to the throne, his daughter Imogen. Cymbeline remarries, only to gain an arrogant idiot stepson, Cloten. Cymbeline then decides he wants Imogene to marry her stepbrother, but unknown to the king, Imogen is in love with her childhood friend Posthumus Leonatus. Knowing she can't defy her father openly, Imogen secretly marries Posthumus. When the king discovers this he banishes Posthumus and confines Imogen to the castle grounds.

Posthumus goes to Rome to stay with his friend, Philario. In walks Iachimo, a mutual acquaintance, who bets Posthumus that he can seduce Imogen. Hurrying to Britain, Iachimo finds Imogen's stalwartness too difficult to overcome, but he must win the bet, not through seductive skill, but guile. He sneaks into her bedroom, steals her bracelet while she sleeps, and returns to Rome. There he convinces the gullible Posthumus that he indeed seduced Imogen.

QUESTION?

Where did Shakespeare get his idea for this play?
Cymbeline seems to be an original play. Though the Iachimo plot, in which a seduction is attempted on a virtuous wife, may have its roots in Boccaccio's *Decameron*, and the scenes in the Welsh wilderness recall fairy tales like "Snow White." Most of the plot and characters are likely directly from Shakespeare's imagination.

Posthumus is distraught that Imogen has cuckolded him and orders his servant Pisanio to kill Imogen. Pisanio can't bring himself to do the deed. Instead, he makes it look like Imogen is dead then takes her to Milford Haven where she disguises herself as a man named Fidele.

In Milford Haven, Imogen (as Fidele) meets her kidnapped brothers, though she doesn't know who they really are, of course. Cloten follows Imogen to Milford Haven wearing Posthumus's clothes, in hopes of tricking her. He gets into a fight with Guiderius, and Guiderius cuts off Cloten's head.

Meanwhile, the Queen tries to trick Pisanio by giving him medicine (which she thinks is poison), hoping he will give it to Imogen or Posthumus as a gift. The Queen figures if Imogen is dead, her son becomes Cymbeline's only heir, and if Posthumus dies, Imogen will be widowed and thus forced to marry Cloten.

In Milford Haven, Imogen falls sick and takes the medicine Pisanio gave her as a present. It is not poison as the Queen believed. The medicine puts Imogen into a deep sleep, and Belarius and sons, believing her dead, lay her beside Cloten's body. When Imogen recovers, she sees the headless body dressed in Posthumus's clothes and thinks that her beloved is dead.

Meanwhile, Caius Lucius demands that Britain pay tribute to Rome and Augustus Caesar. Cymbeline refuses and Lucius declares war on Britain. The Queen gets sick and on her deathbed admits her crimes and sins, including hating Cymbeline. Caius Lucius's army invades Britain, and he comes across Imogen and rescues her from the wild. In the only battle of the war, Cymbeline is captured by the Romans, then rescued by Belarius, Guiderius, and Arviragus, with help from Posthumus. The Britons then capture Posthumus, thinking he is Roman, and take him to Cymbeline. Posthumus has a vision where he is visited by the god Jupiter.

In the rather convoluted last scene of the play, Imogen returns to her father, Iachimo confesses he tricked everyone, Cornelius explains the Queen's "poison," Cloten's death is explained, Belarius admits to kidnapping the princes, Cymbeline allows Imogen and Posthumus to stay married, a soothsayer explains a prophecy in a book left in Posthumus's lap by the god Jupiter, and peace is made with the Romans. Cymbeline does not punish Iachimo or Belarius.

Commentary

Cymbeline is Shakespeare's attempt to tell a fairy tale using the elements of tragedy, and it really doesn't work that well. The language, while rich, is often clumsy, and the mediocrity of certain scenes (notably the appearance of Jupiter) has led a number of critics to suggest that Shakespeare may well have collaborated with a less talented playwright. While the play includes the remarkable Imogen and the entertaining Iachimo, the title character, Cymbeline, is rather two-dimensional, as is a lot of the supporting cast.

Like Helena and Portia, Imogen is a woman whose man does not really deserve her. Posthumus disappears from the action for long periods of time, and the various subplots make the play hard to follow.

The aging Shakespeare seems to have revisited elements of his earlier plays, albeit in a less impressive form. *Cymbeline* feels like a pastiche, as if Hollywood were to make a film that takes the best bits of several successful movies and stitches them together in another framework.

The Imogen-Cymbeline king-daughter relationship suggests Lear and Cordelia in *King Lear*, though Cymbeline is a failure compared to Lear, while Iachimo reminds one of Iago in *Othello*, though he hardly reaches the depths of Iago's villainy, and Posthumus is a poor revisiting of Othello. The sleeping potion and Imogen awakening next to her "husband's" dead body remind us of *Romeo and Juliet*, while Imogen's cross-dressing recalls *As You Like It*, but none of these elements combine into a coherent whole. *Cymbeline* may seem a tragedy, yet disaster never really strikes. Only the wicked characters die, and by the end everyone is reconciled.

In the final scene all the tangled strands of plot are tied together quickly and cleverly. The villains die; Imogen and Posthumus are reunited. Then, perhaps stretching the plot a bit too far, King Cymbeline's abducted sons are restored to him. Overjoyed, Cymbeline declares, "Pardon's the word to all."

Famous Lines

"Hath his bellyful of fighting" (Act II, Scene I).

"As chaste as unsunn'd snow" (Act II, Scene V).

"Some griefs are medicinable" (Act III, Scene II).

"The game is up" (Act III, Scene III).

"I have not slept one wink" (Act III, Scene IV).

The Tempest

Main Characters

Prospero—once the Duke of Milan, overthrown by his brother, Antonio
Alonso—the king of Naples
Gonzalo—a well-meaning elderly counselor of Alonso
Ferdinand—the prince of Naples and Alonso's son
Miranda—Prospero's daughter
Ariel—a spirit Prospero rescued from imprisonment and now controls
Sebastian—Alonso's brother
Antonio—Prospero's brother
Trinculo—Alonso's jester
Stephano—Alonso's butler
Caliban—Prospero and Miranda's slave; the son of a powerful witch
Adrian and Francisco—lords who attend Alonso
Boatswain, Master, and Mariners—seamen

Introduction

The Tempest is considered Shakespeare's last major play (written around 1611). It was likely performed at court as part of the celebration surrounding the marriage of Princess Elizabeth, the daughter of King James I. It contains an unusual amount of "spectacle"—dances, songs, costumed plays-within-the-play—which would have made it especially appropriate as royal entertainment.

Shakespeare seems to have retired from full-time playwrighting after *The Tempest*, although he likely collaborated with others, chiefly John Fletcher, on at least three more plays. As a result, some scholars consider *The Tempest* to be a farewell from a great playwright to his audience and a final, symbolic celebration of the magic of theater. Many people consider Prospero a stand-in for Shakespeare, since he gives up his magic and manipulation of the natural and unnatural world (read, playwrighting) at the play's conclusion.

The Survival of the Sea-Venture

In early June 1609, nine ships carrying around 600 people to strengthen the new English colony in Virginia set out from England. The *Sea-Venture* was the lead ship and carried Sir Thomas Gates, the newly appointed governor of the colony, and Sir George Somers, the admiral of the Virginia Company. On July 25 a violent storm (probably a hurricane) overtook the ships and raged for several days. When the storm had subsided, four of the nine ships found one another and proceeded on to Virginia. Three more eventually made it into port. The *Sea-Venture* never showed up and was presumed to be lost.

FACT

The setting of *The Tempest* draws on chronicles brought back from the early colonization of the Americas by travelers and explorers. Although the magic island of *The Tempest* is supposedly somewhere in the Mediterranean, it actually incorporates many myths and stories about the Bermudas and other American islands.

The news, when it reached England by the fall, created a public sensation. But unknown to the rest of the world, the battered ship had run aground on Bermuda, with all aboard making it safely ashore. The Bermudas had a reputation as a place of devils and wicked spirits, but the colonists found it to be quite pleasant, and they lived there for the next nine months while building a new ship out of native wood under Somers's guidance.

They set sail on May 10, 1610, and reached Jamestown, Virginia, two weeks later. A ship carrying Governor Gates and others left Jamestown two months later and reached England in September. The news of their survival caused another public sensation.

The Tale Told

Several accounts of the wreck and survival of the *Sea-Venture* were rushed into print in the fall of 1610. The first of these, *A Discovery of the Barmudas*, was written by Sylvester Jourdain, who had been aboard the *Sea-Venture* and had returned to England with Gates. A month later *A True*

Declaration of the Estate of the Colonie in Virginia was published. This was edited together from various documents as a piece of pro-Virginia propaganda on behalf of the Virginia Company, the consortium of investors who had underwritten the trip. More important than either publication was William Strachey's *True Reportory of the Wracke, and Redemption of Sir Thomas Gates Knight.* Shakespeare almost certainly read the pamphlets and used them in writing *The Tempest.*

Though it was not officially published until 1625, Strachey's account is dated July 15, 1610, and was circulated among those in the know. Shakespeare had connections to the Virginia Company and Strachey, and it is highly likely that he had access to Strachey's account in manuscript form prior to publication.

A number of later adaptations include John Dryden's *The Enchanted Island*, Thomas Shadwell's opera (1674), and Henry Purcell's score (1690). An 1821 performance of *The Enchanted Island* included music by Purcell, Mozart, and Rossini. It is also the basis of W. H. Auden's long poem, *The Sea and the Mirror.*

The Play

Prospero, a sorcerer and the rightful duke of Milan, lives on an enchanted isle with his daughter, Miranda. Twelve years earlier, Prospero's brother, Antonio, and Alonso, the king of Naples, conspired to usurp his throne. Prospero and Miranda were set adrift in a boat and eventually washed up on the island. Using his magic, Prospero freed a spirit called Ariel from a tree.

As the play begins, Prospero has discovered that a ship carrying his old enemies home from a wedding is sailing nearby. Prospero conjures a storm to wreck their ship. The survivors make it to shore in scattered groups. Among these is Ferdinand, the son of Alonso, who meets Miranda. The two young people fall in love.

Meanwhile, Antonio, Alonso, Sebastian, and Gonzalo search the island for Ferdinand. As they do, Antonio plots with Sebastian to murder Alonso. Ariel thwarts the plot. Elsewhere on the island, Stephano and Trinculo encounter the island's other native inhabitant, Caliban, son of the witch Sycorax. After the three drink together, Caliban convinces the two servants to help him kill Prospero. He even promises Miranda to Stephano. Ariel keeps Prospero apprised of what the various groups are doing.

FACT

The numerous film adaptations of *The Tempest* include at least one classic—the 1956 sci-fi movie *Forbidden Planet*. Those who like interesting "art films" may find Peter Greenaway's *Prospero's Books* (1991), starring Sir John Gielgud, interesting.

Prospero makes Ferdinand work to win Miranda's love; meanwhile, Ariel creates a magical banquet for Antonio and Alonso, which vanishes whenever they try to eat. Prospero also sends Ariel to torment them for their crimes against him.

During a masque to celebrate the upcoming marriage of Miranda and Ferdinand, Prospero decides it's time to put an end to Caliban's plot and sends Ariel to punish him and Stephano and Trinculo as well. The spirit does this by setting other island spirits on them in the shape of hunting dogs that chase them around the island.

Finally, Prospero confronts his brother and Alonso, revealing his true identity as the rightful duke of Milan. He demands that Antonio restore his throne; he also rebukes Sebastian for plotting against his own brother. He reveals Ferdinand as alive and well, playing chess with Miranda. Restored to his natural authority, Prospero abandons his magic and releases Ariel and Caliban from their servitude.

Commentary

The Tempest is simply not a play to be read—it must be seen or at least heard. With this, his last great play, Shakespeare decided to pull out all the stops. It is an inherently visual spectacle, which unfolds in a series of exotic, otherworldly, and sometimes "invisible" characters that the audience can see but other characters cannot. It is best described as a multisensory theatrical experience, with sound and music used to complement a somewhat simple story of retribution, and a lyrical text that is lush with exotic images.

The Tempest does not have the bitterness of the later tragicomedies, and yet it does combine elements of a pastoral (the city folk forced to live as natives in the country) and tragedy (Prospero's revenge) with romantic comedy (the young lovers Miranda and Ferdinand). As in *Measure for Measure*, one of the problem plays, *The Tempest* also poses profound questions that defy easy resolution. There is extraordinary thematic complexity in the play.

FACT

Modern critics often read the Caliban subtext from a postcolonial viewpoint, examining what the play can tell us about European colonization of the Americas in particular, and colonization in general. It is a play of great lyricism and heart that deserves careful and serious study.

Among other things, the play challenges our concepts of reality and illusion and our senses. On one level it is a self-conscious performance overtly orchestrated by the Shakespeare-like "puppet-master" Prospero—the master illusionist, as he and his creator take their final bow. There are a number of themes, notably nature versus civilization or art. From certain perspectives, *The Tempest* tackles an overarching question: What is humanity?

Famous Lines

"I would fain die a dry death" (Act I, Scene I).

"My library
Was dukedom large enough" (Act I, Scene II).

"Fill all thy bones with aches" (Act I, Scene II).

"Full fathom five thy father lies;
Of his bones are coral made;
Those are pearls that were his eyes:
Nothing of him that doth fade

But doth suffer a sea-change
Into something rich and strange" (Act I, Scene II).

"There's nothing ill can dwell in such a temple:
If the ill spirit have so fair a house,
Good things will strive to dwell with 't" (Act I, Scene II).

"Misery acquaints a man with strange bedfellows" (Act II, Scene II).

"Deeper than e'er plummet sounded" (Act III, Scene III).

"Our revels now are ended. These our actors,
As I foretold you, were all spirits, and
Are melted into air, into thin air:
And, like the baseless fabric of this vision,
The cloud-capp'd towers, the gorgeous palaces,
The solemn temples, the great globe itself,
Yea, all which it inherit, shall dissolve,
And, like this insubstantial pageant faded,
Leave not a rack behind. We are such stuff
As dreams are made on; and our little life
Is rounded with a sleep" (Act IV, Scene I).

"Where the bee sucks, there suck I;
In a cowslip's bell I lie" (Act V, Scene I).

The Winter's Tale

Main Characters

Leontes—the king of Sicilia
Hermione—Leontes's queen
Perdita—the daughter of Leontes and Hermione
Polixenes—the king of Bohemia, and Leontes's boyhood friend
Florizel—Polixenes's only son and heir

Camillo—a Sicilian nobleman

Paulina—a noblewoman of Sicily

Autolycus—a roguish peddler

Shepherd—he finds Perdita as a baby and raises her as his own daughter

Antigonus—Paulina's husband

Clown—Perdita's adopted brother

Mamillius—the young prince of Sicilia

Cleomenes—a Lord of Sicilia

Dion—a Sicilian lord

Emilia—one of Hermione's ladies-in-waiting

Archidamus—a Lord of Bohemia

Introduction

The Winter's Tale is one of Shakespeare's last plays, written and performed around 1611. It joins *Cymbeline* and *The Tempest* in the list of genre-defying plays that are usually referred to as tragicomedies or romances.

There is no one source for *The Winter's Tale*, although Shakespeare relied heavily on *Pandosto*, a 1588 prose romance by Robert Greene, a university-trained London writer. In 1592 Green wrote a pamphlet accusing a young Shakespeare of being an untalented, "upstart Crow" who stole from other writers. The story of the abandoned royal baby probably comes from popular folklore, while Hermione's resurrection at the end of the play is obviously from the Greek myth of *Pygmalion*, in which a sculptor's work comes to life.

The Play

Leontes's friend Polixenes of Bohemia thinks he should return to his kingdom after spending time with his old school friend. Leontes asks his wife, Hermione, to try to persuade Polixenes to stay longer. Because Hermione succeeds, Leontes starts to think she is having an affair with Polixenes. His jealousy gets the better of him, and Leontes decides to kill Polixenes.

The play has been a favorite of directors and audiences since it was first presented. In a number of productions the roles of Hermione and Perdita have been played by the same actress, notably Dame Judi Dench in 1969. Other productions have starred Patrick Stewart, Sir Ian McKellen, and Jeremy Irons.

Camillo warns Polixenes and the two men escape to Bohemia. Leontes has Hermione tried for adultery, despite the fact that the Delphic oracle proclaims her innocent. While in prison, Hermione gives birth to a daughter, which Leontes orders killed. He is persuaded to spare the child's life, but orders Antigonus to abandon the baby. Antigonus does so, on the nonexistent "Coast of Bohemia," where he is soon eaten by a bear. (This is the occasion of one of Shakespeare's classic stage directions: "Exit, pursued by a bear.")

Leontes' son, Mamillius, dies from grief over his mother's predicament. Hermione is next reported dead by her maid, Paulina. The shock seems to bring Leontes to his senses. He is overcome by grief and guilt and goes into seclusion.

The abandoned baby, Perdita, is found by a shepherd, who raises her as his daughter. Sixteen years later, Florizel, Polixenes' son meets Perdita, and the two fall in love. Polixenes, however, is not happy that his son is in love with a peasant girl, so Florizel and Perdita decide to flee to Sicilia, aided by old Camillo.

Florizel and Perdita are welcomed at the court of Leontes. Polixenes follows them, and reconciles with Leontes. Perdita is revealed to be a princess, and Leontes and Polixenes are delighted that their children are in love.

Leontes's happiness is tempered by the bitter memory of Hermione's death. Paulina takes Leontes and the court to see a statue of the queen, which magically comes to life. It seems the queen has been hiding for the past sixteen years. Thus Leontes is finally reunited with his wife, daughter, best friend, and closest advisor. Even Paulina regains a husband when Leontes agrees to marry her to Camillo.

Commentary

The Winter's Tale is perhaps Shakespeare's best tragicomedy. It is set in an imaginary world where ancient Greek oracles coexist with Renaissance sculptors, and it offers an *Othello*-like tragedy that magically culminates in the all's well that end's well finale of *A Midsummer Night's Dream* and *The Tempest.*

The play is almost seasonal in structure. The first half is wintry and chilly, emotionally cold, and dominated by a fit of jealous madness and rage that seems so destructive that even an innocent child may not escape.

But sixteen years pass, and Leontes's madness passes. The second half of the play is springlike, and the destruction the king's madness created is ploughed under. Through coincidence, goodwill, and the magic of growth and renewal, a statue of his dead wife comes to life and embraces him.

The problem plays deal with death and the power of evil, and in *The Winter's Tale*, we are given an ending where death is literally banished from the stage.

Like *King Lear*, this play deals with the anarchy unleashed because of the main character's self-absorbed madness. When Leontes is told that there is "nothing" between Hermione and Polixenes, he declares, "Why, then the world and all that's in 'tis nothing." When he finally comes to his senses, all Leontes can offer by way of explanation for his behavior is, "I have drunk, and seen the spider."

If Leontes is a potential tragic hero, Perdita is clearly a fairy-tale princess reared among commoners who falls in love with a prince and discovers her nobility quite naturally. The miracle of Hermione's resurrection at the play's close is an appropriate ending to a play about death (winter) and rebirth (spring).

Famous Lines

"They say we are
Almost as like as eggs" (Act I, Scene II).

"To unpathed waters, undreamed shores" (Act IV, Scene IV).

CHAPTER 14

Shakespeare's Tragedies

A few of Shakespeare's tragedies can be considered meditations on the spiritual conflict in the soul of man and woman, as in *Romeo and Juliet* and *Antony and Cleopatra*. These title characters are defined not by their tense interior as seen in *Hamlet* and *Othello*. Certainly, Romeo and Juliet lack the psychological depth and complexity, as does Lear. Although not of the power of Shakespeare's greatest tragedies, such as *Macbeth*, the following list of plays are not to be disparaged in favor of the others.

14

Antony and Cleopatra

Main Characters

Mark Antony—Cleopatras' lover and Fulvia's husband; one of the triumvirate of Rome along with Octavius Caesar and Lepidus

Cleopatra—the queen of Egypt and Antony's lover; she once seduced Julius Caesar

Octavius Caesar—Julius Caesar's nephew and adopted son; one of the triumvirate of Rome

Domitius Enobarbus—Antony's loyal supporter

Marcus Aemilius Lepidus—the weakest member of the triumvirate; he tries to keep the peace between Octavius and Antony

Sextus Pompeius—son of a great general who was one of Julius Caesar's partners in power

Octavia—Caesar's sister; she marries Antony in order to cement the alliance of the two triumvirs

Charmian and Iras—Cleopatra's attendants

The Soothsayer—an Egyptian fortuneteller

Dolabella—one of Octavius Caesar's men

Agrippa—one of Octavius Caesar's officers

Canidius—Antony's general

Ventidius—a Roman soldier under Antony's command

Scarus—a brave soldier

Proculeius—one of Caesar's soldiers

Mardian, Alexas, and Diomedes—Cleopatra's servants

Thidias, Gallus, and Maecenas—Caesar's men

Demetrius and Philo—Antony's soldiers in Egypt

Eros—an attendant, serving Antony

Menas, Menecrates, and Varrius—soldiers under Pompey

Seleucus—Cleopatra's treasurer

Clown—an Egyptian who brings the poisonous snake to Cleopatra

Decretas—one of Antony's soldiers

Introduction

Antony and Cleopatra was written about 1606 and is considered Shakespeare's epic tragedy, one of global proportions. Shakespeare's primary source for *Antony and Cleopatra* was the "Life of Marcus Antonius" contained in *Plutarch's Lives of the Noble Greeks and Romans*. It had been translated into English by Sir Thomas North in 1579. Shakespeare had no problem lifting lines from other sources, so North's language found its way into the play with only a few alterations.

On a story of such a grand scale, Shakespeare had to compress a decades' worth of events into a dramatic form of only a few hours on the stage. He also took some literary license with the characters, notably Mark Antony, who is far older here than in *Julius Caesar*. Octavius Caesar, a minor character in the earlier play, now becomes a major part, the man who rises to become the first Roman emperor, Caesar Augustus.

Agatha Christie: "To me, Cleopatra has always been an interesting problem. Is *Antony and Cleopatra* a great love story? I do not think so."

Laurence Olivier: "I never really thought a lot about Antony—as a person, that is, I mean, really, he's an absolute twerp, isn't he?"

The plot of the play does not deviate far from North's story, although characters such as Enobarbus and Cleopatra's attendants are Shakespearean creations. The action of the story is basically a continuation of Shakespeare's earlier play, *Julius Caesar*. The time frame is two years later. The major events of the play are historically accurate.

The historical Cleopatra seems to have been rather plain by Western standards, yet seductive. Portrayals of her by such movie stars as Claudette Colbert and Elizabeth Taylor vividly show her as beautiful and seductive.

The Play

Octavius Caesar, Antony, and Lepidus form the Roman triumvirate that rules the Western world. Lepidus decides to retire, leaving Caesar and Antony in charge. Antony, although married to Fulvia, has abandoned her in Rome to frolic in Egypt with Cleopatra. Disgusted by Antony's lifestyle in Egypt and angry about wars caused by Antony's relatives, Caesar recalls Antony to Rome. Fulvia dies and Caesar and Antony try to make peace through Antony's marriage to Caesar's sister Octavia.

Antony quickly returns to Cleopatra. Caesar vows to wrest Egypt from Antony and Cleopatra. As defeat seems near, Antony's best friend, Enobarbus, deserts him and joins Caesar's army, then filled with guilt, dies of a broken heart near Caesar's headquarters. Facing certain defeat, Antony kills himself by falling on his sword. Cleopatra, in grief over Antony's death, and determined never to be taken in chains to Rome as a prisoner, commits suicide by allowing poisonous asps (snakes) to bite her.

Commentary

Antony and Cleopatra, Shakespeare's final tragedy, is an ambitious epic play with a vast cast and complex politics. The title characters are defined by their awareness of themselves as public figures. "But what about me?" they seem to ask. "When is my duty done? When does my personal happiness come?"

QUESTION?

Were Antony and Cleopatra truly in love?
They were certainly infatuated with each other. Antony left his wife to be with Cleopatra in Egypt. Upon hearing of Antony's death, Cleopatra kills herself. Antony and Cleopatra may lose an empire to Octavius, but in the poetry of their final hours, as they realize their personal ambitions, if only briefly, we are led to feel that their suicides are a victory and they will be united beyond the grave.

Cleopatra is a complex character: deeply in love with Antony, yet willing to consider betraying him. She is a sexually mature seductress with a childlike understanding of war; and above all, a performer on the vast stage of Egypt, a "character" who always "knows her lines," playing herself for the enjoyment of her audience. While other Shakespearean tragic heroes, such as Hamlet or Macbeth, die in despair, Cleopatra and Antony achieve what she calls their "immortal longings."

Famous Lines

"There's beggary in the love that can be reckon'd" (Act I, Scene I).

"My salad days,
When I was green in judgment" (Act I, Scene V).

"The barge she sat in, like a burnish'd throne,
Burn'd on the water; the poop was beaten gold;
Purple the sails, and so perfumed that
The winds were lovesick with them; the oars were silver,
Which to the tune of flutes kept stroke, and made
The water which they beat to follow faster,
As amorous of their strokes. For her own person,
It beggar'd all description" (Act II, Scene II).

"Age cannot wither her, nor custom stale
Her infinite variety" (Act II, Scene II).

"He wears the rose
Of youth upon him" (Act III, Scene XIII).

"I am dying, Egypt, dying" (Act IV, Scene XV).

"I have
Immortal longings in me" (Act V, Scene II).

Coriolanus

Main Characters

Caius Martius—a Roman general who is given the name "Coriolanus" after he defeats the Volscians; he is brave but arrogant

Volumnia—Coriolanus's mother; she dominates her son

Menenius—a friend of Coriolanus

Junius Brutus—a Roman tribune

Sicinius Velutus—Brutus's ally in the plot against Coriolanus

Tullus Aufidius—a Volscian general

Cominius—a friend of Coriolanus

Titus Lartius—an old Roman nobleman

Virgilia—Coriolanus's wife

Valeria—a friend of Virgilia and Volumnia

Young Martius—Coriolanus and Virgilia's son

Introduction

Coriolanus was probably written in 1607 or 1608 and first performed in 1609 at the Blackfriars Theatre in London, although these dates are uncertain. It is the penultimate tragedy written by Shakespeare and follows *Othello, King Lear, Macbeth,* and *Antony and Cleopatra*, all of which Shakespeare probably composed between 1604 and 1606.

FACT

The plot of *Coriolanus* probably came from *The Life of Caius Martius Coriolanus*, written in the first century by Plutarch and translated into English in 1579 by Sir Thomas North. (Another source may have been Livy's *History of Rome*.)

As was *Antony and Cleopatra*, it is a Roman play, but *Coriolanus* takes place early in Rome's history, when it was just one Italian city among many fighting for survival. The play takes place just after the fall of Tarquin, the last Roman king, and highlights the period when Rome moved from being a monarchy to a republic.

Renaissance thinkers were fascinated with Roman history (no doubt in part because of North's rich translation). Poets, playwrights, politicians, and philosophers alike consistently turned to Greece and Rome for inspiration, so Shakespeare's interest in the period makes a lot of sense.

One of the attractions of this play may have been the parallel between the events of the play and politics under the new King, James I. Jacobean London was plagued with radical thought and there was a struggle brewing between King James and Parliament as the middle class demanded more say in the running of their lives. The struggle culminated in 1642 in the English Civil War and the execution of James's son Charles I by Parliamentarians under Oliver Cromwell. For a brief period, England became a republic before the restoration of the monarchy in 1660.

The Play

Caius Martius is a legendary Roman general who considers himself better than other men, though he prefers to be a power behind the throne. He defeats the Volscian defenders of the city of Corioli and nearly beats their general Aufidius in hand-to-hand combat. At the last moment Aufidius flees.

For his accomplishments Marcius is renamed Caius Martius Coriolanus. He returns to Rome, where the patricians want to make him a tribune of the common people (the plebeians). The tribunes Sicinius Velutus and Junius Brutus are afraid that Coriolanus may become too powerful. They convince the plebes to condemn Coriolanus to death, and Coriolanus does nothing to help his cause with his arrogant attitude.

Outraged, Coriolanus flees Rome, abandoning his wife Virgilia and mother Volumnia. Coriolanus heads to the city of Antium to help Aufidius and the Volscians defeat the Roman Empire and seize Rome. With Coriolanus's help, the Volscians plunder the outlying Roman towns and pause at the gates of Rome. Friends and relatives try to dissuade Coriolanus from attacking his own people. Volumnia convinces him to make peace by using Coriolanus's son to play on Coriolanus's emotions.

Aufidius becomes infuriated that Coriolanus failed to sack Rome. He murders Coriolanus in front of the lords of Corioli. Aufidius, though pleased that Coriolanus is dead, orders that he be given a noble memorial.

Commentary

Coriolanus is something of a potboiler, and it has never been one of Shakespeare's most popular plays. It lacks depth, and its characters are somewhat two-dimensional. Yet this is perhaps Shakespeare's most overtly political play.

While Coriolanus's skill in battle would seem to make him an ideal hero for the masses, his contempt for the "blue-collar" mob allows him to be set up as an enemy of the people. While Coriolanus was in part responsible for the expulsion of Tarquin, the last Roman king, Coriolanus is a kingly figure born to command and unwilling to con his way to power. He clearly has no place in the republic that is taking command of his city.

Volumnia is not able to achieve power in her own right in the male-dominated Roman society, so her ambition drives her son's. She alone is able to convince Coriolanus to spare Rome, thus unwittingly sealing his doom.

While Coriolanus may be direct, he is surrounded by manipulative characters, such as his friend, Menenius, and the two tribunes, Sicinius and Brutus. Their manipulation of the masses turns the people of Rome against Coriolanus and almost brings about the city's downfall.

Both the political left and right with equal relish have adopted the play. Depending upon a director's philosophical inclinations, the play's ambiguities continue to fuel discussion.

Famous Lines

"Nature teaches beasts to know their friends" (Act II, Scene I).

"His nature is too noble for the world:
He would not flatter Neptune for his trident,
Or Jove for 's power to thunder" (Act III, Scene I).

Julius Caesar

Main Characters

Julius Caesar—a great Roman general and senator

Marcus Brutus—the tragic hero of the play; a Roman senator

Mark Antony—Caesar's friend

Cassius—a conspirator against Caesar

Octavius Caesar—Caesar's adopted son and appointed successor

Calphurnia—Caesar's wife

Portia—Brutus's wife

Flavius and Murellus—civil servants

Decius Brutus—a member of the conspiracy

Cicero—a famous Roman orator

Cinna—one of the conspirators

Cinna the poet—an innocent man killed by the mob because he has the same name as Cinna the conspirator

Casca, Metellus Cimber, Trebonius, and Caius Ligarius—conspirators against Caesar

Aemilius Lepidus—the third member of the triumvirate with Antony and Octavius

Artemidorus—he tries to warn Caesar of the conspiracy

Soothsayer—he warns Caesar about the Ides of March, but Caesar ignores him

Lucilius, Titinius, Pindarus, and Messala—soldiers in Brutus's army

Varrus and Claudio—Brutus's attendants

Introduction

Julius Caesar is one of Shakespeare's shortest plays. (*The Comedy of Errors* and *Macbeth* are both just a bit shorter). It was written around 1599 and performed at the Globe Theatre, a playhouse owned by Shakespeare's increasingly successful company, the Lord Chamberlain's Men. The only authoritative text of the play is the 1623 First Folio edition. The stage directions suggest this text is based on the theater company's promptbook rather than Shakespeare's manuscript.

Julius Caesar was the earliest of Shakespeare's three Roman plays. As are *Antony and Cleopatra* (which is a sort of sequel) and *Coriolanus*, *Julius Caesar* is a history in that it dramatizes real events. The play is clearly a tragedy because of the tragic character of Brutus, the noble Roman whose involvement in the conspiracy to save the state plunges both him and his country into chaos.

Rome was sharply divided into the patrician citizens, senators, and the growing but under-represented plebeians, or common folk. Citizens who favored republican democratic rule were afraid that Julius Caesar's power would lead to their enslavement. A group of conspirators assassinated Caesar, and the civil war they hoped to avoid erupted anyway. The play follows events leading up to Caesar's death and the civil war.

Elizabethans would have been quick to pick up on the parallels between Ancient Rome becoming an imperial power, and Elizabeth's ability to consolidate the powers of the monarchy.

By 1599, Queen Elizabeth I had been queen for close to forty years and had enlarged her powers at the expense of the aristocracy and the House of Commons. At age sixty-six, particularly old for her time, and with no heirs or named successor, many feared her death would plunge England into the kind of chaos suffered during the fifteenth century. The story of Caesar's downfall provided a perspective on what might happen when accepted methods of distributing power were disrupted.

The Play

Julius Caesar enters as a hero having defeated the Gauls, then Pompey's army. Mark Antony attempts three times to crown Caesar king; however, some senators take this as a threat to Rome. Cassius, in particular, has serious misgivings about Caesar's ambition and is clearly jealous of his achievements. To offset Caesar's popular support, Cassius approaches Marcus Brutus, a nobleman known for his integrity. If Brutus were to support a coup, it will be more acceptable to the citizens of Rome, and equally important, Brutus is also a close friend of Caesar.

During a great storm, Brutus considers his options, realizing that the conspirators may well have to assassinate Caesar. Caesar, already warned by the Soothsayer and Calphurnia, his wife, ignores all advice to the contrary and pays a visit to the Senate. There, he is stabbed to death by Brutus, Cassius, and the others.

Brutus dissuades the conspirators from slaying Antony with Caesar. After the assassination Antony asks to accompany Caesar's body and speak at his funeral. Brutus agrees, and at the funeral he delivers a stirring oratory that explains the reasoning for the assassination. Antony follows with his famous "Friends, Romans, countrymen" speech, and through his masterful use of irony stirs the crowd to the point where they call for the blood of Cassius, Brutus, and anyone else associated with Caesar's death.

FACT

Brutus clearly emerges as the most complex character and the play's tragic hero. He is a powerful public figure, but he is also a loving husband and dignified military leader. His rigid idealism becomes both his greatest virtue and his tragic flaw.

Antony then joins Octavius (Caesar's nephew) and Lepidus to wrest control of Rome by force of arms. Brutus and Cassius raise armies against them. In a final battle, with many of his coconspirators now dead, Cassius kills himself when facing defeat, and he is quickly followed by Brutus, who takes his own life rather than allowing himself to be taken captive. Upon discovering the body, Antony laments the tragic fall of Brutus, calling him the noblest of them all.

Commentary

In a world of self-serving ambition, Brutus is truly "the noblest Roman of them all," but his commitment to principle repeatedly causes him to miscalculate. He ignores Cassius's suggestion to kill Antony as well as Caesar, and then, again against Cassius's advice, he allows Antony to speak a funeral oration over Caesar's body, plunging the city and the country into chaos.

Antony is strong where Brutus is weak. He is impulsive and quick-witted, and he is able to save himself by convincing the conspirators he is on their side, then in enraging the mob against the conspirators. Brutus is noble, to be sure, but Antony proves himself the consummate politician.

Shakespeare explores several themes in *Julius Caesar*. The play raises questions about what in our lives is determined by fate and how much free will we have. Cassius, for example, says, "The fault, dear Brutus, is not in our stars, but in ourselves, that we are underlings." On the other hand, Caesar tells his wife, "Death, a necessary end, will come when it will come." The text explores public self versus private self and inflexibility versus compromise.

Brutus interprets his defeat as the work of Caesar's ghost—empowered by the people's devotion to Caesar—and the legacy of a man who somehow transcended fate. Both Brutus and Caesar are stubborn men who ultimately suffer fatally for it. It is the adaptable people, the ones who have the will to compromise, who survive.

Famous Lines

"The live-long day" (Act I, Scene I).

"Beware the ides of March" (Act I, Scene II).

"Let me have men about me that are fat,
Sleek-headed men, and such as sleep o' nights:
Yond Cassius has a lean and hungry look;
He thinks too much: such men are dangerous" (Act I, Scene II).

"A dish fit for the gods" (Act II, Scene I).

"Cowards die many times before their deaths;
The valiant never taste of death but once.
Of all the wonders that I yet have heard,
It seems to me most strange that men should fear;
Seeing that death, a necessary end,
Will come when it will come" (Act II, Scene II).

"Et tu, Brute!" (Act III, Scene I).

"O, pardon me, thou bleeding piece of earth,

That I am meek and gentle with these butchers!
Thou art the ruins of the noblest man
That ever lived in the tide of times" (Act III, Scene I).

"Cry 'Havoc,' and let slip the dogs of war" (Act III, Scene I).

"Friends, Romans, countrymen, lend me your ears;
I come to bury Cæsar, not to praise him.
The evil that men do lives after them;
The good is oft interred with their bones" (Act III, Scene II).

"If you have tears, prepare to shed them now" (Act III, Scene II).

"This was the most unkindest cut of all" (Act III, Scene II).

"Great Cæsar fell.
O, what a fall was there, my countrymen!
Then I, and you, and all of us fell down,
Whilst bloody treason flourish'd over us" (Act III, Scene II).

"There is a tide in the affairs of men
Which taken at the flood, leads on to fortune;
Omitted, all the voyage of their life
Is bound in shallows and in miseries" (Act IV, Scene III).

"His life was gentle, and the elements
So mix'd in him, that Nature might stand up
And say to all the world, 'This was a man!'" (Act V, Scene V).

Romeo and Juliet

Main Characters

Romeo—a Montague; a teenager who falls in love with Juliet
Juliet—a Capulet; she falls in love with Romeo

Friar Laurence—a wise old priest
Nurse—Juliet's second mother and confidant
Benvolio—Romeo's cousin
Mercutio—Romeo's best friend
Tybalt—Juliet's hot-tempered cousin
Capulet—Juliet's father
Lady Capulet—Juliet's mother
Paris—a nobleman; one of Juliet's suitors
Prince Escalus—the ruler of Verona
Montague—Romeo's father
Lady Montague—Romeo's mother

Introduction

Romeo and Juliet was written early in Shakespeare's career, probably in 1594 or 1595 and was first published in 1597. It is his first nonhistorical tragedy, and despite its poetic naiveté, in many ways it holds the promise of the mature plays Shakespeare would come to write in a few years.

The primary source was a poem titled *The Tragicall Historye of Romeus and Juliet* written in 1562 by Arthur Brooke. This, in turn, was a translation of a poem by a Frenchman, Pierre Boaistuau, published in 1559. The French poem, it seems, was derived from a 1554 story by an Italian writer named Mateo Bandello, who in turn had gotten it from a version by Luigi Da Porto, published in 1530.

While the story of Romeo and Juliet was often told in the second half of the sixteenth century, Shakespeare's version has marked differences. His version has some of the greatest love poetry ever written in the English language, subtle and original characters (such as Mercutio and Tybalt, who are among some of Shakespeare's most memorable early characters), and a fast pace (the action is compressed into five days).

The Play

In Verona, two feuding families, the Montagues and the Capulets, brawl constantly in the streets; the reason for the quarrel is never really made clear.

In response to the constant fighting, the prince of Verona issues an edict imposing the death penalty on anyone caught dueling.

QUESTION?

Was *Romeo and Juliet* based on a true story?
Romeo and Juliet was based on the life of two real lovers who both died for each other and lived in Verona, Italy, in 1303. Both the Capulets and Montagues existed in Verona at this time, and Shakespeare is reckoned to have discovered this tragic love story in Arthur Brooke's 1562 poem titled *The Tragical Historye of Romeus and Juliet*.

Romeo of the house of Montague has been infatuated with Rosaline, a niece of Capulet. He and his friends sneak into a masked ball at Capulet's house so that Romeo can see her. During the ball, Romeo catches sight of Juliet, Capulet's daughter, and quickly forgets about Rosaline.

That same night, Romeo creeps under Juliet's bedroom window and professes his love to Juliet, who is standing on her balcony above him and overhears his sighs of love. She confesses she returns his feelings. With the aid of Friar Laurence, Romeo makes plans with Juliet for them to be married in secret.

Tybalt, Juliet's cousin, discovers that Romeo attended the ball and sets out to teach the young Montague a lesson. He challenges Romeo in the street. Romeo tries to avoid a duel because he is in love with Juliet. However, Romeo's best friend, Mercutio, takes up Tybalt's challenge and is killed by Tybalt. Before he realizes what he is doing, a distraught Romeo draws his sword and kills Tybalt in turn.

As a result of the bloodshed, despite the provocation, the Escalus, the prince of Verona, banishes Romeo. Romeo has time to consummate his marriage to Juliet and bid her goodbye. He hopes that they will soon be reunited.

FACT

The phrase "Romeo, Romeo, wherefore art thou Romeo," is second only to Hamlet's "To be or not to be" as the most famous quotation from Shakespeare. "Wherefore art thou Romeo" does not mean "where"; rather, it means "why" are you from a family that feuds with mine.

Juliet's parents, meanwhile, press her to marry Paris. With Friar Laurence's help, Juliet comes up with a desperate plan to avoid her parent's wishes. She obtains a drug that will make her seem dead for forty-two hours. While she is comatose, Friar Laurence will send word to Romeo so that he can rescue her from her family tomb.

Dame Peggy Ashcroft: "There has been a recent fashion in the theatre to define a certain kind of play as a 'black comedy.' I will define *Romeo and Juliet* as a 'golden tragedy.'"

Friar Laurence's letter never gets to Romeo. Instead he hears that Juliet has died. Grief-stricken, Romeo buys some poison with the intention of killing himself. Friar Laurence discovers that Romeo never got his letter, and in horror he rushes to Juliet's tomb.

Too late. At Juliet's tomb, Romeo encounters Paris, who is mourning for his Juliet. In grief for Juliet's loss, the two men fight and Romeo kills Paris. Entering the tomb, Romeo discovers the "dead" Juliet and, swallowing the poison, commits suicide at her side. Friar Laurence arrives at the scene just as Juliet wakes up. She discovers the body of her beloved Romeo beside her, takes Romeo's dagger and stabs herself in the heart.

The prince and the parents arrive, and Friar Laurence explains what has happened. Faced with the awful price their feud has cost them, the Montagues and Capulets swear to end the bitterness between the two families.

Commentary

This is an early play (1594), written by a young poet with amazing literary talent. Despite its story, it is really quite optimistic, especially when compared to the latter tragedies and dark comedies. In modern times, critics have tended to disparage the play in favor of Shakespeare's great tragedies (*Hamlet, King Lear, Macbeth,* and *Othello*). Certainly, when compared to these plays, *Romeo and Juliet* lacks psychological depth and structural complexity.

More recently, scholars have reconsidered their opinion, opting to judge *Romeo and Juliet* in its own right. Viewed in this light, the tragedy of the star-crossed couple is an extraordinary experimental play, featuring radical departures from long-standing conventions.

Romeo

In Juliet, Romeo finds that rare gift, a soul mate—a lover of such purity and passion that when he learns she has died, he cannot endure life without her. At first blush this may seem an immature reaction. In fact, it can also be seen as a tragic sign of maturity. Romeo is the romantic in this couple. He grows up through "the love of a good woman," grounding his romantic notions, but it is Juliet who is the levelheaded one of the pair.

FACT

The ardor and romantic intensity of *Romeo and Juliet*, as well as its theme of young lovers struggling against the oppressive values of their parents, make it an extremely youthful play. It represents a young playwright's first gropings toward the profound philosophical tragedies of *Hamlet, King Lear,* and *Othello.*

At the beginning of the play, Romeo pines for Rosaline, proclaiming her the paragon of women and despairing of her indifference toward him. His histrionics seem frankly juvenile, and he gets the teasing he deserves from his friends and relatives. Sure enough, Rosaline evaporates from Romeo's thoughts when he first sees Juliet. But Juliet is not just another infatuation.

As Romeo's love matures from shallow desire to a profound passion, he also matures as a person. Against great provocation, he tries his best to avoid fighting with Tybalt, and only when Tybalt manages to include him in the death of his best friend, Mercutio, does Romeo "lose it." If only Romeo had restrained himself from killing Tybalt, or waited even a few hours before killing himself after seeing Juliet lying in her tomb, matters might have ended happily. But the same passions that made his love for Juliet so powerful condemned him to respond as he does in both cases.

Juliet

Juliet is a fascinating character. While Romeo is the romantic, Juliet is determined, strong, and down-to-earth. Her growing love for Romeo propels her toward adulthood with the velocity of a rocket. She learns how to manage the adults on their own terms. She promises her mother, for example, that she will consider Paris as a possible husband with an outward show of obedience that is clearly meant to handle her mother.

FACT

Romeo and Juliet has been interpreted and adapted thousands of times in opera, ballet, novels, on the stage, screen, and television. Even so, the passage of time and changing cultural context does not seem to have diminished the play's innate innocence, youthful rebelliousness, or capacity to shock, delight, and move audiences.

Though profoundly in love with Romeo, Juliet is able to see and criticize Romeo's impetuosity and his tendency to romanticize things. After Romeo is banished, she does not follow him blindly to Mantua, but calmly and rationally decides what the course of action should be for the two of them. She then cuts herself loose from her Nurse and her parents in order to reunite with her husband.

When she wakes up in the tomb to find Romeo dead beside her, she decides to kill herself out of the same intensity of love that overwhelmed Romeo. Juliet's suicide actually requires more nerve, as befits her character: While he swallows poison, she stabs herself through the heart with a dagger. Juliet's development from a wide-eyed teenager to a self-assured, loyal, and capable woman is one of Shakespeare's triumphs of characterization. Juliet is one of his most believable female characters.

Famous Lines

"The weakest goes to the wall" (Act I, Scene I).

"He that is strucken blind cannot forget

The precious treasure of his eyesight lost" (Act I, Scene I).

"True, I talk of dreams,
Which are the children of an idle brain,
Begot of nothing but vain fantasy" (Act I, Scene IV).

"But, soft! what light through yonder window breaks?
It is the east, and Juliet is the sun" (Act II, Scene II).

"See, how she leans her cheek upon her hand!
O that I were a glove upon that hand,
That I might touch that cheek!" (Act II, Scene II).

"O Romeo, Romeo! wherefore art thou Romeo?" (Act II, Scene II).

"What's in a name? That which we call a rose
By any other name would smell as sweet" (Act II, Scene II).

"This bud of love, by summer's ripening breath,
May prove a beauteous flower when next we meet" (Act II, Scene II).

"Good night, good night! parting is such sweet sorrow,
That I shall say good night till it be morrow" (Act II, Scene II).

"These violent delights have violent ends" (Act II, Scene VI).

"Taking the measure of an unmade grave" (Act III, Scene III).

"Not stepping o'er the bounds of modesty" (Act IV, Scene II).

"Eyes, look your last!
Arms, take your last embrace!" (Act V, Scene III).

"Too swift arrives as tardy as too slow" (Act II, Scene VI).

"A plague o' both your houses!" (Act III, Scene I).

Timon of Athens

Main Characters

Timon—a wealthy man who enjoys giving gifts to his friends and sharing his wealth

Apemantus—one of Timon's guests

Alcibiades—an acquaintance of Timon

Flavius—one of Timon's servants

Lucullus, Lucius, Sempronius, and Ventidius—Timon's fair-weather friends

Lucilius, Flaminius, and Servilius—Timon's servants

Caphis, Philotus, Titus, Hortensius—servants of creditors who demand payment of their loan

Poet—one of Timon's hangers-on

Painter—one of Timon's hangers-on

Jeweler—one of Timon's hangers-on

Fool—the Fool appears with Apemantus outside Timon's house while servants of creditors wait for their payments

Bandits—thieves Timon meets in the wilderness

Senators—members of the Athenian Senate

Lords—among Timon's many friends who attend his feasts and accept his gifts

Introduction

Timon of Athens was probably written between 1605 and 1608, but the play is not known to have been produced, probably because, as many scholars argue, it was never finished. An alternative theory is that it focused on too controversial a topic for the years directly after James I's accession to the English throne in 1603.

In the early part of the seventeenth century there was growing condemnation of an almost profligate spendthriftness by the English aristocracy, most of whom could not afford the lifestyles they tried to maintain. Nobles constantly competed to out-lavish one another but lacked the cash to back up their behavior. As a result, a new credit market arose.

QUESTION?

Was this late play, *Timon of Athens*, a collaboration?
Some scholars think Shakespeare coauthored this play with a dramatist named Thomas Middleton. Nevertheless, some Shakespearean characteristics are unmistakable, such as the story's derivation from Plutarch's *Lives of the Noble Greeks and Romans*, one of Shakespeare's favorite sources.

James I was well known for such profligate behavior, giving his friends expensive gifts and generally spending money on fashionable things until he had incurred huge deficits in the royal treasury. Much of the aristocracy followed his example. The play draws attention to the irresponsible behavior of the upper classes, a criticism which no doubt contributed to keeping the play from being sponsored or performed.

The Play

Timon is a generous aristocrat in Athens. Everyone loves him because of his generosity. He just hasn't wanted to hear what his steward Flavius has been trying to tell him. When Timon finds creditors knocking on the door, Flavius is finally able to tell him that he is bankrupt.

Timon then sends his servants to his "friends," only to find no one will lend him money to repay his debts except his steward, who gives what little he has to his master. Incensed at this betrayal, Timon invites everyone to one last feast. The only dish, to everyone's surprise, is warm water. Timon then denounces not only his former comrades but also humankind as a whole.

In the meantime, Alcibiades, a captain of Athens, is banished for pleading for the life of one of his men, under sentence of death by the Senate. Alcibiades seriously considers turning his army against Athens in revenge.

He hears about Timon, who was living as a hermit in the forest, digging for roots to eat when he stumbled upon a buried trove of gold. Alcibiades decides to visit Timon, who in turn offers Alcibiades gold if he will sack Athens. Alcibiades accepts his offer and marches on Athens.

Timon receives more visitors, some of whom are bandits, and pays them gold to wreak havoc on Athens. The bandits accept the gold, but Timon's ranting, ironically, convinces them to quit thieving. Timon also sends away his only loyal friend, his former steward, Flavius, but with gold in his pockets and more kindness than he has shown to anyone else.

FACT

Despite his presumed goodness at the start of the play, Timon is a self-absorbed character who sets himself up as a god of generosity. When he loses his wealth through his own foolishness, he becomes a god of vitriol and revenge, cursing humankind with the same kind of enthusiasm with which he earlier praised it.

Alcibiades takes Athens. Knowing he is a friend of Alcibiades, the Athenians beg Timon for help. Timon offers them a tree outside his cave—on which they can hang themselves. The senators ingratiate themselves with Alcibiades by giving up his enemies and those who refused to help Timon when he was in debt. Alcibiades agrees, vowing peace in Athens. A soldier enters with the sad news that Timon has died alone in his cave.

Commentary

Timon of Athens focuses exclusively on one question: Is material well-being inextricably linked to love and friendship? It is, in some ways, almost a proto-Marxist play and has a number of things to say to counter what some critics see as an American buy-now-pay-later mentality.

A Poor Judge of Character

Timon enjoys sharing his wealth but doesn't pick his friends very well. Almost certainly, the only reasons they have stuck around is the hope that Timon will give them a gift. Apemantus may think Timon's friends are all worthless flatterers, but he hangs around as well, although without eating or accepting gifts, just to see how long things will go on before they come crashing to a halt.

Timon likes his friends' affection and seems to get some form of status merely from spending. Perhaps he believes his generosity will solidify his friendship with the various Athenian lords who surround him. He is astonished to see the intangible bonds of "friendship" disintegrate when he needs more loans from his friends.

Possession and Financial Gain

Apemantus takes the opposite tack to Timon at every stage. He believes people are naturally greedy and that generosity is an attempt to control and influence others and gain a return later. Yet both men believe that possessions, or lack thereof, determine how we think of ourselves.

Like the earlier play *The Merchant of Venice*, *Timon of Athens* concerns itself with the connection between ties of affection and monetary bonds. Timon must discover how much friendship has to do with self-interest, how material goods compare to intangible feelings, and how much people are esteemed for their personal characteristics versus their possessions.

The play is almost exclusively about financial exchanges between men (there is no significant female part), and in a certain light it suggests such dealings are almost depraved roles. The Fool at one point actually draws parallels between those who go to creditors and those who go to prostitutes. The play draws on the ancient portrait of moneylending as a depraved form of unnatural "breeding" of money for interest.

Friends: Fair-weather or True?

Timon begins the play as a generous but foolish man and ends it as an angry and foolish man. He takes the behavior of a few people he should have realized were fair-weather friends as a sign that the whole of humanity is rotten. Yet he fails to see that many people who come to see him in his cave prove his assumption false. Flavius, who echoes Timon's philosophy of generosity but in a sensible way, shares his remaining funds with Timon's servants, proving himself an honorable man. Apemantus and Timon argue, but they clearly enjoy each other's company; and Alcibiades, in a subplot involving a condemned friend, which may have been one of the casualties of an unrevised play, prepares to attack Athens in order to rehabilitate Timon's honor in the city. At the end of the play Timon learns from the senators that many Athenians want to make amends for the way Timon has been treated. Still he rejects them.

When Alcibiades arrives at the gates of Athens with his army, the senators convince him not to attack by saying that those who were cruel to Timon and to Alcibiades make up only a small portion of the population and will be easy to single out and punish. The play suggests that the wholesale villainy Timon thought made up the world is really only limited to some badly chosen friends.

Famous Lines

"Here's that which is too weak to be a sinner,—honest water, which ne'er left man i' the mire" (Act I, Scene II).

"Every man has his fault, and honesty is his" (Act III, Scene I).

"Nothing emboldens sin so much as mercy" (Act III, Scene V).

"We have seen better days" (Act IV, Scene II).

"Life's uncertain voyage" (Act V, Scene I).

Titus Andronicus

Main Characters

Titus Andronicus—general of Rome and tragic hero of the play
Tamora—queen of the Goths, mother of Chiron and Demetrius
Aaron—Tamora's Moorish lover
Lavinia—the only daughter of Titus Andronicus; in love with Bassianus
Marcus Andronicus—Roman tribune; brother of Titus Andronicus
Saturninus—the eldest son of the late emperor of Rome
Bassianus—the younger brother of Saturninus
Lucius—Titus's only surviving son
Alarbus, Chiron, and Demetrius—Goth princes; sons of Tamora
Young Lucius—Titus's grandson, and Lucius's son

Introduction

Elizabethan written accounts testify to audiences with particularly bloody tastes, and *Titus Andronicus* was received with great applause, remaining a favorite for over a decade. However gruesome we find *Titus Andronicus* today, it's worth recalling that competing with the burgeoning theater, blood sports such as public bear-baiting were popular in Elizabethan times. And it is also worth noting how a director like Julie Taymor (also responsible for *The Lion King*, itself inspired by *Hamlet*) can find relevance in this play to our own times, saturated as they are with violence. The play was a huge favorite when it opened.

Saving Shakespeare's Good Name

In 1687, some 100 years after the first performance of *Titus Andronicus*, Edward Ravenscroft adapted the play for a different audience and called it *The Rape of Lavinia.*

In an introduction to his more refined version, Ravenscroft wrote, "I have been told . . . that it was not originally [Shakespeare's], but brought by a private author to be acted, and [Shakespeare] only gave some Master-touches to one or two of the principal parts of characters. This I am apt to believe, because 'tis the most incorrect and indigested piece in all his works. It seems rather a heap of Rubbish than a structure."

What's particularly interesting about Ravenscroft's comment is his need to try and rescue Shakespeare's good name. It's as though an overtly brutal pornographic early novel by Samuel Beckett surfaced and scholars felt compelled to justify something they would otherwise condemn with disdain as low popular trash. *Titus Andronicus* is an Elizabethan *Texas Chainsaw Massacre.* Yet, knowing the author, we can't but think its massive excess seems to be less an imitation of the Elizabethan revenge drama than a parody of that form.

Poet T. S. Eliot had this to say: "*Titus Andronicus* is one of the stupidest and most uninspiring plays ever written."

In some ways this account gives some sense of the history of *Titus Andronicus*. Shakespeare's admirers once halfheartedly tried to deny his authorship of what is probably his most violent play. The debate has gone on for centuries. In 1614, Ben Jonson claimed it was as popular a play as Thomas Kyd's equally bloody *The Spanish Tragedy*. Samuel Johnson theorized that Shakespeare "play-doctored" someone else's work.

If scholars acknowledge the hand of the great master in this work at all, they may point to his youth as an excuse. Shakespeare would have been about twenty-six when he wrote *Titus Andronicus,* and it marked his first attempt at writing tragedy. Yet today *Titus* is as often proclaimed as Shakespeare's first critique of Renaissance England's unquestioning attitude toward all things classical. Francis Meres publicly named Shakespeare as the play's author in *Palladis Tamia* (1598), and the play is included in the First Folio.

Sources

The play was likely written between 1590 and 1593. While there is no clear main source for the story, critics think that they included *Hecuba* by Euripides, *Metamorphoses* by Ovid, and *Thyestes* and *Troades* by Seneca. A tutor to Emperor Nero, Seneca wrote plays that described the grisly horror of murder in elaborate detail. When Elizabethans began translating Seneca's works from Latin in 1559, writers relished them and wrote plays "in the classical style" imitating them. Shakespeare appears to have seasoned *Titus Andronicus* and later, *Macbeth* and parts of *King Lear* with some of Seneca's ghoulish spice.

The poetry of *Titus Andronicus* displays definite Shakespearean traits, and in the character of Aaron we see the seeds of Othello, Iago, and Richard III, while Tamora can be seen as an early version of Margaret in the *King Henry VI* plays. It is the only Shakespeare play, ironically, for which we have a contemporary illustration, by the author Henry Peacham, which shows characters in a mix of Roman and Renaissance costumes.

The Play

Titus, a Roman general, returns to Rome after a victorious campaign against the Goths. In tow as captives are Tamora and her sons, one of whom, Alarbus, is sacrificed by Titus's sons. Saturninus, the newly declared Roman emperor, is feuding with his younger brother, Bassianus. Lavinia, Titus's daughter, chooses Bassianus over Saturninus. The emperor is seduced by the captive Queen Tamora, who is plotting with her Moorish lover, Aaron, to get revenge against Titus.

Demetrius and Chiron come across Bassianus and Lavinia in the woods. They kill Bassianus then rape and mutilate Lavinia, leaving her without a tongue to speak or hands to write. Aaron now frames Titus's sons (Quintus and Martius) for Bassianus's murder, and they are condemned to death. Titus's remaining son, Lucius, tries to rescue his brothers and is banished from Rome.

Aaron tells Titus that the emperor will spare Quintus and Martius if Titus cuts off a hand and sends it to him. Titus does so. His hand is returned to him along with the heads of his two sons. Lucius, meanwhile, raises an army of Goths to sack Rome.

Titus finally is able to communicate enough with a half-crazed Lavinia to discover that Demetrius and Chiron were responsible for attacking her. Titus kills them and serves them to their mother as a pie!

When Tamora and Saturninus arrive to try to convince Titus to call off Lucius and his Goths, Titus serves them dinner, featuring pie as the main course. In the middle of the feast, Titus kills Lavinia to put her out of her misery, reveals the secret ingredient of his pie, then butchers Tamora. Saturninus in turn slays Titus. Lucius, newly arrived, kills Saturninus.

Lucius is elected emperor of Rome and orders Aaron (who refuses to ask forgiveness for his crimes) buried up to his chest and left to starve, and Tamora to be left unburied for the scavengers to feast on.

Commentary

Titus Andronicus falls between two schools of drama: it is neither history (though the characters are drawn from Roman history, the events are not) nor is the play, especially in tone, what we think of as Shakespearean tragedy. It is clearly a melodrama, best described as Elizabethan revenge tragedy, a genre defined by a hero who doggedly and bloodily pursues vengeance and perishes at his moment of success. *Titus Andronicus* also features one of the few genuinely evil characters in Shakespearean literature, Aaron the Moor. Aaron orchestrates all of the evil in the play, and his only regret is that he wasn't able to commit more evil. And yet even this personification of evil has one soft spot, his newborn son.

Titus is a paradoxical character. His behavior is hard for us to understand, but we can admire his concepts of honor and justice. As Rome's greatest general, Titus will allow nothing to compromise his honor or that of his family, even if he has to kill one of his sons to maintain it.

QUESTION?

How can a revenge tragedy be best defined?
The revenge tragedy is not just about Titus getting revenge on those who wronged him and his family. It is also about Tamora getting revenge on Titus because his sons killed her son at the start of the play. She pushes Titus to the point where he has been stripped of all he holds dear, but she fails to administer the coup de grâce, leaving him a wounded and dangerous creature.

While *Titus Andronicus* is clearly an archetypal gore-filled Elizabethan revenge tragedy, the story of *Hamlet* has a superficial resemblance to *Titus Andronicus*. Yet clearly, the more mature playwright who wrote *Hamlet*, with years of theatrical experience and real-life experience (with tragedies like the death of his young son) decided to revisit a popular genre in order to turn it on its head and put the genre to rest. In *Hamlet* he is not content with just piling up the bodies (though there is quite a pile by the play's end). Instead, the horror of *Hamlet* is a spiritual one, and it takes the expectations of an audience for a genre play like *Titus Andronicus* and forces them to consider what all this violence and blood does to our souls.

Famous Lines

"Sweet mercy is nobility's true badge" (Act I, Scene II).

"The eagle suffers little birds to sing" (Act IV, Scene IV).

CHAPTER 15

Shakespeare's Four Greatest Tragedies

Such great heroes as Macbeth, Othello, King Lear, and Hamlet will always fail because their tragedy is that while they are great men capable of great deeds, they cannot withstand the inevitability of the character flaw that will bring about their own destruction. They are tragic heroes, doomed by the perilous conflict within their own hearts.

Hamlet, Prince of Denmark

Main Characters

Hamlet—the Prince of Denmark; son of the late King Hamlet and the nephew of the present King Claudius

Claudius—the King of Denmark; Hamlet's uncle who murdered Hamlet's father to obtain the throne

Gertrude—the Queen of Denmark and Hamlet's mother; after the death of her husband (Hamlet's father), Gertrude married her brother-in-law, Claudius

Polonius—the Lord Chamberlain and father to Laertes and Ophelia

Horatio—Hamlet's friend from Wittenberg

Ophelia—Polonius's daughter

Laertes—Polonius's son

Fortinbras—the Prince of Norway; his father was killed by Hamlet's father, and he intends to attack Denmark to avenge his father's death

The Ghost—Hamlet's recently murdered father

Rosencrantz and Guildenstern—former friends of Hamlet from Denmark

Osric, Voltemand, and Cornelius—courtiers

Marcellus and Barnardo—the officers of the watch who report seeing the Ghost

Francisco—a soldier

Reynaldo—Polonius's servant

Introduction

Hamlet. Who hasn't heard of Hamlet? He is the young Danish prince who—as actor Laurence Olivier once said—"can't make up his mind." *Hamlet* is no doubt the most famous play ever written in the English language. Shakespeare penned it during the first part of the seventeenth century at the close of Queen Elizabeth's reign, and it was probably first performed in July 1602.

Hamlet is the tragic story of a Danish prince whose uncle murders his father and marries his mother. There are several sources for the story of the play: The German *Hystorie of Hamblet*; an English translation of a French prose work (François de Belleforest's *Histoires Tragiques*), and an ancient history of Denmark written by Saxo Grammaticus in the thirteenth century.

> T. S. Eliot: "Bad poets borrow, good poets steal. Shakespeare was the prince of thieves. With the exception of *Love's Labour's Lost, A Midsummer Night's Dream*, and *The Tempest*, not one plot is completely Shakespeare's own invention."

What Shakespeare did with the various sources available to him is no doubt the genesis to write *Hamlet*. But it may have been something else: the death of his eleven-year-old son Hamnet, who died in 1596, several years before the play was written. Perhaps Shakespeare's heart sickness at the loss of his only son is echoed in Hamlet's grief for his father.

The Play

Hamlet, Prince of Denmark begins with Hamlet in a quandary. He is depressed by the death of his father, the ghost of whom now haunts Elsinore, ranting that his brother, Claudius, murdered him. After Hamlet's father's death, Claudius married Queen Gertrude, Hamlet's mother, and assumed the throne of Denmark. Fortinbras of Norway has threatened to invade Denmark.

Hamlet's father's ghost demands that his son take revenge for his murder. To do this Hamlet feigns madness. In this maddened state, he scorns the affections of Ophelia, whom he loves.

Polonius grows concerned over Hamlet's growing insanity and discusses his concern with the king and queen. Meanwhile, Hamlet tries to come to terms with the idea that his uncle may have murdered his father. In an effort to "catch the conscience of the king," Hamlet hires a traveling troupe of actors to act out a play, the core of which is an assassination similar to the murder of his father. Claudius' reaction to the murder scene convinces Hamlet that his father's ghost told him the truth. Still, Hamlet, tormented by the idea of committing murder, can't make up his mind to slay his uncle.

Hamlet starts to torment his mother, Gertrude, by insisting she is sleeping with her husband's killer. Polonius, who hides behind a tapestry in the queen's chamber to eavesdrop, panics and cries for help. Hamlet stabs him, thinking it is his Uncle Claudius.

Claudius sends Hamlet to England with Rosencrantz and Guildenstern, two of Hamlet's childhood friends. He gets Hamlet to carry a letter to the king of England in which Claudius asks the king to kill Hamlet (the bearer of the letter). Hamlet turns the tables on his friends and they are put to death instead.

Is *Hamlet* Shakespeare's greatest play?
Whether *Hamlet* is Shakespeare's greatest play is debatable. It is certainly his most famous. *Hamlet* has been analyzed exhaustively for its aesthetic, moral, political, psychological, historical, allegorical, logical, religious, and philosophical aspects. There are thousands of works devoted to the play and how to understand it.

Driven to madness herself by Hamlet's condition and the death of her father, Polonius, Ophelia drowns herself. Her brother, Laertes, returns from his studies and vows his vengeance upon Hamlet for what the prince has done to his family. Claudius plots with Laertes to kill Hamlet. At Ophelia's funeral Laertes and Hamlet confront one another and Laertes challenges Hamlet to a duel.

Claudius tells Laertes to select a sharp blade instead of a dull one for the duel and to poison the tip so that a wound will kill the prince. Claudius also decides to keep some poisoned wine for Hamlet to drink. Then everything goes wrong.

Laertes thrusts first at Hamlet hoping for a quick kill, but misses. As the duel goes on, Gertrude drinks unknowingly from the poisoned wine. Then, in the heat of the fray, Laertes wounds Hamlet. In a twist of fate, he loses the poisoned rapier to Hamlet. Gertrude collapses from the poison she has consumed. Laertes reveals the plot against Hamlet before he dies, telling him he has "not a half-hour's life" in him. Hamlet stabs Claudius with the poisoned foil, then forces him to drink from the poisoned wine that killed his mother.

Hamlet now collapses and dies in Horatio's arms as Fortinbras enters the castle. Fortinbras is left to rule, as the entire Danish royal family is dead. He tells his men to give Hamlet and the rest proper funerals.

Commentary

Hamlet is one of the most complex and compelling characters of English literature. His actions and thoughts have been analyzed over and over and it is this seemingly bottomless well of possibilities that accounts for Hamlet's enduring appeal.

Hamlet is concerned with the profound truths of human nature and our place in the universe. Things to consider include Shakespeare's questioning of the whole revenge play genre, and the nature of revenge itself and how it affects us. Hamlet's struggle over whether or not to murder Claudius, echoed by the Fortinbras and Laertes subplots, acts as a base from which Shakespeare explores the relationship between thought and action. He ponders this thought: Yes, it is human instinct to want revenge when wronged, but is it right to act on that instinct?

Hamlet is not a man of action deliberately, but a scholar, a man of thought and consideration and learning, and many critics feel the imbalance between his active and passive natures is a tragic flaw that makes his wretched fate inevitable.

FACT

Hamlet is the most performed play in the world, yet it is rarely produced in its entirety. Called the "Eternity Hamlet," it takes four and a half hours to stage. *Hamlet* has more lines than any other character, 1,530, and "To be or not to be" is the most quoted phrase in the English language.

Hamlet is a kind of modern Everyman, and his dilemmas echo those that we all face in some form. We can come to any number of reasonable conclusions about Hamlet, but arriving at a definitive one is very difficult.

Other important themes explored in *Hamlet* include the line between sanity and madness, the nature of political power, the connection between the well-being of the state and the moral condition of its leaders, and the moral questions of living a good life and committing suicide. Hamlet's ghostly father is in agony in purgatory, having died unconfessed and with his sins still heavy on his shoulders. But Shakespeare's Anglican audience would not believe in purgatory if they were orthodox Protestants! Hamlet considers killing himself, but he fears God's wrath in the afterlife. Ophelia, clearly an innocent, in a fit of madness does kill herself, but will she still suffer in the afterlife because of it? Other themes are the relationship between sons and fathers (Hamlet and the Ghost, Laertes and Polonius, Fortinbras and the dead king of Norway), the nature of the family, the inevitability of death, and, against that inevitability, the question of what gives life meaning.

Hamlet's love of learning and reason is pulverized by a growing nihilism, as every truth that is supposed to comfort him (religion, society, philosophy, love) either fails him or proves false. Just how insane Hamlet was and how much he faked it is one of the most hotly contested critical controversies surrounding the play. The likely answer is that he decided to feign madness as a strategic way of covering his deep distress at what the ghost reveals to him without putting himself in danger. Yet there is little doubt that his mind is so troubled, confused, and desperate that his pretense assumes the intensity of real madness for a while as he deals with the enormity of what happened.

Famous Lines

"For this relief much thanks: 't is bitter cold,
And I am sick at heart" (Act I, Scene I).

"A little more than kin, and less than kind" (Act I, Scene II).

"All that lives must die,
Passing through nature to eternity" (Act I, Scene II).

"But I have that within which passeth show;
These but the trappings and the suits of woe" (Act I, Scene II).
"He was a man, take him for all in all,
I shall not look upon his like again" (Act I, Scene II).

"Give thy thoughts no tongue" (Act I, Scene III).

"Neither a borrower nor a lender be;
For loan oft loses both itself and friend,
And borrowing dulls the edge of husbandry.
This above all: to thine own self be true,
And it must follow, as the night the day,
Thou canst not then be false to any man" (Act I, Scene III).

"But to my mind, though I am native here
And to the manner born, it is a custom
More honoured in the breach than the observance" (Act I, Scene IV).

"Something is rotten in the state of Denmark" (Act I, Scene IV).

"There are more things in heaven and earth, Horatio,
Than are dreamt of in your philosophy" (Act I, Scene V).

"Brevity is the soul of wit" (Act II, Scene II).

"Doubt thou the stars are fire;
Doubt that the sun doth move;
Doubt truth to be a liar;
But never doubt I love" (Act II, Scene II).

"Though this be madness, yet there is method in 't" (Act II, Scene II).

"There is nothing either good or bad, but thinking makes it so" (Act II, Scene II).

"A dream itself is but a shadow" (Act II, Scene II).

"What a piece of work is a man! how noble in reason! how infinite in faculty! in form and moving how express and admirable! in action how like an angel! in apprehension how like a god!" (Act II, Scene II).

"The devil hath power
To assume a pleasing shape" (Act II, Scene II).

"To be, or not to be: that is the question." (Act III, Scene I).

"Be thou as chaste as ice, as pure as snow, thou shalt not escape calumny.
Get thee to a nunnery, go" (Act III, Scene I).

"Suit the action to the word, the word to the action; with this special observance, that you o'erstep not the modesty of nature" (Act III, Scene II).

"I must be cruel, only to be kind:
Thus bad begins, and worse remains behind" (Act III, Scene IV).

"When sorrows come, they come not single spies,
But in battalions" (Act IV, Scene V).

"The rest is silence" (Act V, Scene II).

King Lear

Main Characters

King Lear—the aging king of Britain
Goneril—King Lear's ruthless oldest daughter; wife of the Duke of Albany
Regan—King Lear's second daughter, as ruthless as Goneril; wife of the
　　Duke of Cornwall
Cordelia—King Lear's youngest daughter
Gloucester—father of Edgar and Edmund
Edgar—Gloucester's oldest son; he disguises himself as a crazy beggar
　　called Poor Tom
Edmund—Gloucester's younger, illegitimate son
Kent—a nobleman loyal to King Lear
Fool—Lear's fool; he mysteriously disappears during Act III

Duke of Albany—Goneril's husband
Duke of Cornwall—Regan's husband
Oswald—Goneril's steward

Introduction

King Lear is one of Shakespeare's most famous tragedies, and, along with *Hamlet*, one of his most challenging. Written about 1605, between *Othello* and *Macbeth*, it rivals *Hamlet* as Shakespeare's greatest play. (Scholars now even believe that Shakespeare began working on and revising the play as early as 1598.)

King Lear is performed less often partly because its central character is more than eighty years old and because it explores madness, despair, chaos, aging, and death. It is a difficult and disturbing play whose dark psychology and symbolic ambiguity seem relentlessly nihilistic. The scenes in which the mad Lear rages naked on a stormy heath against his deceitful daughters and nature itself are considered by many scholars to be the finest example of tragic poetry in the English language.

If the philosophical questioning of *Hamlet* (written around 1601) arose in part because of the death of Shakespeare's young son some four years earlier, one wonders what dark personal event was in the forefront of the Bard's thoughts when he composed *Lear*? The nihilism and bitterness that invades his later works seems to find its zenith in *Lear*.

The actual text of *King Lear* also presents special problems. The play exists in three very different editions—an early quarto printed in 1608, another quarto printed in 1619, and the Folio version printed in 1623. Today, editions of *King Lear* vary depending upon which version is used. Most often, the two editions of the play are woven together. Scholars now even study the play as distinct, possibly evolving versions of the same work.

The Play

King Lear, the aging king of Britain, decides to split his kingdom among his three daughters: Goneril, Regan, and Cordelia. Goneril and Regan pour flattery on him protesting their love for their father, while Cordelia, sincere in her love of her father, simply says she loves him the way a daughter should. Lear is upset by her response and disinherits her. The king of France says that he will marry her anyway. When Kent, one of Lear's nobles, tries to reason with him, Lear banishes him as well.

Meanwhile, Edmund, Gloucester's bastard son, decides to gain his father's inheritance by tricking him into thinking that Edgar, his legitimate son, is plotting to murder Gloucester. Edgar flees for his life, and disguised as a madman, goes into hiding.

The King's Fall

Lear soon discovers how little Goneril and Regan actually love him. Both daughters demean him and try to take away from him the little dignity and power he has kept for himself. Lear is transformed from a powerful king to an impotent old man with only Kent—who has disguised himself and disobeyed Lear's decree of banishment—and his Fool for company.

In the middle of the play, Lear is driven mad by his grief at his foolishness and the betrayal of his children. On a lonely heath, he rages, naked, at a storm. Lear and Kent meet Edgar, who is disguised as Poor Tom. Gloucester provides them shelter and guides them to Dover to meet Cordelia and the French king, who has landed an army in England to come to Lear's aid. For pitying Lear, Gloucester is betrayed by Edmund; Regan and Cornwall put out Gloucester's eyes. However, a servant is so distressed by the scene that he fatally stabs Cornwall before Regan kills him in turn.

QUESTION?

Why is *King Lear* so difficult for audiences to watch?
King Lear is a tragedy of such power that audiences are left emotionally drained at its conclusion. We can only wonder at the meaninglessness of life after the physical and moral horrors at the play's end. Kent, on seeing Lear reduced to a mad, pathetic creature with the murdered Cordelia in his arms, murmurs, "Is this the promis'd end?"

Now blind, Gloucester meets up with Edgar disguised as Poor Tom. Edgar does not reveal himself but leads his father toward Dover. Meanwhile, Goneril's husband, Albany, has begun to speak up for Lear and Gloucester because his wife is calling him a coward. Both sisters independently start affairs with Edmund.

Father and Daughter United in Death

The English and French armies battle and the English win. Lear and Cordelia are taken prisoner, and Edmund orders them hanged. Edgar tracks down his brother and in a duel stabs Edmund fatally. Goneril poisons Regan to win Edmund from her, then kills herself when she learns of Edmund's fate. Realizing he is about to die, Edmund repents his sins and reveals his plots, including the imminent deaths of Lear and Cordelia.

It is all too late: Lear enters carrying Cordelia's body. Overcome by grief and exhaustion Lear collapses and dies a broken old man beside the only daughter who loved him. Gloucester dies after reconciling with Edgar. Kent and Edgar retire, leaving Albany to rule Britain.

Commentary

While traditional critics of *King Lear* find a heroic pattern in the story, modern directors usually see a nihilistic play about the frailty and futility of the human condition. Even the most powerful are humbled before the forces of fate and nature.

One of the important questions about Lear is whether he learns from his mistakes and becomes more personally aware. Does his humiliation and insanity strip away the hubris that caused his downfall? It seems that while he does not permanently regain his sanity, his values do change for the better by the end of the play. As he is made to realize his insignificance by the awesome natural forces that are unleashed on him, he becomes a humbled yet caring man, finally appreciating Cordelia for the jewel she is, though too late to save either himself or her.

Laurence Olivier: "No, Lear is easy. He's like all the rest of us, really; he's just a stupid old fart. He's got a frightful temper. He's completely selfish and utterly inconsiderate. He does not for a moment think of the consequences of what he has said. He is simply bad-tempered arrogance with a crown perched on top. He obviously wasn't spanked by his mother often enough."

Edmund's change of heart is rare among Shakespeare's villains and can make us wonder if *Lear* is not in some ways a play about the power of love amid carnage. Goneril and Regan, for example, totally lack love until they meet Edmund. How is it possible that they are sisters to Cordelia?

The depth of Cordelia's love for Lear is a counterpoint to the height of the king's arrogance. By banishing her, he abandons his soul and plunges his kingdom into chaos and brutal anarchy. As we watch Goneril and Regan torment and plot against their father, deliberately pushing Lear toward madness, we pray that Cordelia will come back and rescue him from himself and his dreadful fate.

When at last they find each other, their reunion marks the restoration of peace and order in the kingdom and the triumph of love and forgiveness over hatred and spite. This fleeting moment of redemption makes the devastating finale of *King Lear* that much more cruel, as Cordelia, the personification of kindness and virtue, is sacrificed for nothing, depriving Lear's world of the meaning he thought he had found at last.

Famous Lines

"Although the last, not least" (Act I, Scene I).

"Nothing will come of nothing" (Act I, Scene, I).

"How sharper than a serpent's tooth it is
To have a thankless child!" (Act I, Scene IV).
"Striving to better, oft we mar what's well" (Act I, Scene IV).

"Blow, winds, and crack your cheeks! rage! blow!" (Act III, Scene II).

"A poor, infirm, weak, and despised old man" (Act III, Scene II).

"I am a man
More sinn'd against than sinning" (Act III, Scene II).

"Oh, that way madness lies; let me shun that" (Act III, Scene IV).

"The worst is not
So long as we can say, 'This is the worst.'" (Act IV, Scene I).

"Pray you now, forget and forgive" (Act IV, Scene VII).

"Her voice was ever soft,
Gentle, and low, an excellent thing in woman" (Act V, Scene III).

Macbeth

Main Characters

Macbeth—an ambitious Scottish general
Lady Macbeth—Macbeth's wife; a deeply ambitious woman
Banquo—a brave general
King Duncan—the king of Scotland, who Macbeth murders
Malcolm—a Scottish prince; the son of Duncan
Macduff—a Scottish nobleman
The Three Witches—seers who prophesy Macbeth's fate
Hecate—the goddess of witchcraft
Fleance—Banquo's son
Lennox—a Scottish nobleman
Ross—a Scottish nobleman
Siward—an English general and earl of Northumberland
The Murderers—assassins hired by Macbeth to kill Banquo and his children

Introduction

With the possible exception of *Titus Andronicus*, which is considered a lesser play, *Macbeth* is Shakespeare's bloodiest tragedy. It traces the disintegration of a powerful man who longs for more power and will stoop to anything, even murder, to get it.

Macbeth was probably composed perhaps as early as 1605, more probably in late 1606 or early 1607. It is the last of Shakespeare's four great tragedies, the others being *Hamlet, King Lear,* and *Othello. Macbeth's* supernatural element suggests that fate plays with us if we let it. Macbeth chooses to walk the bloody path of ambition in order to attain the glory promised him by the witches.

Macbeth is loosely based on a historic king of the same name who lived from 1005 to 1057. He launched a civil war in his efforts to seize the throne from his cousin Duncan. There is no evidence that his wife, Gruoch, ever incited the real Macbeth to murder, or that his actions led to the turmoil dramatized in the play. The real Macbeth, in fact, reigned peacefully for fifteen years.

FACT

In theater lore, no actor actually calls *Macbeth* by its given name. It is called instead, "The Scottish Play" because it has been associated with bad luck over the centuries. The curse began, it is said, with the first performance of the play when the boy actor playing Lady Macbeth collapsed, apparently from a fever, and died before the play had finished.

An integral part of this theme of ambition is the play's most memorable character, Lady Macbeth. Unlike her husband, who is enticed by supernatural evil (in the form of Hecate and the witches) into pursuing his bloody path, Lady Macbeth's lust for power leads her naturally into the nightmare realm of hallucinations and madness.

The Play

During a thunderstorm on a Scottish moor in the midst of a battle between the Scots and the Norwegians, Macbeth kills the traitorous Scot, Macdonald,

Thane (Earl) of Cawdor. The king hears of the death and promises to make Macbeth thane of Cawdor as soon as he sees him.

On the heath near the battlefield, Macbeth and Banquo come upon three witches. They hail Macbeth as thane of Cawdor, baffling Macbeth, who has not yet learned of his promotion. They also say he will be king one day. They then call Banquo "lesser than Macbeth, and greater," and "not so happy, yet much happier." They tell him that he will never be king but that his children will sit upon the throne.

FACT

The witches lurk as the personification of evil; yet their mischief is due mainly to their ability to exploit the weaknesses of their victims. They play upon Macbeth's ambition like puppeteers, while Banquo resists them.

When Macbeth and Banquo reunite with King Duncan, Macbeth learns that he has been promoted to thane of Cawdor in place of the man he killed in battle. Part one of the witches' prophecy has come to pass. Macbeth begins to consider the possibility that he might be king one day. However, Duncan announces Malcolm as his heir. Publicly, Macbeth declares his joy, but privately he admits his disappointment.

After returning home, Macbeth invites Duncan to dine at his castle and Duncan agrees.

Lady Macbeth

At the castle, Lady Macbeth reads a letter from her husband, announcing his promotion and detailing the promises of the witches. Lady Macbeth fears he is too full of "the milk of human kindness" to do what it takes to become king. If only she were a man, she would do the deeds herself, she says. When Macbeth enters, she tells her husband she has a plan.

Duncan and his retinue arrive. Macbeth ponders his plan to assassinate Duncan. On the one hand, he considers murder morally wrong and admires the king; on the other hand, he is driven by ambition. He tells Lady Macbeth he no longer intends to kill Duncan, who has been kind to him. Outraged, she calls him a coward, unmanly, and convinces him to reconsider.

That night Lady Macbeth puts her plan into action. A tolling bell is the signal that the king's servants are asleep. Macbeth emerges from Duncan's chamber steeped in gore. He is badly shaken and says that as he killed the king he thought he heard a voice cry out that Macbeth would never sleep again.

> Max Beerbohm: "To mankind in general, Macbeth and Lady Macbeth stand out as the supreme type of all that a host and hostess should not be." Humorist James Thurber: "*Macbeth* is a tale told by a genius, full of soundness and fury, signifying many things."

Lady Macbeth tries to steady him but is angry when she notices he has forgotten to leave the daggers with the servants to frame them for the killing. Macbeth refuses to go back into the room. Lady Macbeth takes them herself, calling him a coward once again. When Lady Macbeth returns she tells Macbeth a little water will clear them both of the murder.

Macduff and Lennox arrive asking for the king. Lennox describes storms that have raged during the night. He says no one can remember a night like it. Macduff goes to wake the king, and then returns horrified, crying murder. Chaos reigns. Macbeth goes in to see and returns mourning, declaring that in a grief-stricken rage he killed the servants who murdered Duncan.

Descent into Murder and Madness

Later that evening, Macduff meets with Ross outside the castle and tells Ross that Macbeth has been made king. Macduff adds that, although the servants seem the most likely murderers, suspicion has now fallen on the king's sons as well, because they have fled the scene.

Banquo takes time to think about Macbeth's coronation and the prophecy of the witches who foretold not only that Macbeth would be king, but also that Banquo's sons would sit on the throne. Macbeth, elsewhere, is pondering the same topic. His old friend Banquo is the only man in Scotland he now fears. According to the witches' prophecy, Duncan's murder has simply cleared the way for Banquo's sons to become king. Two murderers now enter. Macbeth asks them if they have the stomach to kill Banquo and his children. The assassins hide in a wooded park outside the palace and ambush Banquo and his son Fleance as they ride in and dismount. Banquo is killed, but Fleance escapes.

At the coronation feast the murderers quietly tell Macbeth what has happened. As Macbeth walks among his guests and goes to sit at the head of the table, he finds Banquo's ghost sitting in his chair. Horror-struck, Macbeth speaks to the ghost, which is invisible to the rest of the company. Lady Macbeth makes excuses for her husband, saying that he occasionally has such "visions" and that the guests should simply ignore his behavior. Macbeth cannot control his "fits," and in the end she has to send the guests away.

Lennox walks with another lord and both confess that they suspect Macbeth in the murders of Duncan and Banquo. The lord tells Lennox that Malcolm and Macduff have fled to England to ask King Edward for aid. Their success has prompted Macbeth to begin preparing for war. Lennox and the lord quietly wish Malcolm and Macduff luck.

Macbeth tells Lady Macbeth that he will visit the witches again in the hopes of learning more. Entering a dark cavern, Macbeth asks the witches to reveal more details of their prophecy to him. They summon horrible apparitions: a floating head tells him to beware Macduff; a bloody child tells him that "none of woman born" can harm him; and a crowned child holding a tree tells him that he is safe until "Great Birnam Wood to high Dunsinane Hill shall come against him." Then a procession of eight crowned kings walks through, the last carrying a mirror. Banquo's ghost is at the end of the line. Macbeth demands to know the meaning of this final vision, but the witches cackle with glee and vanish.

Death to the Macbeths

In Scotland, at night, in the king's palace at Dunsinane, Lady Macbeth enters in a trance bemoaning the murders of Lady Macduff and Banquo. She continually sees blood on her hands even though she has tried desperately to wash it off. She leaves, and the doctor and gentlewoman who are looking after her marvel at her descent into madness. Outside the castle, a group of Scottish lords discuss the military situation; the Scottish army will engage Malcolm's English army near Birnam Wood.

Macbeth boasts that he has nothing to fear from the English army or from Malcolm, since "none of woman born" can harm him. Malcolm and the English lord Siward decide that each soldier should cut down a bough of the forest and carry it in front of him as they march to the castle, thereby disguising their numbers.

While organizing defenses Macbeth is told the queen has killed herself. A messenger now enters with the astonishing news that the trees of Birnam Wood are advancing toward Dunsinane. The witches' prophecy is coming true. The battle commences. On the battlefield, Macbeth slaughters with vigor, reminded that "none of woman born" can harm him. Macduff fights his way toward him. They meet at last. As the fight gets underway Macduff tells Macbeth that he was not of woman born, but rather "from my mother's womb untimely ripp'd." (That is, he was born by Caesarian section.) He kills Macbeth.

Malcolm and Siward capture the castle. Macduff emerges with Macbeth's head in his hand and proclaims Malcolm king of Scotland. Malcolm declares that all his thanes will be made earls, as is the English custom. They will be the first such lords in Scottish history. Cursing Macbeth and his "fiend-like" queen, he invites all to see him crowned at Scone.

Commentary

Macbeth is often interpreted as an examination of what happens when ambition goes unchecked by moral constraints. Macbeth is a brave soldier who is tempted by the devil (Hecate) into becoming the king of Scotland. The bloodbath that results from trying to realize this destiny propels Macbeth and Lady Macbeth into a swift descent into arrogance, madness, and death.

It is not a particularly complicated play, but it is powerful and possibly Shakespeare's most emotionally intense. *Hamlet* and *Othello* explore the intellectual complications of their subjects, and *King Lear* deals with the inner chaos of a deranged mind, but *Macbeth* is like a scythe unerringly mowing down anything in its way, leaving corpse after corpse in its wake from the moment the witches appear. The play is a sharp, jagged sketch of theme and character, and, as such, it has shocked and fascinated audiences of stage and screen for nearly 400 years.

FACT

Macbeth is a powerful critique of political power as it ponders exactly what qualities make a good ruler, and the values or dangers of manliness. Whenever a discussion of manhood takes place during the play, it is swiftly followed by violence and death.

Macbeth starts the play as a noble, courageous warrior; he kills Duncan somewhat against his better judgment, but ends the play in a heat of frantic, boastful madness. Lady Macbeth, one of Shakespeare's most compelling female characters, mercilessly eggs on her husband's butchery without being able to imagine the awful price her ambition will cost both her and her husband.

The play also deals with the dangers of arrogant, testosterone-laden manliness. Lady Macbeth continually manipulates Macbeth by urging him to be a man or by asking him if he is a man. Macbeth encourages the murderers to kill Banquo and his children by questioning their manhood, and Malcolm consoles Macduff after the murders of his wife and children by encouraging him to take the news in "manly" fashion.

Famous Lines

"When shall we three meet again
In thunder, lightning, or in rain?
When the hurlyburly's done,
When the battle's lost and won" (Act I, Scene I).

"What are these
So wither'd and so wild in their attire,
That look not like the inhabitants o' the earth,
And yet are on 't?" (Act I, Scene III).

"If you can look into the seeds of time,
And say which grain will grow and which will not" (Act I, Scene III).

"Nothing is
But what is not" (Act I, Scene III).

"Yet do I fear thy nature;
It is too full o' the milk of human kindness" (Act I, Scene V).

"I dare do all that may become a man;
Who dares do more is none" (Act I, Scene VII).

"Is this a dagger which I see before me,
The handle toward my hand? Come, let me clutch thee.
I have thee not, and yet I see thee still.
Art thou not, fatal vision, sensible
To feeling as to sight? or art thou but
A dagger of the mind, a false creation,
Proceeding from the heat-oppressed brain?" (Act II, Scene I).

"There's daggers in men's smiles" (Act II, Scene III).

"Stand not upon the order of your going,
But go at once" (Act III, Scene IV).

"Double, double toil and trouble;
Fire burn, and cauldron bubble" (Act IV, Scene I).

"By the pricking of my thumbs,
Something wicked this way comes.
Open, locks,
Whoever knocks!" (Act IV, Scene I).

"Out, damned spot! out, I say!" (Act V, Scene I).

"Fie, my lord, fie! a soldier, and afeard?" (Act V, Scene I).
"Yet who would have thought the old man to have had so much blood in
    him?" (Act V, Scene I).

"To-morrow, and to-morrow, and to-morrow,
Creeps in this petty pace from day to day
To the last syllable of recorded time . . ." (Act V, Scene V).

Othello

Main Characters

Othello—a Moor commanding the armies of Venice
Desdemona—the daughter of a Venetian senator, and Othello's bride
Iago—Othello's ensign; perhaps Shakespeare's greatest villain
Cassio—Othello's lieutenant, promoted in place of Iago
Emilia—Iago's wife and Desdemona's attendant
Roderigo—a jealous suitor of Desdemona
Bianca—a courtesan in Cyprus, and Cassio's mistress
Brabantio—Desdemona's father, and a senator in Venice
Lodovico—Brabantio and Desdemona's kinsman
Gratiano—Brabantio's brother
Clown—Othello's servant
Montano—the governor of Cyprus before Othello
The Duke of Venice—the official authority in Venice

Introduction

Othello was likely written in early 1604 and first performed in front of King James I of England on November 1 of that year. The great Richard Burbage played Othello. In 1660, Margaret Hughes played Desdemona, becoming the first woman allowed to perform on the English stage.

Shakespeare's choice of a black African as a hero was strikingly original. Blackness in Elizabethan England was a color associated with moral evil and death, and Moors in the theater, like Jews, were usually stereotyped as villains, such as Aaron the Moor in *Titus Andronicus*, an early play. Othello is a noble, towering figure whose good nature is the means to his downfall, making the play that much more tragic.

Othello is set against the backdrop of the wars between Venice and Turkey that raged in the latter part of the sixteenth century. Cyprus, which is the setting for most of the action, was a Venetian outpost attacked by the Turks in 1570 and conquered by the Ottomans the following year. Shakespeare's information probably comes from *The History of the Turks*, by Richard Knolles, which was published in England in autumn of 1603.

Scholars believe *Othello* is derived from an Italian prose tale written in 1565 by Giovanni Battista Giraldi in his collection *Hecatommithi*, although there seems to have been no English translation at the time Shakespeare wrote *Othello* (prompting the thought that he may well have been able to read some Italian). The original story concerns a Moorish general who is deceived by his ensign into believing his wife is unfaithful.

The Play

Othello, a celebrated Moorish general of Venice, has promoted Cassio as his lieutenant instead of Iago. Iago is incensed and plots against Cassio and Othello to get his due. Othello and Desdemona, the beautiful daughter of Brabantio, fall in love, elope, and marry. Brabantio is deeply upset by the deceit and the marriage. When Othello is posted to Cyprus by the Duke of Venice, Iago escorts Desdemona.

Framing Cassio

Arriving in Cyprus, Iago immediately begins plotting. He tricks Cassio into getting drunk, then has Roderigo, a former suitor of Desdemona who is upset at her marriage, pick a fight with Cassio. Cassio ends up getting arrested and subsequently demoted. Iago then encourages Cassio to call on Desdemona, saying that if she speaks up for him with her husband, Othello may reinstate him.

Iago now goes to Othello, and as they watch Desdemona and Cassio talk, recalling her father's accusations of her betrayal of trust, Iago plants the seeds of jealousy in Othello. Iago suggests that Cassio and Desdemona are having an affair.

By chance, because his wife Emilia is Desdemona's maid, Iago gets hold of a handkerchief Othello gave Desdemona as a token of his love for her.

Iago plants the handkerchief in Cassio's room and then tells Othello that he saw Cassio with it. When Othello asks Desdemona about the handkerchief, she tells him that it was lost. Cassio, meanwhile, gives it to a courtesan with whom he is intimate. Iago then gets Othello to overhear a conversation whereby Othello thinks they are discussing Desdemona, when in fact they are talking about Bianca, the courtesan.

Iago's evil is the antithesis of the love that Othello and Desdemona share. The purity of their passion is perhaps one of the strongest portrayals of romantic affection in any tragedy, including *Romeo and Juliet*. It is this deep love that Iago hates so much because he is incapable of it, and his awareness of his weakness provides him with the key to destroying Othello.

George Bernard Shaw, who more than once vented his critical anger at Shakespeare's plays, said of *Othello*, "It has a police court mentality and commonplace thought."

Based on Iago's misinformation, Othello reacts. He tells Iago to kill Cassio and then angrily confronts Desdemona. Despite Desdemona's protests of innocence and Emilia's vouching for her, Othello is now convinced she is sleeping with Cassio.

The Scheme Unravels

Iago gets Roderigo to murder Cassio. Roderigo only wounds him, and Iago kills Roderigo so Roderigo can't betray his machinations. Othello hears the commotion in the street and thinks Iago has kept his part of their bargain. Now it is time to strangle Desdemona in her bed.

When Emilia discovers the crime, Desdemona, with her dying breath, refuses to accuse her husband. Emilia becomes distraught and accuses the Moor of being a murderous villain. She refuses to believe that Iago has so evilly manipulated Othello. Iago's appearance and subsequent answers make Emilia realize her husband is responsible for this tragedy.

Letters found on Roderigo's body confirm Iago's villainy. Faced with the shame of having murdered an innocent Desdemona and confronted by

Venetian emisaries, Othello delivers a famous soliloquy which leads to his suicide. He dies stabbing the "heathen" within himself.

Commentary

Othello is an intense, fast-paced play with most of the action compressed into a twenty-four-hour period. Scenes begin in midconversation, and subplots are pretty inconsequential. Everything plays to the domestic tragedy, centering on the three principle characters manipulated by Iago. Indeed, in no other tragedy does a single figure have so much control over events.

The horror of the play is its inevitability. We know what Iago is planning, and we are forced to watch it unfold. The audience shares in the fate of Desdemona and Othello—caught in Iago's trap.

FACT

We suffer with Iago's victims because he manages to use the purity of Othello and Desdemona's love against them. They, and we, are helpless against the chaos that Iago represents. Indeed, Othello says of Desdemona, "When I love thee not, Chaos is come again." And chaos, embodied in "honest Iago," seems to win the day.

The swiftness with which Iago manages to destroy Othello is stunning. He needs only two conversations and a missing handkerchief to convince the Moor that Desdemona has been unfaithful. Iago's "evidence" reminds Othello of her father's parting words: "Look to her, Moor, if thou hast eyes to see. She has deceived her father, and may thee."

Once Othello snaps, Shakespeare delays Desdemona's murder, and we can hope that she may be saved at the last moment. Instead, Iago tries to make Othello suffer even more. Once his plan has borne its bitter fruit, the play is ended.

Famous Lines

"We cannot all be masters, nor all masters
Cannot be truly follow'd" (Act I, Scene I).

"I will wear my heart upon my sleeve
For daws to peck at" (Act I, Scene I).

"Reputation, reputation, reputation! Oh, I have lost my reputation! I have
  lost the immortal part of myself, and what remains is bestial" (Act II,
  Scene III).

"O God, that men should put an enemy in their mouths to steal away their
  brains!" (Act II, Scene III).

"How poor are they that have not patience!" (Act II, Scene III).

"Good name in man and woman, dear my lord,
Is the immediate jewel of their souls:
Who steals my purse steals trash; 't is something, nothing;
'T was mine, 't is his, and has been slave to thousands;
But he that filches from me my good name
Robs me of that which not enriches him
And makes me poor indeed" (Act III, Scene III).

"O, beware, my lord, of jealousy!
It is the green-eyed monster which doth mock
The meat it feeds on" (Act III, Scene III).

"Trifles light as air
Are to the jealous confirmations strong
As proofs of holy writ" (Act III, Scene III).

"He that is robb'd, not wanting what is stolen,
Let him not know 't, and he's not robb'd at all" (Act III, Scene III).

"Take note, take note, O world,
To be direct and honest is not safe" (Act III, Scene III).

" 'Tis neither here nor there" (Act IV, Scene III).

"Put out the light, and then put out the light:
If I quench thee, thou flaming minister,
I can again thy former light restore
Should I repent me; but once put out thy light,
Thou cunning'st pattern of excelling nature,
I know not where is that Promethean heat
That can thy light relume" (Act V, Scene II).

"So sweet was ne'er so fatal" (Act V, Scene II).

"Then, must you speak
Of one that loved not wisely but too well;
Of one not easily jealous, but being wrought
Perplex'd in the extreme; of one whose hand,
Like the base Indian, threw a pearl away
Richer than all his tribe; of one whose subdued eyes,
Albeit unused to the melting mood,
Drop tears as fast as the Arabian trees
Their medicinal gum" (Act V, Scene II).

CHAPTER 16

Shakespeare's Histories

Today, Shakespeare's histories are not as popular as his tragedies and comedies. Many people assume they are tedious textbook re-creations. Elizabethans, on the other hand, totally enjoyed them. Audiences were familiar with the events that unfolded on the stage and could readily identify the various political factions and complex family relationships depicted in the plays.

King Henry IV, Part II

Main Characters

King Henry IV—the ruling king of England

Prince Hal—also called Prince Henry, Harry, Prince Harry, Harry Monmouth, the Prince of Wales, and, after his father's death, King Henry V

Princes John, Duke of Lancaster; Humphrey, Duke of Gloucester; and Thomas, Duke of Clarence—Prince Hal's younger brothers

The Lord Chief Justice—the most powerful law official in England

Earl of Warwick, Earl of Surrey, Earl of Westmoreland, Gower, Harcourt, and Sir John Blunt—King Henry IV's allies and advisors

Sir John Falstaff—sometimes called Jack; Prince Hal's mentor and close friend

Page—a boy who serves Falstaff

Poins, Peto, and Bardolph—friends of Falstaff and Prince Hal

Ancient Pistol—a soldier (ancient meant "ensign" in Elizabethan English)

Mouldy, Shadow, Wart, Feeble, and Bullcalf—army recruits

Scroop—Archbishop of York; a powerful clergyman who leads the rebellion against King Henry IV

Mowbray and Hastings—two lords who conspire with the Archbishop of York

Henry Percy—Earl of Northumberland, brother of Worcester, and father to Hotspur who have recently been killed in battle against King Henry IV. Also called Harry

Travers—Northumberland's servant

Hotspur—Northumberland's son and a leader of the rebellion against the king

Lord Bardolph—an ally of Northumberland (not to be confused with Falstaff's friend Bardolph)

Owen Glendower—a Welsh rebel leader

Mistress Quickly (the Hostess)—proprietor of the seedy Boar's Head Tavern in Eastcheap, London

Doll Tearsheet—Falstaff's favorite prostitute and a good friend of Mistress Quickly

Fang and Snare—incompetent policemen

Justice Shallow and Justice Silence—justices of the peace (minor judges)
Davy—Justice Shallow's servant

Introduction

King Henry IV, Part II is the third part of Shakespeare's four-part series dealing with the rise of the English royal house of Lancaster. (It is preceded by *King Richard II* and *King Henry IV, Part I* and followed by *King Henry V.*) The play was probably written around the year 1598.

The Play

The Earl of Northumberland (Henry Percy) learns that his son Hotspur has been killed in battle and that Richard Scroop, the archbishop of York, is continuing the rebellion against Henry IV.

Back in London, the Lord Chief Justice criticizes Falstaff for his wicked ways and tells the old knight that King Henry IV has decided to separate Falstaff from Prince Hal by sending Falstaff with Prince John of Lancaster (Hal's brother) to fight Scroop and Northumberland. Prince Hal returns from fighting the Welsh and meets with some of his friends to discuss his father's sickness and a pompous letter Falstaff has written to Hal complaining about being abandoned by his friend.

Northumberland's wife and his daughter-in-law convince him to flee to Scotland. The Earl of Warwick (with the Earl of Surrey and Sir Walter Blunt) assure the king that Northumberland will be defeated, though Henry repeats Richard II's prediction that Northumberland, who helped Henry IV to the throne, would eventually revolt and defeat Henry.

FACT

There are no good contemporary film versions of either of the *Henry IV* plays, but people who have read them might get a kick out of *My Own Private Idaho*, a 1992 film by Gus Van Sant based loosely on the *Henry IV* plays.

On his way to battle, Sir John Falstaff arrives at Justice Shallow's home seeking old friends to be soldiers. Falstaff conscripts Mouldy, Shadow, Wart, Feeble, and Bullcalf, though Bullcalf and Mouldy bribe Bardolph (Falstaff's friend) to avoid having to fight.

At the battlefield, Scroop, Mowbray, and Hastings learn that Northumberland will not help them. Prince John yields to Scroop's demands, granting protection to the rebelling nobles, who quickly tell their armies to disperse. Westmoreland and Prince John now betray Hastings, Scroop, and Mowbray, and arrest them for treason. Falstaff stumbles on Sir John Coleville of the Dale (a rebel) and captures him without a fight.

Hal arrives while Henry IV is asleep and tries on his father's crown. Henry wakes and rebukes Hal for wishing him dead and taking the crown. Hal claims he thought his father was dead and wanted to protect the crown.

Back in London, Henry IV vows to go on a crusade to the Holy Land if the rebellion is suppressed. When it is, he is distressed that Hal is still associating with criminals. Henry IV advises Hal when he is king to wage foreign wars to occupy Britain's time and to increase Hal's popularity. Henry IV then dies. Hal becomes King Henry V and swears to be kind to all, even the chief justice who once jailed Prince Hal.

Falstaff returns to London, hoping to receive favors from King Henry V, his alehouse friend. However, during a coronation march, Falstaff and his gang are banned from approaching Henry V within ten miles, after which Falstaff is arrested for his crimes.

Commentary

In contrast with the earlier *King Henry IV*, this sequel is concerned with justice, sickness, and betrayal. The play is sometimes described as the battle between vice and virtue for the soul of a king, and although Hal banishes Falstaff, Falstaff's philosophy offers an alternative view to the serious and the rational.

The play captures the entire English national life from the country to the town and from lowly drinking houses to the anguish and responsibilities of kings. It reflects Shakespeare's own experience—the country boy who came from Stratford, then lived in the taverns of London, then made a success of his life by writing plays that are presented to kings, queens, and nobility.

Famous Lines

"I do now remember the poor creature, small beer" (Act II, Scene II).

"Uneasy lies the head that wears the crown" (Act III, Scene I).

"We have heard the chimes at midnight" (Act III, Scene II).

"A man can die but once" (Act III, Scene II).

King Henry VI, Part I

Main Characters

King Henry VI—king of England and various regions in France; the son of Henry V

Charles—the Dauphin of France

Gloucester—regent until Henry is old enough to rule; he and Winchester are in a feud

Winchester—head of the English church; Gloucester's nemesis

Richard Plantagenet—later known as York; his father once had a claim to the throne of England before Henry IV killed him

Talbot—English general of the troops in France; Talbot is so feared by the French that, when he is captured, they have archers guard him while he sleeps

Joan—also known as Joan of Arc

Somerset—an English lord who argues with Richard Plantagenet

Suffolk—an English lord

Edmund Mortimer—Richard Plantagenet's uncle; Earl of March

Burgundy—a French lord

Bedford—an English general

Alençon—a French lord

Reignier—Duke of Anjou

Bastard of Orléans—a French lord

Exeter—an English lord; Exeter becomes a kind of chorus, remarking on the problems caused by internal dissension and strife in England and abroad

Warwick—an English lord
Salisbury—an English soldier
Gargrave—an English soldier
Glansdale—an English soldier
Vernon—one of Somerset's men
Basset—one of York's men
Sir William Lucy—a messenger
John—Talbot's son
Margaret—Reignier's daughter, captured by Suffolk
Countess of Auvergne—a French woman
Sir John Fastolf—a cowardly English soldier (not the same as Falstaff)
Woodville—the warden of the Tower of London
Master Gunner—a French soldier
Governor—the governor of Paris
General—the general of Bordeaux
Shepherd—Joan's father

Introduction

King Henry VI, Part I, written about 1592, is one of Shakespeare's earliest plays. True to historical events, it begins seven years after the Battle of Agincourt. King Henry V is dead, replaced by his son, Henry VI. This play centers on the Wars of the Roses and covers the events that caused the loss of Britain's territories in France.

FACT

The authorship of the play was once in question. A few scholars have hypothesized that Thomas Nashe wrote parts of *King Henry VI, Part I*; others believe Shakespeare wrote only the scene in the Temple Garden and the battle scenes. The questions to be asked are: Why would the playwright collaborate with other writers so early in his career? Why would authors want to work with a new playwright?

Shakespeare was fascinated with the roles of kings in history and wrote two more plays about Henry VI: *King Henry VI, Part II* and *Part III*. Interestingly, Shakespeare had no problem with chronology: the second two plays are said to have been written first, although the later publication of the plays does not reflect their order of composition.

For a young playwright to take on such a formidable task as writing a series of historical plays must have been daunting. Perhaps he honed his stagecraft skills with *The Comedy of Errors*. Yet, most scholars agree that he crafted *King Henry VI* first, then followed that success with plays that traced the years after Henry VI's death. Later in his career Shakespeare decided to add to his portfolio of kings and wrote about the history prior to Henry VI's kingship, including that of his father Henry V.

The writing of historical plays was one of the reasons for Shakespeare's theatrical success. The Elizabethan public held a fascination for kings of the past, and to see their lives unfold on the stage became a treasure that helped mold patriotic sentiment.

Once again Shakespeare probably used Raphael Holinshed's *Chronicles of England, Scotland, and Ireland* as his primary source, focusing on the history of the houses of York and Lancaster in the Wars of the Roses.

The Play

Henry V, king of England and parts of France, has died, and his young son Henry VI is on the throne. Charles, the Dauphin of France, is nurturing a rebellion across the channel, and rifts among the nobles in England are festering, notably between the houses of York and Lancaster (which will eventually become the Wars of the Roses). Emboldened by the exploits of Joan of Arc, the French attack Talbot at Orléans. Henry VI manages to retake Orléans by night in a surprise attack.

In England, Richard Plantagenet and the Duke of Somerset have a disagreement concerning the letter of a law. The two men ask others to show their support for their respective positions: those supporting Richard pick a white rose, and those supporting Somerset pick a red one. After talking with his uncle, Edmund Mortimer, Richard is convinced that the throne more rightfully belongs to the house of York than young King

Henry. Meanwhile, Winchester and Gloucester, guardians of the young king, continue a feud of their own.

Back in France, Joan drives the English from Rouen, but an English counterattack gets it back. Joan now convinces the Duke of Burgundy to switch over to the French side. Talbot marches against him, and Henry orders Richard and the Duke of Somerset to reinforce Talbot in the battle. Somerset and Richard continue to feud however, and while Talbot fights valiantly, he is slain in the combat when the reinforcements never arrive.

Richard and Somerset set aside their differences long enough to capture Joan of Arc and burn her as a witch. In the meantime, Gloucester tries to set up a match between Henry and Margaret, the daughter of a French lord, in order to force a peace between France and England. The Earl of Suffolk, however, introduces another Margaret (of Anjou) to Henry in an attempt to get him to marry her. Suffolk hopes to use her to control Henry, which leads to the action of *King Henry VI, Part II*.

Commentary

King Henry VI, Part I depicts England's struggle to retain its military and political control over French territories gained by Henry V. The play compresses early events of the early reign of Henry VI, including the feuding of English lords and the eventual loss of half the French lands.

While Shakespeare drew on historical records, he condensed dates and events, reordering things to create drama. For example, Henry VI was actually only nine months old when he became king, while in the play he is a teenager. What's more, one of the play's most striking scenes, in the Temple Garden, in which the followers of Richard Plantagenet and Somerset pick white and red roses as emblems of their opposing views, is complete fabrication. It does explain the origin of the Wars of the Roses, an affair whose actual origins are boring and complicated.

Shakespeare gives equal voice to two predominant theories on the cause of fifteenth-century British turmoil: (1) history is the result of human choices and actions, and (2) the violence of the fifteenth century was some sort of divine punishment for the murder of King Richard II.

The warrior culture of King Henry V is changing around Henry VI. After Henry V's death, lords abandon a unity for the sake of king and country and return to plotting their own advancement. War loses its chivalrous quality. The deaths of Talbot and his son signal the death of "romantic" chivalry.

While *King Henry V* (which was written later) portrays a man who claims his birthright and lives up to the full potential of his masculinity, *King Henry VI, Part I* acknowledges the potential weaknesses of men. Sometimes, as in the case of Queen Elizabeth I, a woman must step up to the plate and take charge even if it means usurping a traditional male role.

Famous Lines

"Halcyon days" (Act I, Scene II).

"She's beautiful, and therefore to be wooed;
She is a woman, therefore to be won" (Act V, Scene III).

King Henry VI, Part II

Main Characters

Henry VI—king of England

Humphrey—the Duke of Gloucester; Henry's uncle, regent until Henry is old enough to rule

Duke of Somerset—Somerset stands for the red rose, against York and those who wear the white rose

Duke of Buckingham—a lord who joins Somerset, Suffolk, Beaufort, and Margaret to plot against Gloucester

Beaufort—head of the English church. In *King Henry VI, Part I* he was called Winchester

Duke of York—called Richard of Plantagenet in the earlier play; he is heir to Edward III's third son, while Henry is heir to Edward III's fourth son

Duke of Suffolk—a lord of the court

Earl of Salisbury—a lord of the court; Salisbury supports York

Earl of Warwick—a lord of the court; Warwick supports York

Margaret, Queen to King Henry—also referred to as Margaret of Anjou

Eleanor, Duchess of Gloucester

John Hume—a priest and procurer of conjurers and witches

Peter Thump—a working man

Thomas Horner—an armourer; accused by Peter of treason

Margery Jordan—a witch; hired by the duchess, she helps raise a spirit

Roger Bolingbroke—a conjurer

Simpcox—a poor man who pretends he has been blind since birth

Jack Cade—hired by York to cause trouble in England while York is away

Walter Whitmore—one of the Captain's men; he kills Suffolk

Rebels—common people led by Jack Cade

Butcher—one of Jack Cade's men

Weaver—another of Jack Cade's men

The Staffords—two nobles of the court who challenge Jack Cade; Stafford and his brother die, and their bodies are dragged behind Cade's horse to London

Lord Say—sought and killed by Jack Cade

Sergeant—husband of the woman the Butcher rapes

Lord Clifford—a lord of the court who convinces Jack Cade's troops to surrender

Alexander Iden—a noble who kills Cade

Edward—York's son; he will be the next king of England

Richard—York's son; he will become Richard III

Introduction

Some editors think *King Henry VI, Part II* was written before *King Henry VI, Part I*, probably in 1591, making it one of Shakespeare's earliest plays. It takes place after the French wars, when the English lost and regained most of the lands originally won by Henry V. During the wars, depicted in King *Henry VI, Part I*, disagreements between Somerset and York led to the creation of two factions, those who supported the red rose and those who supported the white, setting the stage for the civil wars known as the Wars of the Roses.

Shakespeare no doubt used Raphael Holinshed's *Chronicles of England, Scotland, and Ireland* for details of Cade's rebellion, modeling it on the revolt by Wat Tyler in the Peasant's Rebellion of 1381 during the reign of Richard II.

King Henry VI, Part II concerns the continued power struggles between Gloucester and Beaufort, and York and Somerset. This infighting and the popular uprising by Jack Cade show what happens when a king is too weak to rule. The play charts the rise and fall of many lords and lesser figures within the kingdom.

A version of the play was first published in 1594, while a longer version appeared in the First Folio in 1623. The relationship between these two texts has been a long-debated point in Shakespeare scholarship.

One well-known quote from the play is: "The first thing we do, let's kill all the lawyers."

Some scholars have suggested that the shorter version was a reconstruction of the play prepared by actors, who remembered as much of the play as they could for publication. Others think the 1594 version may have been an early draft, and the later published play a more polished version. Most editors agree that actors, scribes, publishers, and censors all had a hand in altering the play as it moved onto the stage. The Oxford editors decided to use the later, longer version of the play, but incorporated lengthy stage directions and lines from the earlier version.

The Play

The action picks up from the end of *Part I*. Humphrey, Duke of Gloucester is unhappy with Margaret's lack of dowry and with Henry's giving up territory in France. Suffolk, who introduced Margaret to Henry in the hopes of controlling her, and thus the king, sets plots into motion against Gloucester. He sets up Gloucester's wife to be arrested for witchcraft. Meanwhile, York bides his time, convinced of the legitimacy of his claim to the throne.

Gloucester is eventually arrested on trumped-up charges. During Gloucester's trial, York is sent to Ireland to put down a revolt. While in Ireland, York encourages Jack Cade to muster support among the common folk for York to depose Henry. If Cade succeeds, York has an army at his back to use against Henry when he returns from Ireland.

Gloucester is murdered at Suffolk's behest. Henry banishes Suffolk. En route to France, Suffolk is captured by pirates and summarily put to death.

Cade's rebellion gathers support, and he marches on London leaving brutality and havoc in his wake, with Henry retreating before him. Buckingham confronts his force with an army and extends pardons to all who abandon Cade. After a five-day flight without food, Cade is killed while foraging in a private garden. In the wake of Cade's failed uprising, York returns from Ireland and demands that the king arrest Somerset before York's men lay down their arms.

The king does so, but Margaret, now queen but Suffolk's lover, frees him almost immediately. York declares war on King Henry, determined to take the crown by force if necessary. At the Battle of St. Albans, Richard, son of York, slays Somerset. The Yorkists then set out in pursuit of the fleeing Henry and Margaret.

Commentary

It is Henry's weakness as a king and leader that is the focus of the play. If Henry were stronger, he would not have agreed to the imprisonment of an innocent man. Yet Henry seems powerless to resist his nobles and his wife. Suffolk arrests Gloucester, Beaufort orders him taken away, and the others all accuse him. And though the nobles agree that they have no real proof of wrongdoing, they agree he should be killed immediately, without a trial. Similar to Cade's rampage through the countryside, the nobles play out their own version of mob rule, removing their enemies from office and killing them without reason.

King Henry VI, Part III

Main Characters

Richard Plantagenet—the Duke of York

Henry VI—king of England

Edward—the Earl of March, York's eldest son; soon to be Edward IV

George—Edward's younger brother; soon to be Duke of Clarence

Richard—soon to be Richard III; a younger brother of Edward and George, most noted for his physical deformities, including a humpback, lame leg, and shriveled arm

Warwick—One of York's allies, who switches his allegiance to Henry

Queen Margaret—Henry's French wife

Prince Edward—Prince of Wales; son of Margaret and Henry

Edmund, Earl of Rutland—York's youngest son, killed by Clifford

Lord Clifford—he kills York's young son Rutland, then York himself

Marquess of Montague—one of Warwick's relatives

Duke of Westmoreland—one of Henry's supporters

Duke of Exeter—one of Henry's supporters

Duke of Norfolk—one of Henry's supporters

Duke of Somerset—one of Edward's supporters

Earl of Northumberland—one of Henry's supporters

Lady Bona—sister of Louis, king of France

Lady Grey—Edward propositions her, but she refuses; then she agrees to become queen

Earl of Oxford—one of Henry's supporters

Rivers—one of Edward's supporters, brother of Lady Gray

Hastings—one of Edward's supporters

Montgomery—one of Edward's supporters

Richmond—the young Henry, Earl of Richmond (soon to be Henry VII)

Introduction

King Henry VI, Part III has attracted attention for its boldness in adapting a complex historical narrative to the requirements of the theater and is considered one of Shakespeare's earliest plays. It was first published in 1595 in an octavo volume under the title *The True Tragedy of Richard Duke of York and the Good King Henry the Sixth*.

Some scholars believe that the first version was an early draft of a later folio edition. Other editors believe that the octavo version was reconstructed from memory by actors, which explains its shorter length. Editors think the folio version is based on Shakespeare's own manuscript before he gave it to his players, while the octavo version may have been based on a prompt book for the actual production. Most editors use the longer folio version with occasional additions from the octavo.

FACT

Shakespeare again likely referred to fifteenth-century histories as well as Raphael Holinshed's *Chronicles of England, Scotland, and Ireland* and Edward Hall's *Union of the Two Noble and Illustre Families of Lancaster and York* (1548) when researching the play.

King Henry VI, Part III is a continuation of the depiction of the Wars of the Roses, begun in *King Henry VI, Parts I* and *II*, which trace the struggles between the Lancastrians (red rose) and Yorkist (white rose) descendants of Edward III. The third part depicts some of the many significant battles fought during that civil war.

The Play

Part III picks up from the end of *Part II*. Following his victory at St. Albans, York is now set to take the Crown of England. Henry VI presents York an offer: Henry will rule England until his death, and then the Crown will pass to the house of York.

York agrees, but Queen Margaret is irate because her son, the Prince of Wales, should be the next king. Margaret fights a battle that kills the duke of York and his youngest son, Rutland. The Yorkists rally, however, and Margaret and Henry have to flee the country. Edward, eldest son of York, now becomes king.

Henry secretly returns to England but is captured by Edward and put in the Tower of London. Margaret petitions the king of France for help. However, Warwick tries to outmaneuver her by attempting to broker a marriage between Edward and the French king's sister-in-law, Bona. This plan falls apart when word comes that Edward has married Lady Grey.

Back in England, Warwick manages to capture Edward, temporarily restoring Henry to the throne. Richard, now duke of Gloucester, rescues Edward. Edward and the Yorkists then defeat and kill Warwick at the Battle of Tewksbury. Margaret and the Prince of Wales are captured and while the prince is killed, Edward grants Margaret mercy.

Richard pays a visit to the Tower of London to see Henry, who is a prisoner. When Henry foretells Richard's bloody future, Richard kills him. Edward now holds the throne as King Edward IV, but his brother Richard plots to usurp the Crown for himself. The story picks up in *King Richard III*.

Commentary

Some critics have seen *King Henry VI, Part III* as a flawed play, perhaps showing Shakespeare's weariness with the dramatization of the Wars of the Roses, or the difficulty of getting so much historical matter on the stage. Yet contemporary productions have been successful, particularly in depicting the ruthless Margaret and the increasingly alienated and enraged Richard, who emerges as the play's antihero.

Famous Lines

"The smallest worm will turn, being trodden on" (Act II, Scene II).

"Didst thou never hear
That things ill got had ever bad success?
And happy always was it for that son
Whose father for his hoarding went to hell?" (Act II, Scene II).

King Henry VIII

Main Characters

King Henry VIII—king of England
Cardinal Wolsey—the king's right-hand man

Queen Katharine—married to King Henry VIII's brother before marrying Henry

Duke of Buckingham—a lord of the court; he is accused of plotting to gain the throne

Anne Boleyn—Spelled "Anne Bullen" in the play; Henry's future wife who dies giving birth to the child Elizabeth

Cranmer—archbishop of Canterbury

Cardinal Campeius—an emissary from the pope

Duke of Norfolk—a lord of the court; at first he doesn't believe Buckingham's criticism of Cardinal Wolsey and urges Buckingham to hold his tongue

Duke of Suffolk—a lord of the court

Lord Chamberlain—a lord of the court

Lord Chancellor—a lord of the court

Cromwell—a friend of Cardinal Wolsey; he is devastated by Wolsey's demise, yet Wolsey encourages him to go back to the king and continue serving the state

Lord Sands—a lord of the court, also called Walter Sands

Sir Thomas Lovell—a lord of the court

Gardiner—Cardinal Wolsey's former secretary

Sir Henry Guildford—a lord of the court

Sir Nicholas Vaux—a lord of the court

Earl of Surrey—Buckingham's son-in-law

Lord Abergavenny—Buckingham's friend

Brandon—Sergeant at arms

Sir Anthony Denny—a lord of the court

Doctor Butts—the king's doctor

Surveyor—surveyor to Buckingham

Old Lady—Anne Boleyn's attendant

Griffith—Queen Katharine's attendant

Capucius—an ambassador from the king of Spain

The Child—christened Elizabeth, she will later become Queen Elizabeth I

Prologue—a character who introduces the play to the audience

Epilogue—a character who ends the play for the audience

Gentlemen—people in the streets

Introduction

King Henry VIII was written in 1613 and combines the genres of history play with tragicomic romance, a genre gaining new popularity in the early seventeenth century. The play focuses on the instabilities of the royal court from roughly 1530 to 1533 when Elizabeth is born. The king of England, when Shakespeare wrote the play, was James I (James VI of Scotland), who was the son of Mary, Queen of Scots, the daughter of Henry VIII's sister who married a Scottish king. James, though a Stuart, is a direct descendent of the Tudors. The play centers on Henry VIII's break with Rome and the Catholic Church.

In 1531, disappointed that his wife Catherine of Aragon (spelled "Katharine" in this play) had not given him a male heir, Henry decided to divorce her. His advisors argued that because she had been his brother's widow the marriage was invalid, but the pope ruled against the divorce.

Henry nevertheless went forward with the divorce and married Anne Boleyn ("Anne Bullen" in the play) in 1533. The pope excommunicated Henry, and Henry declared himself the head of the Church of England and dissolved the monasteries and seized their wealth.

The rest of Henry's reign was plagued by rebellions of groups who wanted to restore Catholicism or who were supporters of various religious reformation groups. The actual break with the pope is not dramatized in the play, but we see Henry's advisors discuss ways to negotiate a legal divorce. We even see Cardinal Wolsey urge the pope to refuse the divorce. But the actual break is only alluded to.

The years following Henry's death were wracked with religious disagreement and rebellions. When Queen Elizabeth finally came to the throne, she returned England to Protestant rule, although the religious unrest continued. The frequent public executions that took place following Henry's break with Rome and during the reigns of Edward, Mary, and Elizabeth are foreshadowed by the execution of Buckingham.

No one believed Henry's reason for wanting to divorce Katharine resulted from a flare-up of his conscience about the legality of his marriage. Everyone knew he wanted to marry Anne because she could give him a son and heir. Despite a compliment to King James at the end of the play, criticism of Henry as an inattentive ruler was probably also aimed at King James, who was known to neglect affairs of state.

The Play

Cardinal Wolsey, advisor to King Henry VIII, has arranged the arrest of the Duke of Buckingham on charges of treason. Henry's wife, Queen Katharine, pleads on Buckingham's behalf with no success. Buckingham is tried and executed.

At a party hosted by Wolsey, Henry meets and is smitten with Anne Bullen, a lady-in-waiting to Queen Katharine. Henry decides he needs a new wife and seeks Wolsey's advice. Henry's argument is that Katharine is the widow of his brother, which makes the marriage one step removed from incest—never mind that Henry and Katharine have been wed for almost twenty years.

Wolsey has become despised for taxes he has levied in King Henry's name, as well as for his role in Buckingham's death. He is now further despised because Henry wishes a divorce. Wolsey agrees to have the pope send a representative to render a decision on the matter. Katharine, however, views her marriage as sacred.

FACT

King Henry VIII recounts the fall of the three main figures of King Henry VIII's early court, and the near fall of a fourth. The traditional Renaissance idea of a wheel of fortune is at work here: What rises must inevitably fall.

Wolsey endures a series of political stumblings that present him in an unflattering light to King Henry. Most damning is Wolsey's meddling in the king's divorce. Wolsey is disgraced, and Henry divorces Katharine and marries Anne in secret regardless of the pope's opinion. Wolsey dies soon after, and Katharine (who is in poor health) follows him to the grave.

The new archbishop of Canterbury, Cranmer, becomes the focus of a plot by Gardiner, Wolsey's secretary. Cranmer is brought to trial in much the same manner as Buckingham, but he enjoys the king's protection. Henry exonerates Cranmer and has him christen his and Anne Bullen's new daughter, Elizabeth. At the christening, Cranmer prophecies a noble reign for Elizabeth and glory for England in her time.

Commentary

The merging of romance and history suggests that fate somehow helped shape English history and the most important of these fateful events is the birth of Elizabeth, future queen of England, who had died by the time the play was produced. In order for the birth to take place, a complex set of events must be put into motion, and anyone who stands in the way must be gotten rid of.

Unlike other histories that dealt with the fate of kings, this play deals with the rise and fall of lesser court figures such as Buckingham, Katharine, Wolsey, and Cranmer. Each downfall—or near downfall—is played out in scenes of pageantry.

With the exception of Cranmer, each must go because he or she prevents Elizabeth's being born. Buckingham believes he has a claim to Henry's throne; Katharine is queen and can't give Henry a male heir; and Wolsey opposes Henry's marriage to Anne. If Elizabeth's birth is ensured, then so is the legitimacy of the succession of the king who was currently on the throne when Shakespeare wrote the play—James I, who was Elizabeth's successor.

It's a mystery why Cranmer survives his trial. He suffers from the same kind of negative rumor mill that brings down the other characters. Yet the king clearly wants to save him. We can conjecture that the cycle of lords blaming each other had to stop somewhere or it threatened to spin out of control and into civil conflict. But history reveals that Cranmer was later executed anyway.

Famous Lines

"Heat not a furnace for your foe so hot
That it do singe yourself" (Act I, Scene I).

"Press not a falling man too far!" (Act III, Scene II).

"Had I but served my God with half the zeal
I served my king, he would not in mine age
Have left me naked to mine enemies" (Act III, Scene II).

"To dance attendance on their lordships' pleasures" (Act V, Scene II).

King John

Main Characters

King John—the king of England, the third son of Henry II; his older brother, Richard the Lionheart, was king before him

Eleanor—John's mother

Philip—the king of France; Arthur's champion

Arthur—son of Geoffrey; John's elder brother

The Bastard—Philip, the illegitimate son of Richard the Lionheart and a chorus for the play

Louis—Philip's son

Pandulph—a messenger from the pope

Hubert—one of John's men

Constance—Arthur's mother

Earl of Pembroke—one of John's followers

Earl of Salisbury—one of John's followers

Lymoges—Duke of Austria; one of Philip's men, killed by the Bastard

Blanch of Spain—John's niece; she marries Louis, thus cementing a bond between John and Philip

Earl of Essex—one of John's followers

Lord Bigot—one of John's followers

Melun—one of Louis's men

Robert Faulconbridge—the Bastard's younger (legitimate) brother

Lady Faulconbridge—the Bastard's mother

Chatillon—a messenger from France

Prince Henry—John's son; he becomes King Henry III at John's death

Introduction

King John was written about 1596 or earlier and stands as the odd play out in the early histories that trace the Wars of the Roses. It was published in the First Folio of 1623. Chronologically, it is the earliest of the history plays, covering the period of John's reign from 1199 to 1216.

While parallels oversimplify the facts, they nevertheless capture the themes Shakespeare wanted to emphasize in this play. John's claim to the throne is based on his older brother Richard the Lionheart's will. Elizabeth's father, Henry VIII, made Elizabeth his heir by will, despite disputes about the legality of appointing successors. Also, the pope excommunicated both John and Elizabeth for disobedience.

John's rival to the throne was Arthur, the son of Geoffrey, John's elder brother, in much the same way that Elizabeth's rival, Mary, was the daughter of Henry VIII's older sister who married into the Scottish line of kings. (Her son, James VI of Scotland, became James I of England on Elizabeth's death.) Because succession traditionally passed to the son of the oldest child, both John's and Elizabeth's claims to the throne were weak. Arthur's cause was championed by King Philip of France, while Mary's claims were supported by King Philip II of Spain.

John brought about Arthur's death, regrets his decision, and tries to distance himself from it, just as Elizabeth ordered Mary's execution and then distanced herself from it. Arthur's death provided an excuse for a French invasion; Mary's death provoked Philip II to launch the Spanish Armada. What's more, the invasion against John in England is wrecked by a storm that shipwrecks the French reinforcements, while a storm also saved England from the brunt of the Spanish Armada in 1588.

The Play

King John's nephew, Arthur, believes he is the rightful heir to the throne of England and is backed by Philip of France in a rebellion. Refusing the king of France's demand that he surrender his throne, John sends an army to France under the command of Philip Faulconbridge (also known as Philip the Bastard), illegitimate son of Richard I and Arthur's half-brother.

The English army clashes with the French at Angiers, but neither can claim a decisive victory. John proposes peace, ceding Philip some English territory in France and arranging for the dauphin (the French King's son) to wed his niece, Blanch.

The pope excommunicates John over a dispute concerning the appointment of the archbishop of Canterbury. Pandulph, the pope's legate, orders the French to resume their war with King John. John's army beats back the French and captures Arthur. John wishes him executed. His chamberlain,

Hubert, disobeys the order, but Arthur later plunges to his death while trying to escape. Ironically, the nobles suspect John of murder, his original intent, and desert him for the French. Meanwhile, John arranges peace with Pandulph, to whom he turns over the Crown of England. He will receive it back, therefore becoming a vassal of the church.

Now that John is back in the fold of Mother Church, Pandulph tries to stop the war. The French won't play ball, and the armies clash at St. Edmundsbury. During the battle, a French noble named Melun warns the turncoat English noblemen that the king of France will have them executed as soon as John has been conquered. The nobles, seeing the winds of fortune shift, return their allegiance to King John.

Without his allies, the French king comes to terms with Pandulph and John. John is hardly able to enjoy his victory. While staying at Swinstead Abbey he is poisoned by one of the monks. His son will ascend the throne as King Henry III.

Commentary

King John focuses on historical events, but the events in *King John* seem repeatedly to get in the way of intention and outcome—the characters are continually thwarted by historical accident and adversity. It is almost the antithesis of Cassius's famous speech in *Julius Caesar*, "The fault, dear Brutus, is not in our stars, But in ourselves, that we are underlings": in other words, we control what happens to us. In *King John*, it seems that no one controls things.

FACT

King John treats history as an unpredictable unfolding of events. Decisive moments seem insignificant episodes in a haphazard universe. Elizabethan audiences would have picked up on King John's comment on the contemporary debate about Queen Elizabeth I's legitimacy to the throne, as opposed to that of Mary, Queen of Scots.

While John thinks he can secure his hold on the throne by killing Arthur, his lords turn against him, proving him wrong. Arthur is actually spared, only to panic and kill himself by accident. John is again foiled by fate.

Famous Lines

"I would that I were low laid in my grave:
I am not worth this coil that's made for me" (Act II, Scene I).

"Talks as familiarly of roaring lions
As maids of thirteen do of puppy-dogs!" (Act II, Scene I).

"Grief fills the room up of my absent child,
Lies in his bed, walks up and down with me,
Puts on his pretty looks, repeats his words,
Remembers me of all his gracious parts,
Stuffs out his vacant garments with his form" (Act III, Scene IV).

"Life is as tedious as a twice-told tale
Vexing the dull ear of a drowsy man" (Act III, Scene IV).

"Make haste; the better foot before" (Act IV, Scene II).

King Richard II

Main Characters

King Richard II—the king of England
Henry Bolingbroke—the Duke of Herford, occasionally referred to by his
nickname, "Harry"; King Richard's cousin and the son of Richard's
uncle, John of Gaunt
John of Gaunt—the Duke of Lancaster; called either "Gaunt" or "Lancaster"
Edmund of Langley—the Duke of York; called "York"; Richard's uncle, and
a brother of John of Gaunt
Duke of Aumerle—the Earl of Rutland and son of Edmund of Langley; also
called "Rutland"
Thomas Mowbray—the Duke of Norfolk; called "Norfolk"
Bushy, Bagot, and Greene—Richard's friends and supporters
Henry Percy, Earl of Northumberland, nicknamed Hotspur; Lord Ross; and
Lord Willoughby—noblemen who join Bolingbroke's rebel army to
fight against King Richard

Duchess of York—the wife of Edmund of Langley and mother of Rutland

Duchess of Gloucester—sister-in-law of John of Gaunt and Edmund of Langley

Queen to King Richard

Lord Berkeley—the ruler of Berkeley Castle in Gloucestershire

Earl of Salisbury—a nobleman loyal to King Richard

Bishop of Carlisle—a clergyman loyal to Richard

Sir Stephen Scroop—a nobleman loyal to Richard

Abbot of Westminster—a clergyman loyal to Richard

Sir Piers Exton—a nobleman who assassinates King Richard

Introduction

King Richard II was probably composed around 1595, and certainly no later than 1597. It is set around the year 1398 and documents the fall of the last Plantagenet king, Richard II, and the rise of the first Lancastrian king, Henry IV.

Richard came to the throne as a young man. He chose his counselors unwisely and was detached from the people, wasting too much time spending money on his close friends and raising taxes to fund his pet wars in Ireland and elsewhere.

FACT

King Richard II is chronologically the first play in Shakespeare's second "history quartet," or, as scholars phrase it, "tetralogy," a series of four plays that dramatizes the Wars of the Roses, an English civil war between the houses of Lancashire and Yorkshire that lasted close to 100 years. (Its sequels, although written earlier, are *King Henry IV, Parts I* and *II*, and *King Henry V.*)

He "rented out" pieces of English land to wealthy noblemen, and seized the lands and money of the Duke of Lancaster on his death (the father of Henry Bolingbroke who will take the throne from Richard) in order to raise funds for a war, which upset both commoners and nobles alike. Bolingbroke, in particular, is incensed to learn that Richard has stolen his inheritance.

The Play

Henry Bolingbroke and Thomas Mowbray, the Duke of Norfolk, get ready to settle an argument through trial by combat. Bolingbroke feels that Norfolk is responsible for the murder of Richard's uncle, the Duke of Gloucester. At the last moment, King Richard decrees that both men are to be banished. Soon after, Bolingbroke's father, John of Gaunt, the Duke of Lancaster, dies. Richard seizes the estates in order to raise an army for a campaign in Ireland.

Bolingbroke returns to find that the Earl of Northumberland has joined with other disaffected nobles against Edmund of Langley, the Duke of York, Richard's regent while the king is in Ireland. When Richard returns, he discovers that Bolingbroke has not only reclaimed the lands stolen from him but also dispersed Richard's army and executed two of Richard's favorites.

Richard flees to Flint Castle for his own protection. Bolingbroke overtakes him and brings him back to London as a prisoner. Richard is made to confess crimes against the state and abdicate the crown to Bolingbroke, who becomes King Henry IV.

The Duke of York's son, Aumerle, loyal to Richard, conspires against King Henry. Aumerle is granted clemency, but Richard is imprisoned in Pomfreet Castle. Sir Piers of Exton murders Richard because he thinks King Henry wants him dead. Henry disavows the deed when he hears of it but promises a Crusade to atone for Richard's death.

Commentary

Richard's poetic and metaphysical musings on the nature of kingship and identity mark a new direction for Shakespeare and his histories. Some scholars feel that *King Richard II* reads like a dry run for the mature *Hamlet*.

King Richard II is stylized and in sharp contrast to the "Henry" plays that follow it (though they were written before *King Richard II*), and it contains virtually no prose. The play is replete with grand metaphors, such as the famous comparison of England to a garden, and of its reigning king to a lion or to the sun.

Famous Lines

"In rage deaf as the sea, hasty as fire" (Act I, Scene I).

"The tongues of dying men
Enforce attention like deep harmony" (Act II, Scene I).

"This royal throne of kings, this sceptred isle,
This earth of majesty, this seat of Mars,
This other Eden, demi-paradise,
This fortress built by Nature for herself
Against infection and the hand of war,
This happy breed of men, this little world,
This precious stone set in the silver sea,
Which serves it in the office of a wall
Or as a moat defensive to a house,
Against the envy of less happier lands,—
This blessed plot, this earth, this realm, this England" (Act II, Scene I).

"The ripest fruit first falls" (Act II, Scene I).

"Let's talk of graves, of worms, and epitaphs" (Act III, Scene II).

"And nothing can we call our own but death
And that small model of the barren earth
Which serves as paste and cover to our bones.
For God's sake, let us sit upon the ground
And tell sad stories of the death of kings" (Act III, Scene II).

"Comes at the last, and with a little pin
Bores through his castle wall—and farewell king!" (Act III, Scene II).

"As in a theatre, the eyes of men,
After a well-graced actor leaves the stage,
Are idly bent on him that enters next,
Thinking his prattle to be tedious" (Act V, Scene II).

King Richard III

Main Characters

Richard—the Duke of Gloucester; deformed in body and twisted in mind

Duke of Buckingham—Richard's right-hand man

Sir Richard Ratcliff and Sir William Catesby—two of Richard's supporters

Sir James Tyrrel—a murderer whom Richard hires

King Edward IV—older brother of Richard and Clarence

George, Duke of Clarence—the trusting middle brother of Edward and Richard

Queen Elizabeth—the wife of King Edward IV

Dorset, Rivers, and Grey—kinsmen and allies of Elizabeth

Lady Anne—the young widow of Prince Edward, son of the former king, Henry VI

Duchess of York—widowed mother of Richard, Clarence, and King Edward IV; not to be confused with Margaret

Margaret—widow of the dead King Henry VI. Mother of the slain Prince Edward

The Princes (in the Tower)—the two young sons of King Edward IV, Prince Edward and the young duke of York

Elizabeth—daughter of the former Queen Elizabeth who was married to Edward IV

Richmond—challenges Richard for the throne and becomes Henry VII

Lord Hastings—a lord who supports the Yorkist cause

Lord Stanley—Lord Stanley, Earl of Derby; stepfather of Richmond

Lord Mayor of London—a gullible and suggestible fellow

Sir Thomas Vaughan—a friend of Elizabeth, Dorset, Rivers, and Grey

Introduction

King Richard III is the last of the four plays in Shakespeare's first quartet of history plays. It concludes a dramatic chronicle started in *King Henry VI, Part I* and then moving through *King Henry VI, Part II*, and *King Henry VI, Part III*. The entire four-play saga was composed early in Shakespeare's career, and most scholars date *King Richard III* to about 1591 or 1592.

King Richard III is a dramatization of historical events that concluded in 1485 with the defeat of King Richard III at the battle of Bosworth, when the Tudors replaced the Plantagenet family as rulers of England. Shakespeare often plays fast and loose with the facts, stretching and altering the timeline. The events of this civil war—including the murders of King Henry and Prince Edward by the York brothers, and the earlier killing of Rutland by Henry's family—are an important background to *King Richard III*. In Shakespeare's version, both Henry and Edward leave widows: Margaret and Lady Anne. Although Anne mourns Henry VI's death, she nevertheless becomes Richard's wife.

FACT

Richard III is a fascinating figure, in the same way that we are entranced by the charismatic malevolence of a Hannibal Lecter. Audiences for generations have found themselves seduced by Richard's eloquence and cunning emotional manipulation, even as they are repelled by his evil.

When *King Richard III* begins, Edward IV is growing old. His malicious and deformed younger brother, Richard, is plotting to get his hands on the throne. But a great many people stand between him and the kingship. When Edward dies, he leaves behind two sons who are in line for the throne before Richard. They are still children, though, and Richard has them murdered while they live in captivity in the Tower of London. Their young sister, Elizabeth, becomes an important pawn in bringing peace to the realm.

Richard's ambition is also blocked by his older brother and Clarence's two children, all of whom Richard must get rid of in order to seize the throne. Once on the throne, Richard soon finds himself besieged by his second cousin, Henry, the Earl of Richmond, who has been gathering strength overseas. Henry believes he has a rightful claim to the throne, and in preparing to challenge Richard sets up the final conflict of the Wars of Roses.

The Play

The play picks up from the end of *King Henry VI, Part III*. Richard's brother is now King Edward IV. In order to gain the crown himself and eliminate his brothers, Richard pits his older brother George, Duke of Clarence, against Edward. He convinces Edward that George is guilty of treason and has him arrested. He also brazenly woos Anne, widow of the murdered Edward, the Prince of Wales, in the midst of her husband's funeral procession.

FACT

Shakespearean audiences would have thought of the "wicked Italian" Machiavelli when watching this play, because Richard is the epitome of the amoral, power-hungry courtier made famous by the French in their corrupted version of the book *The Prince* (1532) by the Renaissance Italian writer Niccolò Machiavelli. (The French version was translated into English long before the original would be.)

Edward IV, who is deathly ill at the beginning of the play, dies. Richard has already arranged for his brother George to be murdered while in prison, and now he becomes regent until Edward's son (also named Edward, Prince of Wales) comes of age.

In order to "protect" the Prince of Wales and his younger brother, Richard puts them in the Tower of London. He then executes Edward's loyalist lords: Vaughan, Rivers, Hastings, and Grey. With the aid of Buckingham, Richard has Edward's sons declared illegitimate. Buckingham "offers" the throne of England to Richard, who pretends to be reluctant to accept. Few are fooled by his false modesty. Even his mother curses him as a bloody tyrant.

Richard hires a murderer to kill the princes in the tower because Buckingham has refused to help him. Having married Anne, who conveniently dies, Richard proposes marriage to Princess Elizabeth, King Edward's daughter. Her mother Elizabeth (Edward's widow) pretends to go along with the match but actually arranges for her daughter to marry Henry, the Earl of Richmond instead.

Richmond is raising an army in France to fight Richard. Buckingham, out of favor with Richard because he refused to go along with the murder of the young princes, gives his allegiance to Richmond. Buckingham is captured and Richard has him executed.

Richmond finally lands with his army and marches for London. The French and English armies get ready to fight near Bosworth Field. The night before the battle, the ghosts of the people he has killed visit Richard, and all prophesy his death.

During the battle Richard is thrown from his horse ("A horse! a horse! my kingdom for a horse!"). He and Richmond fight, and Richmond prevails, killing Richard. Richmond is crowned King Henry VII. The Battle of Bosworth is the final engagement of the Wars of the Roses and marks the founding of the Tudor dynasty of kings and queens.

Commentary

King Richard III is a chronicle of bloody deeds and atrocities, and modern audiences can find it difficult to follow the complex political intrigue, family relationships, and personal vendettas. The play is as much melodrama as history, and Richard is a self-professed villain of monstrous proportions comparable only to Iago in *Othello*, or to a lesser extent Edmund in *King Lear*. Richard's ambition makes Macbeth look like an amateur by comparison. He is a totally Machiavellian creature, able to splinter and nearly destroy the forces opposing him, until Richmond finally defeats him.

Richard is clearly ambitious and sadistic, but no clear reason for his motivations or his hatred is given. It is as if he decides early on in life that he will be as bitter and twisted inside as he is out because that is the only joy he can ever really expect to have. Like the character the Devil from medieval morality pageants who represented evil, Richard does not even try to justify what he does.

Richard was probably no more murderous than the kings who came before or after him. He was more the rightful king of England when he died in battle than Richmond. History is written by the victors, and at the time Shakespeare was writing, England was ruled by Queen Elizabeth—granddaughter of King Henry VII, the man who defeated Richard. The official "party line" was that Richard had been a monster who was not the legitimate king of England. To suggest anything else would have been thoroughly dangerous for Shakespeare.

FACT

Modern historians are split on whether the real Richard murdered the young princes or whether he even had a humpback. History reports that Richard came to be known as "Humpty," and historians say the nursery rhyme Humpty Dumpty is about Richard's defeat at the Battle of Bosworth.

Famous Lines

"Now is the winter of our discontent
Made glorious summer by this sun of York,
And all the clouds that loured upon our house
In the deep bosom of the ocean buried.
Now are our brows bound with victorious wreaths,
Our bruised arms hung up for monuments,
Our stern alarums changed to merry meetings,
Our dreadful marches to delightful measures.
Grim-visaged war hath smoothed his wrinkled front;
And now, instead of mounting barbed steeds
To fright the souls of fearful adversaries,
He capers nimbly in a lady's chamber
To the lascivious pleasing of a lute.
But I, that am not shaped for sportive tricks,
Nor made to court an amorous looking-glass;
I, that am rudely stamped, and want love's majesty
To strut before a wanton ambling nymph;
I, that am curtailed of this fair proportion,
Cheated of feature by dissembling nature,
Deformed, unfinished, sent before my time
Into this breathing world, scarce half made up,
And that so lamely and unfashionable

That dogs bark at me as I halt by them,—
Why, I, in this weak piping time of peace,
Have no delight to pass away the time,
Unless to spy my shadow in the sun" (Act I, Scene I).

"O, I have passed a miserable night,
So full of ugly sights, of ghastly dreams,
That, as I am a Christian faithful man,
I would not spend another such a night,
Though 't were to buy a world of happy days" (Act I, Scene IV).

"Lord, Lord! methought, what pain it was to drown!
What dreadful noise of waters in mine ears!
What ugly sights of death within mine eyes!
Methought I saw a thousand fearful wrecks,
Ten thousand men that fishes gnawed upon,
Wedges of gold, great anchors, heaps of pearl,
Inestimable stones, unvalued jewels,
All scattered in the bottom of the sea:
Some lay in dead men's skulls; and in those holes
Where eyes did once inhabit, there were crept,
As 't were in scorn of eyes, reflecting gems" (Act I, Scene IV).

"Off with his head!" (Act III, Scene IV).

"An honest tale speeds best, being plainly told" (Act IV, Scene IV).

"I have set my life upon a cast,
And I will stand the hazard of the die:
I think there be six Richmonds in the field" (Act V, Scene IV).

"A horse! a horse! my kingdom for a horse!" (Act V, Scene IV).

CHAPTER 17

Shakespeare's Two Top Histories

King Henry IV, Part I is an epic play and has been called Shakespeare's greatest history play. Its three-dimensional characters and overt politics have been the subjects of many books and critical essays. *King Henry V* is also the most popular of Shakespeare's history plays. It is rife with colorful characters, noble speeches, battles, and a young king (Henry) who is brave, modest, and fiercely focused, yet with a sense of humor.

King Henry IV, Part I

Main Characters

King Henry IV—the ruling king of England; he feels guilty about the murder of Richard II and is also irritated by the irresponsible antics of his eldest son, Prince Hal

Prince Hal, the Prince of Wales—he will become King Henry V; he is sometimes called "Harry" or "Harry Monmouth"; he is the heir to the throne of England but spends all his time hanging around the bad side of London, wasting his time with highwaymen, robbers, and barflies

Hotspur—the son and heir of the Earl of Northumberland; his real name is Henry Percy

Sir John Falstaff—a fat old knight, a rogue, and Prince Hal's closest friend

Earl of Westmoreland—allied with King Henry

Prince John of Lancaster—son of King Henry

Sir Walter Blunt—serves as a messenger of King Henry

Thomas Percy—the Earl of Worcester; the mastermind behind the Percy rebellion

Henry Percy—the Earl of Northumberland; Hotspur's father

Edmund Mortimer—the Earl of March

Owen Glendower—the leader of the Welsh rebels

Archibald—the Earl of Douglas; usually called "the Douglas" (a traditional way of referring to a Scottish clan chief); the leader of the large army of Scots allied with the Percys

Sir Richard Vernon—allied with the Percys

Richard Scroop—the archbishop of York

Ned Poins, Peto, Bardolph, and Gadshill—criminals and highwaymen who drink with Falstaff and Prince Hal in the Boar's Head Tavern

Mistress Quickly—hostess of the Boar's Head Tavern, a seedy dive in Eastcheap, London

Introduction

King Henry IV, Part I, written between 1596 and 1597, is one of Shakespeare's four-part series of the Kings of England. It deals with the rise of the house of Lancaster. The play takes place during the war years of 1400–3

Like writers of historical movies and plays of today, Shakespeare significantly altered or invented history to better the dramatic story line. He also altered or melded historical characters like Hotspur, who was not the same age as Prince Hal. Mortimer is a fictional character metamorphosed from two different historical people.

The Play

King Henry IV is tormented by guilt over the murder of Richard II, but he is also disillusioned with the escapades of his older son Prince Hal, the heir to the throne. Hal has little use for his princely trappings and spends most of his time in taverns in the squalid part of London, hobnobbing with prostitutes and vagrants. His closest friend is a fat old knight named Falstaff

FACT

Falstaff is one of the most famous of Shakespeare's creations. Falstaff can also be considered the best comic figure in all of Shakespeare, one with a vile tongue, as we can see from his capacity for swearing: "'Sblood, you starveling. You eel-skin, you dried neat's tongue, you bull's pizzel, you stock-fish!" It must have given Shakespeare great joy to write lines for Falstaff.

King Henry IV has far more political problems than worrying about the conduct of his son, Hal. There is discontent fermenting with the Percys, families of noblemen, who feel they have not been properly rewarded for helping the king come to power. This anger becomes so strong that they plot a rebellion. Harry Percy, known as Hotspur, leads the Percy forces. Although the same age as Prince Hal, Hotspur is the complete opposite of the young prince, shunning the tavern life in which Hal has enmeshed himself. Hotspur as also respected for his bravery in battle, where Hal has yet to engage in battle.

The Percys gather a formidable army from Scotland and Wales, including English nobles and clergymen who have grievances against King Henry. The king, realizing his kingdom is in danger, prepares for war, enlisting one unlikely choice: his son. With the threat upon him, Prince Hal reforms and rides to the battlefield in front of an army to defeat Hotspur.

At the Battle of Shrewsbury, Prince Hal saves his father's life, winning his father's approval. Hal also defeats Hotspur in single combat and most of the leaders of the Percy family are put to death. Falstaff, a glutton and a coward, manages to survive the battle by steering clear of the clashing of swords. Powerful rebel forces remain in Britain, however, so by play's end the ultimate outcome of the war has not yet been resolved.

Commentary

King Henry IV, Part I is more than a battlefield epic; it parallels two worlds—the courtly world of King Henry IV and that of the low-class reprobates who spend their days guzzling beer in taverns. Bridging the worlds is Prince Hal, who has now eschewed his life of frivolity and develops an unorthodox plan to prepare for the throne by becoming close to the people he will eventually rule.

FACT

King Henry IV, Part I refers to its "prequel," *King Richard II*. Its source was once again Raphael Holinshed's *Chronicles of England, Scotland, and Ireland*.

The play mixes history (the king) and comedy (Falstaff), moving from the realm of political intrigue to the debased world of rogues who spend their days in taverns or thievery. Thematically, the play is concerned with the nature of kingship, honor, and loyalty. King Henry is politically shrewd, unlike his predecessor, Richard II. But because he came to the throne as a usurper responsible for the death of God's anointed king, Richard, Henry's ability to rule is diminished, and the country is inevitably plunged into chaos.

Shakespeare explores this concept of honor through the characters of Hotspur, Falstaff, and Prince Hal. It is upon the shoulders of Prince Hal to balance the two extremes—Hotspur's obsession with honor and Falstaff's lack of it—so that he may become an honorable king.

Famous Lines

"He will give the devil his due" (Act I, Scene II).

"I know a trick worth two of that" (Act II, Scene I).

"Out of this nettle, danger, we pluck this flower, safety" (Act II, Scene III).

"O, monstrous! but one half-pennyworth of bread to this intolerable deal of sack!" (Act II, Scene IV).

"Exceedingly well read" (Act III, Scene I).

"Two stars keep not their motion in one sphere" (Act V, Scene IV).

"The better part of valour is discretion" (Act V, Scene IV).

King Henry V

Main Characters

King Henry V—the young, recently crowned king of England
Duke of Exeter, Earl of Westmoreland, Earl of Salisbury, and Earl of War-
    wick—advisors to the king
Duke of Clarence, John Duke of Bedford, and Humphrey Duke of Glouces-
    ter—Henry's younger brothers
Archbishop of Canterbury and Bishop of Ely—wealthy and powerful
    clergymen

Earl of Cambridge, Lord Scroop, and Sir Thomas Grey—three conspirators against King Henry

Duke of York and Duke of Suffolk—cousins who die at the Battle of Agincourt

Charles VI—the king of France

Isabel—the queen of France

Lewis, the Dauphin—the son of the king of France and heir to the throne

Katherine—the king of France's daughter

The Constable of France, the Duke of Orléans, the Duke of Britain, the Duke of Bourbon, Lord Grandpré, Lord Rambures, the Duke of Burgundy, and the Governor of Harfleur—French noblemen and military leaders

Sir Thomas Erpingham—a veteran soldier

Fluellen, Macmorris, Jamy, and Captain Gower—captains of Henry's troops

Pistol, Bardolph, and Nym—commoners from London who serve with King Henry's army

Boy—formerly in the service of Falstaff, the nameless Boy leaves London after his master's death and goes with Pistol, Nym, and Bardolph to the war in France

Michael Williams, John Bates, and Alexander Court—common soldiers with whom King Henry argues (while in disguise) the night before the Battle of Agincourt

Mistress Quickly—the keeper of the Boar's Head Tavern in London; she is married to Pistol

Alice—Princess Katherine's maid

Montjoy—the French herald

Monsieur le Fer—a French soldier

Chorus—the character who narrates the play

Introduction

King Henry V is the last part of the four-part series that deals with the historical rise of the English royal house of Lancaster. *King Henry V* was probably composed in 1599 and is one of the most popular of Shakespeare's history plays. It is rife with colorful characters, noble speeches, battles, and a young king (Henry) who appears to be brave, modest, and fiercely focused, yet with a sense of humor.

FACT

This is a stirring play, and when you watch it, it's useful to keep the paradoxes of morality and character in mind. The brilliance of Henry's speeches and his wit make him a Kennedy-esque kind of inspiring leader.

The Play

Worried over impending legislation that would effectively rob the Church of England of its power and wealth, the Archbishop of Canterbury convinces Henry V to instead lay claim to France. When he does so, however, Lewis, the dauphin, sends an insulting response, balls—a gift of tennis balls—that convinces Henry that the French want war. He puts together an army to invade France. But before he can leave, he must sort out the last of the rebels against his father and his house.

Lords Cambridge, Scroop, and Grey conspire to assassinate Henry (they are paid by the French). The plot is discovered and Henry arrests them personally and oversees their public execution. The army then lays siege to Harfleur, France, capturing it after heavy losses.

The night before a battle where the English face overwhelming odds, Henry disguises himself as a commoner in order to mingle with his troops. He talks candidly with his men and discovers that they may be unsure of their king, but they are steadfast in their willingness to beat the French.

The morning of the Battle of Agincourt, St. Crispin's Day, Henry makes a stirring speech, knowing his army is outnumbered five to one. His expert archers help Henry rout the French who are forced to ask for peace, which Henry grants on his own terms. He signs the Treaty of Troyes, marries Princess Katherine of France, and insists he is named heir to the French throne, thus uniting England and France in peace.

Commentary

The play is harder to analyze than it seems. Henry appears a model hero but for all his patriotism—or land lust, depending on your point of view—he invades a nonaggressive country and slaughters thousands. He sentences former friends and prisoners of war to death, paying lip service to mercy; and he never accepts any responsibility for the bloodshed he has initiated.

King Henry V concludes the saga begun in *King Henry IV, Part I*—the making of a king. At the end of *Part I*, Hal seems to have evolved from profligate prince to mature heir to the throne. Yet in *Part II*, while Prince Hal has become Prince Harry, he still appears to shun the responsibilities of his father's court in favor of Falstaff's clearly defined and "honestly" declared licentiousness. Prince Harry, caught trying on the crown while his father lies dying, intuitively understands (and fights against) the knowledge that "uneasy lies the head that wears the crown." Falstaff's anarchic, irresponsible world is hard to resist, particularly when the alternative is a kingdom embraced by vicious politics and feuding strife.

It is only at his father's deathbed that Prince Harry finally resolves the doubts that have plagued him. He recognizes that the crown, though blemished on his father's head because it was illegally wrested from Richard II, will sit comfortably on his own, because he will inherit it lawfully.

Prince Harry becomes Henry V, transforming himself finally into the great king who will defeat the French at Agincourt and win for England her lost dominions. But before making the last leg of this great journey, he must reject the disreputable and dishonorable anarchy of Falstaff's world, which he does with a chilling firmness: "I know thee not, old man. Fall to thy prayers."

Famous Lines

"Turn him to any cause of policy,
The Gordian knot of it he will unloose,
Familiar as his garter: that when he speaks,
The air, a chartered libertine, is still" (Act I, Scene I).

"Even at the turning o' the tide" (Act II, Scene III).

"Once more unto the breach, dear friends, once more,
Or close the wall up with our English dead!
In peace there's nothing so becomes a man
As modest stillness and humility;
But when the blast of war blows in our ears,
Then imitate the action of the tiger:
Stiffen the sinews, summon up the blood" (Act III, Scene I).

"I would give all my fame for a pot of ale and safety" (Act III, Scene II).

"Men of few words are the best men" (Act III, Scene II).

"This day is called the feast of Crispian:
He that outlives this day and comes safe home,
Will stand a tip-toe when this day is named,
And rouse him at the name of Crispian" (Act IV, Scene III).

"We few, we happy few, we band of brothers" (Act IV, Scene III).

CHAPTER 18

Shakespeare's Last— and Lost—Plays

When Shakespeare retired to Stratford-upon-Avon in 1611, we can assume it was to bask in the sun in his garden at New Place, to have time to read what must have been his favorite books. Perhaps he wanted to be with his wife, Anne, his daughters, Judith (unwed at age twenty-five), and Susanna, who had married a Stratford doctor, John Hall, as well as his grand-daughter, Elizabeth. Yet, he could not stop what he had done all his life—write. With a young playwright, John Fletcher, and George Wilkins, he may have coauthored the following five plays: *Cardenio* (1613? termed the lost play), *King Edward III* (1596, but not attributed to Shakespeare until 1998), *King Henry VIII* (1613), *Pericles, Prince of Tyre* (1607), and *The Two Noble Kinsmen* (1613).

Cardenio

Main Characters

The Tyrant—usurped the king's throne
Govianus—the king; in love with the Lady
The Lady—Govianus's love, and pursued by the Tyrant
Helvetius—the Lady's father
Memphonius, Sophonirus, and Bellarius—nobles of the court
The Wife—wife of Anselmus
Anselmus—brother-in-law of Govianus
Votarius—Anselmus's best friend
Leonella—the Wife's servant

Introduction

A mystery surrounds the play *Cardenio*—a mystery of authorship and text. Although it is now considered to be a lost play by William Shakespeare, it took centuries to find its true author. It is thought to have been written around 1613 (with John Fletcher) when Shakespeare lived in Stratford-upon-Avon. The play was not attributed to Shakespeare until it appeared until 1728. It was then that Lewis Theobald published a play called *Double Falsehood*; or *The Distressed Lovers*, which he said was based on the story of Cardenio and Lucinda in Cervantes's *Don Quixote*. Theobald said that he had revised the play and "adapted to the stage" from an old manuscript "originally written by Fletcher and Shakespeare."

What we do know about *Cardenio*'s history is that that on May 20, 1613, John Heminges, who ran the King's Men, was presented a sum of money for performing six plays, one of which was titled *Cardenio*. It did not list the playwright's name. Then, in 1653, the printer Humphrey Moseley entered in the Stationers' Register several plays, including "*The History of Cardenio*, by Mr. Fletcher and Mr. Shakespeare." Even earlier, in 1612, one scholar argues that an untitled, anonymous, handwritten draft of a play was delivered to Sir George Buc, the Master of the Revels to King James I. Confused by the lack of a title, or a playwright's name, he referred to it as "this *Second Mayden's Tragedy*." That play might have been *Cardenio*.

Yet, the story is not complete, as it had not been positively attributed to Shakespeare. Some of those who examined the manuscript concluded that it was the work of Thomas Midddleton. Then in 1994, historian Charles Hamilton published the script, along with 140 pages of testimony (*Shakespeare with John Fletcher: Cardenio; or The Second Maiden's Tragedy*. New York: Marlowe & Company, 1994). The final analysis of this extended inquiry stated that the play, *Cardenio*, was coauthored by Shakespeare and Fletcher. *Cardenio* was now the first play—perhaps the last—to be added to the Shakespearean canon since the publication of the Fourth Folio more than 300 years ago.

The Play

Cardenio has two distinct plots that are linked by the relationships of the main characters. One plays against the other in a scene-by-scene progression that neatly uses one plot to contrast with, and comment on, the other.

Act 1 opens in the midst of a coup, as Govianus, the rightful king, loses his throne to an obsessive Tyrant. Rubbing salt in an open wound (and recalling Richard III and Lady Anne), the Tyrant proceeds to woo Govianus's love, referred to in the play only as the Lady.

QUESTION?

Why is John Fletcher considered to be the coauthor of the play?
It is well known that John Fletcher was a great admirer of Cervantes, and he was probably able to read *Don Quixote* in its original Spanish. Shakespeare and Fletcher might well have written a play based on the Cardenio episodes in volume 1 of *Don Quixote*.

She remains steadfast in her devotion to Govianus, even in the face of her own father's appeals to make things easier for everyone by simply appeasing the Tyrant and giving him what he wants. Govianus and the Lady are imprisoned. Frustrated by the Lady, the Tyrant sends his soldiers to force her to submit to him. Rather than be "borne with violence to the Tyrant's bed," she begs Govianus to kill her.

He can't bring himself to do that, so she kills herself instead. Undeterred and angry that the Lady has managed to thwart him, the Tyrant steals her corpse from its tomb intent on making her his queen anyway. Govianus is released, finds his way to court, and avenges her death. Restored to the throne, Govianus returns her body to the tomb.

In the subplot, a jealous lord, Anselmus, brother-in-law to Govianus, convinces his best friend, Votarius, to seduce his wife as a test of her fidelity. Surprised by their unexpected passion for each other, Votarius and the Wife begin a clandestine affair. To divert her husband's suspicions, the Wife and Votarius plot to have Anselmus overhear a conversation in which the Wife will seemingly spurn Votarius' advances with a sword. The Wife's servant, however, has poisoned the sword's tip, and the Wife unwittingly kills her lover. As the various plots and deceptions are revealed, all are slain.

Commentary

Those who want to pursue the authorship question should start with Charles Hamilton's *Cardenio; or The Second Maiden's Tragedy* and Anne Lancashire's *The Second Maiden's Tragedy*.

For those who consider the play a lost Shakespeare piece, the evidence is seen in the characterizations, particularly of the women, such as the Lady herself, who seems to continue the lineage of the spiritually powerful princesses of *Cymbeline*, *The Winter's Tale*, and *Pericles, Prince of Tyre*. The language also seems to be Shakespeare's by its delight in new words and powerful imagery.

FACT

For each list of arguments that tries to link Shakespeare's and Fletcher's works to *The Second Maiden's Tragedy*, an equally persuasive list of comparisons can be made with the plays of Thomas Middleton.

Proving a play's authorship is something of a detective game. Hamilton, for example, based part of his evidence on handwriting analysis. The manuscript contains stage directions, censor's cuts, and slips of paper with textual corrections in the same hand as the body of the text, leading some scholars to conclude that the manuscript was handwritten by the playwright, while others believe it is a copy, prepared by a professional scribe. Particularly puzzling is that there is no character named Cardenio in *The Second Maiden's Tragedy*.

King Edward III

Main Characters

King Edward III—king of England
Queen Philippa—Edward's wife
Prince Edward—Prince of Wales
Earl of Salisbury
Countess of Salisbury
Earl of Warwick
Sir William Montague
Earl of Derby
Lord Audley
Lord Percy
Sir John Copland
Lodowick—Edward's confidant
Robert of Artois
Earl of Montfort
Gobin de Grey
King John II (the Good)—king of France
Prince Charles (of Normandy)—John's son
Prince Philip—John's son
Duke of Lorrain
Lord Villiers—a French lord
King of Bohemia—aid to John
Polonian captain—aid to John
King David II of Scotland
Earl Douglas
Scottish messenger

Introduction

For over 400 years everyone but a handful of renegade critics have classified *King Edward III* as an anonymous play. First printed in 1596 by the London bookseller and publisher, Cuthbert Burby, the play's title page told Elizabethan readers that "it hath bin sundrie times plaied about the Citie of London," but Burby credited no author. The play was likely successful at the time, for Burby published another edition in 1599, again without naming an author. Capell re-edited the play in his *Prolusions* (1760) and first put forward the claim that Shakespeare wrote the play.

Capell's assertions received some support in the nineteenth century, most significantly from the poet Tennyson, and in the twentieth century by distinguished Shakespearean Kenneth Muir. Still, the play has remained in the "apocrypha" sections of Shakespeare anthologies—that is, material reputed to be written by Shakespeare but unproven to be so.

FACT

Three problems hindered the play's acceptance: it was not mentioned in Francis Meres's book *Palladis Tamia* (1598), a work that listed Shakespeare's early plays; John Heminge and Henry Condell did not include the play in the First Folio of 1623; and the play is considered by some scholars not to display Shakespeare's writing ability.

Over the last few years critics have reassessed the play's merits and are beginning to argue that "hollow and insincere" passages are not reason enough to deny that Shakespeare wrote the drama. The writing in *King Edward III* measures up to Shakespeare's early work in the *King Henry VI* trilogy and *King John*.

In 1998, the Arden Shakespeare series (the leading publisher of William Shakespeare's works), the Cambridge University Press, and American Riverside Press included the play in their collected Shakespeare editions. Various publishers have used computer analysis of the play's text and language to verify its main source of authorship. *King Edward III* could yet prove a major addition to the Shakespearean canon, and while no one claims Shakespeare is the sole author (John Fletcher may have collaborated when

Shakespeare retired in Stratford), he is considered the author of a significant part of the play.

King Edward III tells the story of the first campaigns of the Hundred Years' War and is likely one of Shakespeare's earliest works. Written in verse, the play opens with a scene similar to the first scene of *King Henry V.* The preparations for King Edward's campaign in France quickly give way to the romance of the king and the Countess of Salisbury.

QUESTION?

Why, if Shakespeare wrote *King Edward III*, did it become a forgotten play and why was it omitted from the First Folio?

This is pure speculation, of course, but it can be considered an early play, possibly even his first. It's possible Shakespeare shelved the play because he was unhappy with it and decided to use parts of it for other plays. As a result it did not become part of the repertoire that Shakespeare revised and revived, and actors Heminges and Condell, who collected the plays for the First Folio, did not know the play was his.

The Play

King Edward opens the play by rejecting his political obligations to the French king and claiming the French Crown. The king instructs Prince Edward to prepare to invade France, while he himself repulses the Scots besieging the Roxborough castle in the north. The prince is eager to do the job right, and his youthful idealism is in contrast to his father's political opportunism.

Distracted by a Woman

Edward's campaign against the Scots is put on hold when he meets the Countess of Salisbury. He knows she is the wife of one of his loyal lords, but he becomes besotted with her nevertheless. Edward never confronts the Scottish king, forsaking war for lustful adultery. He commissions a poem from Lodowick, the court secretary, who seems to deliberately misunderstand the situation. Edward tries wooing her, but the Countess says she realizes he is only testing her honor.

The dramatic tension of *King Edward III* is built on the contrast between King Edward and his son Prince Edward, the Black Prince. The king is a somewhat passive, less-than-honorable father, while the prince is a genuinely honorable warrior son.

Edward exacted a thoughtless oath of loyalty from the Countess's father, the Earl of Warwick, and now asks him to win over the Countess to his adulterous desires. Warwick is reluctant to break his oath and discusses the matter with his daughter who, to his relief, rejects the king's proposition.

While Edward has been besieging the Countess, the prince has assembled an army to invade France. He then gets a message that the Countess is against war with France, and Edward now sees the invasion of France as a sin worse than adultery. The Countess demands that both her husband Salisbury and Queen Philippa be put to death. Edward says he can't do that because what she wants is "beyond our law," and the Countess tartly replies, "So is your desire [for me]."

Edward reluctantly agrees, and the Countess pulls out two daggers, gives one to the king, and proposes that they kill their spouses by killing themselves, since they both carry the images of their spouses in their hearts. The Countess now adds that if he doesn't leave her alone, she'll kill herself right now. Edward realizes that while the Countess's suicide would certainly embarrass him politically, the war in France is a much better bet.

Returning to War

In France, Prince Edward becomes his father's steward in the battle. At one point the prince is surrounded and in trouble, but the king refuses to help him. If the prince can "redeem" himself he will "win a world of honour." If not, the king says, "we have more sons than one, to comfort our declining age." Happily, the prince enters in triumph. The French king, however, escapes to Poitiers, and King Edward sends the prince to pursue him. The king, meanwhile, decides to wait at Calais.

In Poitiers, Prince Edward is surrounded by the French and is in danger of being killed. King Edward, meanwhile, captures Calais by insisting that the six richest men in the city throw themselves on his mercy. How Edward will treat these merchants is a mystery, but things do not look good.

The old knight Audley tells the prince they are surrounded by four French armies. The prince, characteristically optimistic, replies, not so, we have one army; they have one army: "One to one is fair equality."

Against great odds, the prince faces death bravely. The Battle of Poitiers ends in defeat for France's John II, whose army is cut to ribbons by Prince Edward of England. Edward, a badly wounded Audley, and their captives set out for King Edward at Calais.

King Edward, meanwhile, tells his men to put all to sword "and make the spoil your own." The six wealthy men of Calais beg for peace and mercy. Edward decides to take possession of the city in peace but decides to drag the six men around the walls of the city, "and after feel the stroke of quartering steel."

Edward's queen, Philippa, who has just arrived at Calais, talks him into being merciful. The king agrees, claiming, somewhat ironically, "that we as well can master our affections as conquer others by the dint of sword."

At this point Copeland enters with King David of Scotland as his captive. Salisbury enters to announce that the prince has (apparently) fallen at Poitiers. But then the prince enters triumphant, with the French king and his son in tow.

Commentary

Ironically, King Edward goes north to relieve the siege of Roxborough, only to passively become the besieger of the Countess of Salisbury and Calais. His son becomes the active warrior who wrests great victories from daunting odds at Crécy and Poitiers. The king acts for political gain; the prince acts for honor and national pride, and without the prince, there would be, in this play, no conquest of France.

Written in verse throughout, the play opens with a scene similar to the first scene of *King Henry V.* No sooner are the preparations for the invasion put underway than we get King Edward's romantic besieging of the Countess of Salisbury. Finally, when the king conquers his adulterous passion, the military conquest takes place, with the honorable Prince Edward of Wales as its hero.

Pericles, Prince of Tyre

Main Characters

John Gower—a chorus
Antiochus—king of Antioch
Daugher of Antiochus
Thaliard—a villain hired by Antiochus to kill Pericles
Pericles—husband of Thaisa and father of Marina
Helicanus—one of Pericles's advisors in Tyre
Aeschines—another of Pericles's advisors
Cleon—governor of Tarsus, a city beset by famine
Dionyza—fife of Cleon
Simonides—king of Pentapolis; father of Thaisa
Thaisa—daughter of Simonides; mother of Marina
Marina—daughter of Pericles and Thaisa
Leonine—murderer hired by Dionyza to kill Marina
Lychordia—Thaisa's nurse, later Marina's nurse
Cerimon—a kindly physician in Ephesus
Philomon—Cerimon's assistant
Lysimachus—governor of Mytilene
Pander—a brothel keeper
Bawd—a madam who takes care of the prostitutes, probably Pander's wife
Master—the master of the fishermen who takes Pericles to the jousting
    competition on Pentapolis
Knights—suitors for Thaisa's hand at the jousting competition in Pentapolis
Boult—servant to Pander and Bawd
Diana—goddess of chastity
Shipmaster—captain of the ship on which Thaisa allegedly dies

Introduction

Pericles, Prince of Tyre, probably written around 1607, came late in Shakespeare's career. As in most of Shakespeare's plays (and those of his contemporaries), Shakespeare drew on earlier authors and common stories as source material for the play. The fourteenth-century poet John Gower, who appears in the play as a kind of chorus, wrote the most important direct source for *Pericles* in his *Confessio Amantis*; he himself had derived the story from one by Apollonius of Tyre. The story probably dates back to fifth-or sixth-century Latin texts, and before that perhaps even a Greek romance influenced by Homer's *Odyssey*, which it cursorily resembles.

Authorship

Scholars have long debated whether Shakespeare wrote *Pericles* alone. It is likely that another playwright named George Wilkins wrote the first nine scenes and Shakespeare wrote the remaining thirteen. Dual authorship is a good explanation for the stylistic differences between the two parts of the play. In the first part, the language closely reflects John Gower's fourteenth-century language rather than that of Shakespeare or his contemporaries.

Though both Wilkins and Shakespeare use iambic pentameter, Wilkins uses more rhyming couplets to end lines, while Shakespeare relies on his characteristic use of enjambment, where a phrase or idea doesn't end at the end of a line, but carries over to the next. Structurally, the dual-author theory works as well, since the actions of the first half of the play repeat themselves for the most part in the second half.

Source Text

Another interesting problem about *Pericles* is the unreliability of its source text. Almost all of Shakespeare's other plays, first published in quarto form, draw directly on the author's manuscript or the actor's promptbooks. *Pericles*, however, exists only as a quarto so poor that it is assumed to have been assembled out of reports from actors and spectators. Elizabethan citizens and actors lived in a world where far less printed text was available, so memorization was common. For this reason no authoritative text of *Pericles* exists.

Various editors have tackled this problem by making the greater or lesser efforts to increase the intelligibility of the play. Editors of the Oxford edition of the plays, for example, which many further adaptations draw from, decided to use a First Quarto version of this play, largely unchanged. Other editors have drawn on another of Wilkins's plays about *Pericles* to add more to the story. But if the First Quarto edition was already based on reported speech, then any edition that tries to further reconstruct what the original *Pericles* may have been probably strays even farther from any "original text."

FACT

It's important to remember that none of Shakespeare's texts is really word-for-word originals. Shakespeare worked in collaboration with a company of actors, and so his plays were constantly changing. Most likely what he first wrote changed substantially during rehearsals and again during performances.

The Play

Pericles goes to Antioch to court the princess. He is given a riddle to solve and correctly guesses that it reveals that Antiochus, the king, and his daughter are involved in an incestuous affair. Realizing that Pericles has guessed his secret, Antiochus determines to kill Pericles. His life in peril, Pericles runs for his life.

Antiochus is determined to destroy Pericles. Knowing this, Pericles appoints his counselor Helicanus to rule as regent and then sails from Tyre for Tarsus, where he saves the people by bringing them much-needed supplies and wins the gratitude of the governor, Cleon, and his wife, Dionyza. He then sets sail for Pentapolis. On the way, the vessel is shipwrecked, and Pericles is the sole survivor.

At Pentapolis, Pericles participates in a tournament for the hand of Thaisa, daughter of Simonides. He wins the tournament, and Pericles and Thaisa marry. In the meantime, news arrives that Antiochus is dead and that the people of Tyre want their prince back. Pericles and Thaisa, who is now pregnant with their child, set sail for Tyre. During a storm, Marina, their daughter, is born. Thaisa is believed to have died in childbirth. She is sealed in a watertight coffin and buried at sea. The coffin washes up on the shores of Ephesus, where Cerimon manages to revive Thaisa, who assumes that Pericles is lost at sea and promptly becomes a votaress (or "nun") in the Temple of Diana. Pericles leaves the baby Marina at Tarsus with Cleon and Dionyza, and continues on to Tyre.

Sixteen years later, Dionyza becomes jealous of Marina and resolves to have her murdered. Dionyza's servant takes her to the shore but cannot carry it out. As he stands there indecisively, pirates capture Marina. The servant reports back that Marina is dead, and Cleon mournfully raises a monument to her memory. Pericles encounters the tomb on a visit to Tarsus and falls into a deep despair.

Pericles sails into Mitylene still depressed about losing his daughter. He encounters Marina and eventually recognizes her as his daughter. The two are happily reunited. Lysimachus, the governor, asks for Marina's hand, which Marina accepts. Then, Pericles is visited by a dream that instructs him to travel to Ephesus. There he is reunited with Thaisa (who is now the head priestess of Diana), and the whole family is together again.

Commentary

Pericles is not one of Shakespeare's best works. The style of the play is so uneven, scholars suspect it is not the work of a single author. Yet the play was popular in its day and has been successfully performed since.

FACT

Unlike many of Shakespeare's works, there is little connection made in this play between the nobility and peasants. The fishermen who help Pericles are forgotten, despite his promise to remember them. In the brothel in Mytilene, Marina constantly proves she is better than those who would lord it over her by virtue of her royal blood. Lower-class characters are caricatures.

Ben Jonson, one of Shakespeare's contemporaries, attributed the success to its use of "scraps out of every dish"—touches of fairy tales, the Bible, *The Tempest*, incest, a lost daughter and a wife presumed dead, several storms, several contests for the hand of a princess, and innumerable kingdoms ruled by men of greater or lesser stature.

Structurally, the play divides in two. In the first nine scenes, Pericles falls into unfortunate circumstances and his luck changes. In the final thirteen scenes, he repeats this pattern. One explanation for this repetition is that the authors shift after scene nine.

Pericles's Sufferings

Pericles himself seems something of a cipher, largely because Shakespeare does not delve into the workings of his psyche as he did with characters in the tragic plays he wrote immediately before. Overall, the play suggests that, like Job, enduring miseries heaped one on another, Pericles ultimately gets his reward: his family reunited.

Pericles and his cohorts live in a pagan world, where even the goddess Diana becomes a character. Yet the complex plot is unwoven at the end to reveal a version of Christian providence, masquerading as the workings of the Greco-Roman gods. The trajectory from suffering to triumph is Christian in content.

Redemption

The journey to self-knowledge from a place of unawareness is a repeating narrative for Shakespeare's characters. But Pericles leaves one kingdom in fear for his life because of a contest for the hand of the princess, only to enter an identical contest quite soon after. He loses his wife whom he barely knew and then makes sure he won't know his daughter by leaving her in a different kingdom. At the end everyone is reunited, but Pericles divides the family again by sending Marina to Tyre and going to Pentapolis with Thaisa.

Meanwhile, most of Gower's monologues merely repeat the plot of scenes just past or narrate events that take place offstage. Only through Gower's conclusion are we given a sense of any kind of redemption in the plot. He explains to us, finally, that Antiochus and his daughter and Cleon and Dionyza are punished because they did evil, whereas Pericles and his family are rewarded. Gower also explains the role of the minor characters, who were living embodiments of their various virtues, such as loyalty (Helicanus) and charity (Cerimon).

The Two Noble Kinsmen

Main Characters

Theseus—the Duke of Athens

Palamon—nephew of the king of Thebes

Arcite—nephew of the king of Thebes

Pirithous—an Athenian general

Artesius—an Athenian captain

Valerius—a noble of Thebes

A Jailer—oversees the imprisonment of Palamon and Arcite

A Doctor—ordered by Theseus to tend to the wounds of Palamon and
Arcite

Gerrold—a schoolmaster

Hippolyta—wife of Theseus

Emilia—Theseus's sister

Three Queens—their husbands were killed by Creon, ruler of Thebes

Jailer's Daughter—in love with Palamon; frees him from the jail

Introduction

The Two Noble Kinsmen was written at the end of Shakespeare's career, as a collaboration with the rising young dramatist John Fletcher. Chaucer's story of Palamon and Arcite was based on Boccaccio's *Teseide*. Boccaccio in turn based his work on material by Statius. Richard Edwards wrote *Palamon and Arcyte* as early as 1566, and it was performed before Elizabeth I by Oxford students on the occasion of the queen's visit to the university that year. The account of this lost comedy, published in John Nichols's *Progresses of Elizabeth*, suggests that it was a very different kind of play from *The Two Noble Kinsmen*. Nothing is known of the *Palamon and Arsett* mentioned by Henslowe as having been acted at the Newington theater in 1594.

The Two Noble Kinsmen was first published in 1634 in quarto format, although scholars date it to sometime around 1613. The title page ascribes the play to "the memorable Worthies of their time; Mr. John Fletcher, and Mr. William Shakspeare" [sic]. Most modern critics accept this attribution.

Because the play was excluded from the 1623 First Folio some critics dispute Shakespeare's role in the play's composition. However, *Pericles* was also excluded from the First Folio, and *Troilus and Cressida* was included in only some editions, having been stitched into the binding between *King Henry VIII* (another coauthored play) and *Coriolanus*, and is subsequently absent from the title pages of those editions. When the second Beaumont and Fletcher folio was published in 1679, an additional eighteen plays were included, including *The Two Noble Kinsmen*.

It was not included in a complete Shakespeare edition until 1841 (*The Pictorial Shakespeare*) and only during the twentieth century has it been included in most of the major modern collections of Shakespeare's works: the Oxford, Riverside, Arden, Norton, Cambridge, and Penguin editions.

FACT

Curiously, of all the single-edition versions of the play in the twentieth century, only one, the Regents Renaissance Drama edition (edited by Richard Proudfoot, 1970), bears the names of both Shakespeare and Fletcher on the front cover. Now the New Arden edition of that play overcomes that silence with its twenty-first-century edition.

The Play

The Two Noble Kinsmen is essentially an adaptation of Chaucer's *Knight's Tale*. In this story, the two kinsmen are Palamon and Arcite, who are captured while fighting for Thebes against Athens. While imprisoned, the two cousins find themselves attracted to Emilia, Theseus's unmarried sister-in-law. Their professed "eternal friendship" is severely tested as the two cousins woo her. Theseus finds out what's going on, exiles Arcite from Athens, and leaves Palamon in jail.

Once he is free, Arcite disguises himself as a peasant in order to keep an eye on Emilia. Meanwhile, the Jailer's Daughter has fallen in love with Palamon and helps him to escape and hide in the forest.

He runs into Arcite again, and the two men resume their argument over Emilia. They decide to fight a duel for her. However, as they prepare for the duel, the two cousins are discovered by Theseus. He condemns both to death, but after pleading from both Emilia and her sister Hippolyta, the duke decides to banish them both.

FACT

The Two Noble Kinsmen is a play that needs to be seen for the masque-like splendor of some of its scenes to be fully realized. It contains elements of classic legend, medieval romance, Elizabethan comedy, and Jacobean masque, and in the union of these varying elements, we can recognize the genius of a dramatist who could subdue all things to harmony.

Both Palamon and Arcite refuse. Theseus tells Emilia she must choose between them, and the loser will be put to death. Emilia, however, can't make up her mind, so Theseus declares that the matter will be settled by combat after all. In one month, Palamon and Arcite will fight for Emilia's hand, and the loser will be executed.

Meanwhile, the Jailer's Daughter has gone mad because of her unrequited love for Palamon. Theseus pardons the Jailer, realizing he had no part in Palamon's escape, and forgives his deranged daughter. A doctor tries to help restore her sanity by getting her fiancé to pretend he's Palamon.

The time for the contest comes about, and Arcite defeats Palamon. However, while Palamon awaits execution, a messenger arrives bringing news that Arcite's fatally injured himself in a horse-riding accident. Arcite gives Emilia's hand to Palamon before he dies.

Commentary

Neglected until recently by directors and teachers, the play deserves to be better known for its moving dramatization of the conflict of love and friendship. While one of the kinsmen braces himself for execution, the shocking accident that frees him seems to make nonsense of the belief that we are responsible for our own fates. This concept is reinforced by Theseus's closing speech in the last scene, where he tries to convince us that Palamon had the better right to the lady because he saw her first. The enduring impression the play leaves is that humans are but puppets of fortune.

The Two Noble Kinsmen follows Chaucer's *Knight's Tale* closely, but the dramatists, deferring to the seventeenth-century taste for a realistic subplot to a romantic theme, added the story of the Jailer's Daughter. The play has problems. Palamon and Arcite are not particularly distinguished from each other; Theseus is a stilted and a vacillating figure; and Emilia is a poor copy of Chaucer's "Emelye the sheene." Finally, the subplot reminds us of a poorly revisited Ophelia (in *Hamlet*).

The authorship is clearly a problem. But to the play's credit, it's tough to say who wrote what exactly. Critics are agreed that one of the two authors was Fletcher, and that to him may be allotted most of acts II, III, and IV. This includes the whole of the subplot, with the possible exception of the two prose scenes, but that is only a small, and comparatively unimportant, part of the main story.

The whole of the first act, the first scene in act III, and almost the whole of the last act are clearly not by Fletcher, and the choice of authorship seems to fall to Shakespeare. The profusion of striking metaphors, the profound thoughts, and the extreme conciseness of writing the scenes bear a marked resemblance to Shakespeare's later plays.

APPENDIX A

Additional Resources

Books

All these book titles are available at Amazon.com or from your local bookseller.

Acting Shakespeare, by John Gielgud

Acting with Shakespeare: The Comedies, by Janet Suzman

Adaptations of Shakespeare: A Critical Anthology, edited by Daniel Fischlin and Mark Fortier

The Arden Dictionary of Shakespeare Quotations, compiled by Jane Armstrong

The Arden Shakespeare Complete Works, edited by Richard Proudfoot, Ann Thompson, and David Scott Kastan

The Art of Shakespeare's Sonnets, by Helen Hennessy Vendler

Brightest Heaven of Invention: A Christian Guide to Six Shakespeare Plays, by Peter J. Leithart

Bulfinch's Mythology, by Thomas Bulfinch

The Cambridge Companion to Shakespeare, edited by Margreta De Grazia and Stanley W. Wells

The Cambridge Companion to Shakespeare on Film, edited by Russell Jackson

The Children of Henry VIII, by Alison Weir

Clues to Acting Shakespeare: Skills Clarified for the Actor, Student, and Reader, by Wesley Van Tassel

Cleopatra, by Michael Grant

Coined by Shakespeare: Words and Meanings First Used by the Bard, by Jeffrey McQuain and Stanley Malless

A Companion to the Shakespearean Films of Kenneth Branagh, by Sarah Hatchuel

Daily Life in Elizabethan England, by Jeffrey L. Singman

Dictionary of Classical Mythology, by John Edward Zimmerman

A Dictionary of Shakespeare, by Stanley Wells and James Shaw

The Friendly Shakespeare: A Thoroughly Painless Guide to the Best of the Bard, by Norrie Epstein

From Shakespeare to Existentialism, by Walter Kaufmann

Greek Gods and Heroes, by Robert Graves

The Greek Myths, by Robert Graves

Henry V, War Criminal? and Other Shakespeare Puzzles, by John Sutherland, et al.

Heroes, Gods and Monsters of the Greek Myth, by Bernard Evslin

A History of Shakespeare on Screen: A Century of Film and Television, by Kenneth S. Rothwell and Kenneth J. Rothwell

Interpreting Shakespeare on Screen, by Deborah Cartmell

Lectures on Shakespeare, by W. H. Auden

The Lives of the Kings and Queens of England, by Antonia Fraser

The Military Campaigns of the Wars of the Roses, by Philip A. Haigh

The Merchant of Venice: Choice, Hazard and Consequence, by Joan Ozark Holmer

The Merchant of Venice Study Guide, by Bethine Ellie

Mythology: Timeless Tales of Gods and Heroes, by Edith Hamilton

Othello: A Guide to the Play, edited by Joan Lord Hall

Shakespeare's Kings: The Great Plays and the History of England in the Middle Ages: 1337–1485, by John Julius Norwich

Orson Welles, Shakespeare, and Popular Culture, by Michael Anderegg

The Purpose of Playing: Shakespeare and the Cultural Politics of Elizabethan Theatre, by Louis Montrose

The Reader's Encyclopedia of Shakespeare, edited by Oscar James Campbell and George Quinn

Romeo & Juliet Study Guide, by Bethine Ellie

Shakespeare's England: Life in Elizabethan and Jacobean Times, by Ron Pritchard

Shakespeare's Globe Rebuilt, edited by J. R. Mulryne and Margaret Shewring

A Shakespeare Glossary, by C. T. Onions

Shakespeare: The Invention of the Human, by Harold Bloom

Shakespeare and the Jews, by James Shapiro

Shakespeare Lexicon and Quotation Dictionary, by Alexander Schmidt

Shakespeare in the Movies: From the Silent Era to Shakespeare in Love, by Douglas C. Brode

Shakespeare's Sonnets: Critical Essays, edited by James Schiffer

Shakespearean Tragedy: Lectures on Hamlet, Othello, King Lear and Macbeth, by A. C. Bradley

Shakespeare's Women in Love, by Alice Griffin

Shakespeare, the Movie: Popularizing the Plays on Film, TV, and Video, edited by Lynda E. Boose and Richard Burt

Shakespeare's Mystery Play: The Opening of the Globe Theatre 1599, by Steve Sohmer

Shakespeare's Theatre, by Andrew Langley

Staging in Shakespeare's Theatres, by Andrew Gurr and Mariko Ichikawa

Shakespeare After Theory, by David Scott Kastan

Tempest: Complete Study Edition, edited by Sidney Lamb

Thy Father Is a Gorbellied Codpiece: Create over 100,000 of Your Own Shakespearean Insults, by Barry Kraft

Twelfth Night: A User's Guide, by Michael Pennington

Understanding Hamlet, by Don Nardo

Understanding Hamlet: A Student Casebook to Issues, Sources, and Historical Documents, by Richard Corum

Understanding Macbeth: A Student Casebook to Issues Sources, and Historical Documents, by Faith Nostbakken

Understanding The Merchant of Venice: A Student Casebook to Issues Sources, and Historical Documents, by Jay L. Halio

Understanding Othello: A Student Casebook to Issues Sources, and Historical Documents, by Faith Nostbakken

Understanding Romeo and Juliet, by Thomas E. Thrasher

Understanding Romeo and Juliet: A Student Casebook to Issues Sources, and Historical Documents, edited by Alan Hager

Understanding Shakespeare's Julius Caesar, by Thomas J. Derrick

Welcome to the Globe: The Story of Shakespeare's Theatre, by Peter Chrisp (children's book)

William Shakespeare and the Globe, by Aliki

William Shakespeare: The Man Behind the Genius: A Biography, by Anthony Holden

What Happens in Hamlet, by John Dover Wilson

Will in the World: How Shakespeare Became Shakespeare, by Stephen Greenblatt

In Search of Shakespeare, by Michael Wood

A Year in the Life of Shakespeare: 1599, by James Shapiro

Shakespeare: The World as Stage, by Bill Bryson

Shakespeare: The Biography, by Peter Ackroyd

Shakespeare on the Web

There are quite literally thousands of Web sites about Shakespeare. Following are a handful of sites that are interesting and useful. They have been categorized by topic to help you find your way around. No doubt your search will find many more.

Complete Texts

www.ipl.org/reading/shakespeare/shakespeare. html

http://shakespeare.about.com/mbody.htm

Summaries and Plot Guides

A. C. Bradley's Shakespearean Tragedy
www.clicknotes.com/bradley/welcome.html

All Shakespeare
Shakespeare Resource Center—Synopsis Index
www.bardweb.net/plays/index.html

Shakespeare Magazine
www.shakespearemag.com

SparkNotes Shakespeare
www.sparknotes.com/shakespeare

The Seven Ages of Shakespeare's Life
http://ise.uvic.ca/Library/SLTnoframes/life/life subj.html

Shakespeare Play Summaries-Synopses
*www.unc.edu/~monroem/shakespeare/
    shakespeare.html*

Shakespeare Study Guide with Plot Summaries
http://sites.micro-link.net/zekscrab

Shakespeare Performed

Romeo and Juliet
www.romeoandjuliet.com

IMS William Shakespeare, HarperAudio
*http://town.hall.org/Archives/radio/IMS/Harper
    Audio/020994_harp_ITH.html*

Shakespeare Wired for Books
www.tcom.ohiou.edu/books/shakespeare

Village Story Tapes
www.storytapes.net/index.html

Shakespeare and the Globe Then and Now
http://search.eb.com/shakespeare/index2.html

The Play's the Thing audio files and information
www.eamesharlan.org/tptt/audio.html

A Taste of Shakespeare
www.atasteofshakespeare.com

Virtual Globe Theatre—Opening Page
*www.holycross.edu/departments/theatre/
    wrynders/globe/globe.htm*

The Official Royal Shakespeare Company (RSC)
    Web site
www.rsc.org.uk

Shakespeare's Globe Theatre, Bankside, South-
    wark, London
www.shakespeares-globe.org

APPENDIX B

Shakespeare on Film

There is nothing that compares to watching a wonderfully envisioned and acted version of a Shakespeare play. Type in Shakespeare at the Internet Movie Database (*www.imdb.com*) and you will get many listings for Shakespeare on DVD and videotape going back to a silent version of *King John* in 1899, directed by Sir Herbert Beerbohm Tree. Most of this is available for rent or purchase. A great resource to start with is your local library, many of which now have movie rental sections and can get interlibrary loans for movies they don't have, in some cases. If you are interested about the portrayal of Shakespeare's plays through the television age, pick up a copy of *The History of Shakespeare on Screen: A Century of Film and Television*, by Kenneth S. Rothwell.

When watching Shakespeare on film, you will enhance your experience if you pay attention to the following ten viewers' clues:

1. Things happen in a live performance that are sometimes unrehearsed and unscripted. But everything in a film is meant to be there. If something stands out, chances are it was supposed to, so pay attention. In general, ask yourself why a director would use that music or focus on that thing.

2. Watch the film a couple of times and then follow it with a copy of the original play on your lap. Try and spot which scenes have been cut or merged, and which lines cut or reordered. Play performances are often rearranged and edited as well, but not to the same degree. What is the director trying to tell you about the play? To really see the difference a director can make, watch two different versions of the same play.

3. Who's in the cast? Are they popular actors? Do they specialize in something? For

example, is Ice-T playing Othello? How does this affect the way you see this character? Is the director relying on star appeal? Shock appeal? Can you explain any of the director's casting decisions?

4. Where is the film set? In what era? Does the play need a historically "accurate" setting for example, Renaissance England rather than Fascist Italy in the 1930s for *Richard III*?

5. What do the costumes tell you? Are they being used to convey a general impression or to establish a historical era or both?

6. How knowledgeable are we expected to be about the original play? Have any subplots or characters been dropped for this film? Why?

7. Has the genre of the film been changed? *Hamlet* became Disney's *The Lion King*; *The Tempest* became the 1956 sci-fi classic *Forbidden Planet*. What does this change tell you about the play that you hadn't thought of before?

8. What does the music in the film tell you about it? Music speaks to the emotional undercurrent in the story. How does the score affect how you experience the dialogue? Is it intrusive?

9. What did this film teach you about this play? What would you change?

10. When a new film comes out, watch how it's promoted. Catch interviews with the cast and the director. What they thought they were doing and what actually ended up on film may be very different.

The following is a partial list of films of Shakespeare plays, of dramas inspired by his plays, or about Shakespeare, that are worth watching.

The Taming of the Shrew (1929), featuring Douglas Fairbanks and Mary Pickford

Romeo and Juliet (1936), directed by George Cukor

A Midsummer Night's Dream (1935), directed by Max Reinhardt and William Dieterle

As You Like It (1936), directed by Paul Czinner

Swingin' the Dream (1939), featuring Louis Armstrong and Benny Goodman (based on *A Midsummer Night's Dream*)

Henry V (1945), directed by Laurence Olivier

A Double Life (1947), directed by George Cukor, starring Ronald Coleman (based on *Othello*)

Macbeth (1948), directed by Orson Welles

Hamlet (1948), directed by Laurence Olivier

Othello (1952), directed by Orson Welles

Julius Caesar (1953), directed by Joseph L. Mankiewicz

Romeo and Juliet (1954), directed by Renato Castellani

Richard III (1955), directed by Laurence Olivier

Forbidden Planet (1956), directed by Fred M. Wilcox (based on *The Tempest*)

West Side Story (1961), starring Natalie Wood and Richard Beymer (based on *Romeo and Juliet*)

Hamlet (1964), starring Richard Burton and directed by Bill Colleran and John Gielgud

Hamlet (1964), directed by Grigori Kozintsev

Chimes at Midnight (1965), directed by Orson Welles (a fictional biography of Falstaff, lifted from the histories)

Othello (1965), starring Laurence Olivier, Maggie Smith, and Frank Finlay

The Taming of the Shrew (1967), starring Elizabeth Taylor and Richard Burton, and directed by Franco Zeffirelli

Romeo and Juliet (1968), directed by Franco Zeffirelli

King Lear (1971), directed by Peter Brook

King Lear (1971), directed by Grigori Kozintsev

Macbeth (1972), directed by Roman Polanski

Antony and Cleopatra (1974), starring Patrick Stewart and Ben Kingsley, and directed by Trevor Nunn and John Schoffield

Comedy of Errors (1978), starring Judi Dench and Francesca Annis, and directed by Philip Casson and Trevor Nunn

Richard II (1978), starring Derek Jacobi, John Gielgud, and Wendy Hiller

Hamlet, Prince of Denmark (1980), starring Patrick Stewart, and directed by Rodney Bennett

The Merry Wives of Windsor (1982), starring Ben Kingsley, and directed by David Hugh Jones

The Tempest (1982), directed by Paul Mazursky

Ran (1985), directed by Akira Kurosawa (based on *King Lear*)

King Lear (1987), directed by Jean-Luc Godard

Henry V (1989), directed by Kenneth Branagh

Rosencrantz and Guildenstern Are Dead (1990), featuring Richard Dreyfuss (based on *Hamlet*)

Romeo and Juliet (1990), directed by Armando Acosta II, starring Francesca Annis, Vanessa Redgrave, and Ben Kingsley

Hamlet (1991), directed by Franco Zeffirelli, starring Mel Gibson, Glenn Close, Ian Holm, and Helena Bonham Carter

Prospero's Books (1991), directed by Peter Greenaway (based on *The Tempest*)

As You Like It (1992), directed by Christine Edzard

Much Ado about Nothing (1993), directed by Kenneth Branagh, starring Kenneth Branagh, Emma Thompson, Denzel Washington, Keanu Reeves, and Michael Keaton

Othello (1995), directed by Oliver Parker, starring Lawrence Fishburne and Kenneth Branagh

Richard III (1995), directed by Richard Loncraine, featuring Sir Ian McKellen

Hamlet (1996), directed by Kenneth Branagh, starring Kenneth Branagh, Richard Attenborough, Judi Dench, Billy Crystal, and Kate Winslet

Twelfth Night (1996), directed by Trevor Nunn, starring Helena Bonham Carter, Nigel Hawthorne, Ben Kingsley, Imogen Stubbs, and Mel Smith

Looking for Richard (1996), directed by Al Pacino

Romeo + Juliet (1996), directed by Baz Luhrmann, starring Leonardo DiCaprio and Claire Danes

Shakespeare in Love (1998), directed by John Madden, starring Gwyneth Paltrow, Joseph Fiennes, Geoffrey Rush, and Judi Dench

10 Things I Hate about You (1999), directed by Gil Junger, starring Julia Stiles and Heath Ledger (based on *The Taming of the Shrew*)

A Midsummer Night's Dream (1999), directed by Michael Hoffman, starring Calista Flockhart and Michelle Pfeiffer

Titus (1999), directed by Julie Taymor, starring Anthony Hopkins and Jessica Lange

Love's Labour's Lost (2000), directed by Kenneth Branagh

William Shakespeare's The Merchant of Venice (2005), directed by Michael Radford, starring Al Pacino, Jeremy Irons, and Joseph Fiennes

Index

Literary works cited are by William Shakespeare unless otherwise noted.